CREATIVITY TIPS

FOR

SCRAPBOOKERS

A TREASURY OF FAVORITES
PRODUCED EXCLUSIVELY FOR LEISURE ARTS

FOUNDING EDITOR	Lisa Bearnson
EDITOR-IN-CHIEF	Tracy White
MANAGING EDITOR, SPECIAL PROJECTS	Leslie Miller
MANAGING EDITOR	Sharon Stasney
EDITOR-AT-LARGE	Jana Lillie
SENIOR WRITERS	Denise Pauley, Rachel Thomae
SENIOR EDITORS	Brittany Beattie, Vanessa Hoy
ASSOCIATE EDITOR	Jennifer Purdie
ASSOCIATE WRITER	Lori Fairbanks
COPY EDITOR	Kim Sandoval
EDITORIAL ASSISTANTS	Joannie McBride, Fred Brewer, Liesl Russell
CREATIVE DIRECTOR	Brian Tippetts
ART DIRECTOR, SPECIAL PROJECTS	Erin Bayless
GRAPHIC DESIGNER	Gaige Redd
VICE PRESIDENT, GROUP PUBLISHER	David O'Neil

LEISURE ARTS, INC.

VICE PRESIDENT AND EDITOR-IN-CHIEF	Sandra Graham Case
EXECUTIVE DIRECTOR OF PUBLICATIONS	Cheryl Nodine Gunnells
SENIOR PUBLICATIONS DIRECTOR	Susan White Sullivan
SPECIAL PROJECTS DIRECTOR	Susan Frantz Wiles
DIRECTOR OF DESIGNER RELATIONS	Debra Nettles
DIRECTOR OF MARKETING AND PHOTOGRAHY	Amy Vaughn
PHOTOGRAHY MANAGER AND GRAPHIC DESIGNER	Katherine Atchison
SENIOR DIRECTOR OF PREPRESS	Mark Hawkins
PUBLISHING SYSTEMS ADMINISTRATOR	Becky Riddle
PUBLISHING SYSTEMS ASSISTANTS	Clint Hanson, John Rose
	Brian Richardson and Janie Wright

CHIEF OPERATING OFFICER	Tom Siebenmorgen
DIRECTOR OF CORPORATE PLANNING AND DEVELOPMENT	Laticia Mull Dittrich
VICE PRESIDENT, SALES AND MARKETING	Pam Stebbins
DIRECTOR OF SALES AND SERVICES	Margaret Reinold
VICE PRESIDENT, OPERATIONS	Jim Dittrich
COMPTROLLER, OPERATIONS	Rob Thieme
RETAIL CUSTOMER SERVICE MANAGER	Stan Raynor
PRINT PRODUCTION MANAGER	Fred F. Pruss

Library of Congress Control Number: 2006937257
White, Tracy
Creating Keepsakes: Creativity Tips for Scrapbookers
"A Leisure Arts Publication"

Softcover ISBN 1-57486-607-9

Page 221

editor's
note

WOW! LOOKING THROUGH THIS BOOK IS AMAZING. You'd think that as Editor-in-Chief of *Creating Keepsakes* magazine, all of this stuff would be old-hat to me. After all, this is the "best of the best" from the last couple years of the magazine. However, it always surprises me how many really cool ideas and tips we have in the magazine that I seem to forget as time goes by. As I look through the pages, I keep thinking "Oh, oh, oh, I want to try that."

I'm sure you'll be thinking the same thing as you look through the ideas in this book. We've gathered some of the best tips on creativity, design and organization from the last two years of *Creating Keepsakes* magazines and special issues and put them in this one single volume. Here you'll find tips on everything from how to find more inspiration in the things around you to how to stretch your scrapbooking budget just a bit further. Plus, you'll be inspired by the fabulous scrapbook pages featured in each article.

I'm confident that you'll be as excited as I am to break out your scrapbooking supplies and get started scrapbooking. Good luck, and remember that it is all about creating those precious keepsakes that your family will love—and having a great time doing it. ❤

Tracy White

Page 252

contents

heidi's
7 habits
for successful scrapbooking

here's the method to my madness...

BY HEIDI SWAPP

Structure? I like as little of it as possible. Still, after having countless people ask how I accomplish so much in scrapbooking, I realized there really is a method to my madness. Following are seven habits I've picked up that make my obsession possible. They can help you succeed, too!

1. Organize your resources...

Store your photos and supplies in systems that are easy to access, make "sense" for the way you scrapbook, and are systems you can maintain with little effort. If you can't find the right system, create your own!

I organize my photos by grouping them by category or event, then stacking them chronologically. I get rid of any photos I know I'll never use. Index prints, negative sleeves and computer programs are all tools that help me stay organized.

I love Apple's iPhoto software—it's so easy to sort photos into folders, then burn the images to CD. I use a Sharpie to note the categories stored on each CD, as well as the date. I keep the CDs in a big binder, organized chronologically.

heidi's 5 storage solutions

I own a ton of supplies, and it's easy to forget what I have. It's also hard to keep things organized. To help, I've come up with five quick, easy and accessible ways to store my favorite supplies.

1 • ribbon on rings

I own a *lot* of ribbon, but just a small amount of each type. To keep it organized, I put each strand in a 3" zip-lock baggie and punch a hole in the top. I organize the ribbons by color on book rings and hang the rings on hooks on my wall.

2 • serious stuff caddy

I know I'm serious about a project when I pull out supplies like dyes, modeling paste and decoupage materials. I keep these items in a cleaning caddy. If I'm "getting serious," I want fast access to all my serious stuff!

3 • travel journal kit

I'm always on the go, so I've compiled a little collection of scrapbooking necessities and keep it at the ready. As long as I have my kit handy, I can get things accomplished! The travel journal kit is a quick grab for a trip, class or crop with friends.

4 • ice-cube trays

The smallest items can top off a project just right. I have an ice-cube tray that holds my favorite tiny embellishments. To choose an accent, I simply pull out my tray and set it next to the project I'm working on.

5 • paint holder *(not shown)*

I use acrylic paint often and need a quick way to see what I have available. My solution? I've taken an old drawer and mounted it to the wall for a shelf.

☆ Invent a system that makes sense to you!

2. Shop for inspiration...

The best scrapbookers draw inspiration from the world around them. They look everywhere—at bookstores, restaurants, department stores and other favorite locations. They "case" catalogs, product packaging, bags or purses, ads, stationery, cards, advertising and Internet sites.

☆ buy stuff that inspires you—
keep it with you; hang it up...
let it "Muse" you!

I like to know what's hot in fashion, whether I buy or not. It's important to keep up on the latest trends and color combos.

Tissue paper is elegant and play-ful, and I couldn't wait to use it here. I cut each flower out of three layers of tissue, then sewed the flowers to the layout at their centers. *Note:* If archival safety is a concern, treat your tissue paper with deacidification spray before including it on your layout.

Supplies *Textured cardstock:* Bazzill Basics Paper; *Patterned paper:* SEI; *Label holder and cardstock:* Making Memories; *Ribbon:* May Arts; *Silk ribbon:* Bucilla; *Paper flowers:* Anthropologie tissue paper; *Acrylic paint:* Delta Technical Coatings.

create an inspiration book

Get a little book you can jot notes in. (Make sure it's a good size to carry around!) Draw sketches as ideas come to mind and write quotes or cute one-liners you read or hear. Tear out ideas from other places and staple the ideas into your book.

3. Take effective photos

Think like a photojournalist—your pictures should help tell a story and re-create emotions. Cover:
- who
- what
- where
- when
- why

be thoughtful

Be thoughtful and focus on capturing what you want to remember. The other day, I recorded my kids "surfing" down the stairs on a crib mattress.

plan ahead

Plan ahead. Consider lighting and what people in your pictures will be wearing. You want them to look good!

create a "memory list"

Create a "memory list" for your photos. I cut a 4" x 6" piece of cardstock and jot down details about a particular event. I answer the five Ws first, then add a bullet-point list of items I don't want to forget. I keep the list with my group of photos.

Answer the 5 "W" questions with your photos: who, what, where, when, why?

4. TRY something new...

Take classes at your local scrapbook store, attend CKU, or sign up for art or photography classes. Another fun idea? Get a group together, then take turns teaching each other cool techniques.

See what you can discover from hobbies like sewing, needlework, jewelry or bookmaking.

Subscribe to several magazines, whether they're scrapbook-related or not. I regularly flip through stamping, home décor, surf and skateboarding, wedding, fashion and computer magazines.

just One of many in Alyssa's beach-Summer Wardrobe...

cute suit

Alyssa

summer

just turned four

2004

I've loved flamingos for months now and have looked for an excuse to use them. When I saw this ad in an *Anthropologie* catalog, I couldn't help myself. I bought a hot-pink printed gift box, freehanded and cut out flamingo images, then sanded the edges for a distressed look!

Supplies *Foam stamps, ribbon and acrylic paint:* Making Memories; *Index tabs:* Avery; *Photo corners:* Paper Source; *Other:* Post-it tabs and chipboard box, purchased at Target.

⭐ Anything can be incorporated into a scrapbook page! ...find a way...

5. Tell the story

Think about your audience and what your page "says." Make sure everything is easy to follow and understand. Remember, your photos need to tell the story as much as your journaling.

Don't stop short when including important facts or cool details. You can always include them in hidden journaling or fold-out books.

Use a photo sequence. I couldn't wait to snap pictures of my expressive son, Cory, getting his face painted. I included pictures of the process in accordion pages, then put a photo of him after the transformation on the cover of the fold-out book. Cory was thrilled!

Supplies *Iron-on letters:* Jo-Ann Crafts; *Letter stamps:* From *stamp-out-cute.com*; *Acrylic paint:* Making Memories; *Electrical tape:* Home Depot; *Chipboard gift box and star stickers:* Purchased at Target.

☆ think about your audience...what would they want to know (details!)

6. work on what moves you ...

Ideas to note: I used the jigsaw number as a mask for painting. I created the black-and-white polka dot paper with a stencil. I used a paper piercer to scratch into the photographs.

Remember, there aren't really any rules in scrapbooking. You can work on whatever you're drawn to—what you find exciting and fun. You don't have to follow a chronological order or get bogged down in items you're not interested in at the time.

Supplies *Foam stamps and jigsaw and rub-on alphabets:* Making Memories; *Spray paint:* Krylon; *Patterned paper and player sticker:* Rusty Pickle; *Dots paper:* Heidi's own design.

7. it has to be FUN...

Enjoy the process and discover more about yourself and those you love. When you create a scrapbook page, share your work. Open that album, post your layout online, or make a copy for someone else.

Hang a favorite layout to add personalized flair to your surroundings.

don't get stuck in a rut

Once you've got the "hang" of these seven habits, pat yourself on the back. You and I are on the path to successful scrapbooking! ❤

Scrapbook Your Way

Do what works best for you

A few weeks ago, I was scrapbooking with my seven-year-old daughter, Jaeme. As she flipped through photos, I kept exclaiming, "Oh, you have to write the story about that picture on your page!" She gave me *that* look and said, "Or, I could scrapbook this picture in my own *artistic* way."

I stopped and put down my pen, realizing that we both like to scrapbook in entirely different ways. While I write my story before embellishing it with photos and embellishments, Jaeme enjoys using her art supplies to create unique page accents.

I was reminded of an important scrapbooking lesson: there is no right or wrong way to scrapbook. It doesn't matter how you start a page. The most important thing is taking the time to create a layout that's meaningful to you.

Here are five starting points for creating scrapbook pages that reflect who you are and what you love to do. Use them to discover your favorite way to scrapbook—I've included permission slips to get you going!

by Rachel Thomae

Photographs as a Starting Point

Photography might be your starting point if:

- Friends and family members ask you to take informal family portraits for them.
- The people at your local photo lab know you by name.
- You know your camera manual backward and forward.
- You design your scrapbook pages so your photographs shine.
- You love taking photography classes and reading books on the topic.
- You always have at least one camera with you, no matter where you go.
- You enjoy reading articles on how to take better photographs and set up your own photo shoots.

Tell your story with photographs.

Annie Weis believes that in Tuscany, there is "a poetry in the landscape that leaves you breathless." With beautiful detail and vibrant colors (see layout), she captures a sense of what she calls "a magical place." Annie tells a story with her pictures. Here's what she did on her layout (you can, too):

1 Extended her large focal photo across both pages.

2 Featured photos of shapes, lines and textures at left.

3 Printed her journaling in a horizontal column across the bottom of the page to keep the focus on her pictures.

4 Experimented with taking photographs from a variety of angles.

5 Thought about how she wanted to convey through her pictures the joy she feels when viewing America's beautiful landscapes.

There is no place in the world I'd rather travel to than Tuscany. There is something magical about the sunny fields, the rolling hills, the cypresses, the olive groves, the vineyards, the sunflowers, the farm houses, the ancient towns, the tiny villages, the gorgeous food and the fabulous views. There is serenity and beauty there – a poetry in the landscape that leaves you breathless. When you are there, you feel it. The world suddenly seems right. Your life has harmony and peace. This is Tuscany.

tuscany

"Tuscany" *by Annie Weis.* **Supplies** *Textured cardstock:* Linen Paper; *Patterned paper:* 7gypsies; *Stickers:* American Crafts; *Computer font:* Bell MT, downloaded from the Internet.

Permission Slip

○ Enlarge that favorite photograph and feature it prominently on a two-page spread.

○ Take pictures of signs and macro shots of images you think would make great page titles and accents. Organize the photographs into a file on your computer for easy access.

○ When ordering pictures, choose a favorite image and request it in all the sizes available from the lab. Play with the pictures and move them around on your layout.

Supplies as a Starting Point

Supplies might be your starting point if:

- As a child, you loved going to the fabric store with your mom and touching all the fabrics and colorful ribbon.

- Friends and family members mention your ability to accessorize an outfit with just the right belt or the perfect necklace.

- You love spending an hour at your local scrapbook store (and you've got the supplies to prove it!).

- Your favorite *Creating Keepsakes* column is Three Products, Five Scrapbookers.

- When shopping for a new dress, you can't help but notice how the fabric matches the new line of paper you picked up at your local scrapbook store.

- You enjoy the "mix and match" process of combining patterned papers, stickers, computer fonts and more.

Tell your story with supplies.

Linda Albrecht enjoys "celebrating the colors and traditions" of each season. Through carefully selected and thoughtfully combined supplies (15 in all on this page!), she reinforces her description of the leaves beginning to show "a tinge of red."

Linda tells a story with her supplies. Here's what she did on her layout (you can, too):

1 Selected three pieces of patterned paper with an assortment of fall colors.

2 Unified her page design with the use of dark denim blue (see page corner, title, paisley patterned paper and page tag) while drawing attention to her son's picture.

3 Added a silk flower tinted with the same prominent colors in her leaf photograph to draw the viewer's eye across the page.

4 Played with mixing and matching a variety of different supplies.

5 Used her supplies to create a unique title to convey her message.

"Prelude" *by Linda Albrecht.* **Supplies** *Patterned papers:* Chatterbox, Deluxe Designs, The Paper Loft and Mustard Moon; *Rivets, nails, stitched envelope and letter stencil:* Chatterbox; *Canvas ringer tag and letter stamps:* Creative Imaginations; *Brad:* Making Memories; *Acrylic paint:* Jo Sonja's; *Embossing powder:* Ultra Thick Embossing Enamel, Ranger Industries; *Computer fonts:* Jefferson and Vanthian, downloaded from 1001Fonts.com; *Other:* Silk flower.

Permission Slip

○ Celebrate finding and using scrapbooking supplies creatively. It's more than OK to be inspired by your favorite supplies!

○ Use as many embellishments as needed to tell the story you want to tell.

○ See a new piece of patterned paper you want for your stash? Buy it!

Design as a Starting Point

Design might be your starting point if:

- As a child, you enjoyed drawing designs on your Etch A Sketch.

- You've got an eye for color and friends often ask you which colors look best on them.

- Friends and family members often compliment your home décor.

- You love going to flea markets, thrift stores and garage sales, and you always pick out hip, cool items.

- You believe in "a place for everything" and "everything in its place."

- You are happiest when your scrapbook pages tell a story in a neatly organized way.

- Your favorite *Creating Keepsakes* column is Becky's Sketch.

Tell your story with design.

This year, Deb Perry would love to apply for freelance art jobs, maintain consistent health and take her kids to Hawaii. Her layout here is a visual summary of 18 different hopes and dreams. Here's what she did (you can, too):

1 Sketched a design that let her feature three categories on her page: goals, hopes and dreams.

2 Balanced her page by dividing it into two vertical columns.

3 Maximized her journaling by writing each thought on a paper square.

4 Found a piece of patterned paper with "our lives, new beginnings" text that supports her page theme.

5 Personalized her page look and feel by combining her own handwriting with photographs, patterned paper, rubber stamping and paper squares.

"Dreams" *by Deb Perry.* **Supplies** *Patterned paper:* Déjà Views, The C-Thru Ruler Co.; *Transparency and number stickers:* Creative Imaginations; *Black marker:* Zig Writer, EK Success; *Decorating chalk:* Craf-T Products.

Permission Slip

○ Take your favorite Becky Higgins sketch and copy it exactly or modify it.

○ Repeat a winning page design as many times as you'd like in your album.

○ Carry a sketchbook. When people see you sketching the menu board at your favorite espresso shop, they'll admire your creativity.

Art as a Starting Point

Art might be your starting point if:

- As a child, you loved finger painting, drawing with sidewalk chalk, or spending hours coloring with crayons, markers and colored pencils.

- You are happiest when you're experimenting with new scrapbooking techniques.

- Your favorite *Creating Keepsakes* columns are Featured Artist and Tips & Tricks.

- Friends and family members compliment you on non-scrapbooking crafts like painting, quilting and needlework.

- You love spending an hour in the art section of your favorite craft store.

- When you look out your window, you can't wait to grab your favorite pastel crayons and re-create the sunset.

- The creative process of scrapbooking appeals to you just as much as the completed page.

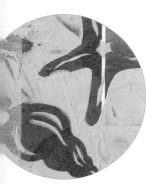

Tell your story with art.

On a trip to the beach, Nicole Gartland's daughter experienced playing with sand for the first time. She loved feeling the texture in her fingers and making footprints. As a scrapbooker, Nicole enjoys discovering new techniques that can help capture the essence of an experience.

Nicole's layout illustrates its story with an art technique. Here's what she did (you can, too):

1 Experimented with texture medium. (Nicole placed die-cut seashells on her page, brushed texture medium over the die cuts, then carefully peeled them from the medium.)

2 Colored the texture medium with acrylic paint to create the look of sand.

3 Played with two pen types to create a certain handwritten look for her title and journaling.

4 Explored the idea of brushing texture medium directly over her photographs.

5 Overlapped her handwritten page title onto her photograph.

"Exploring Sand" *by Nicole Gartland.* **Supplies** *Patterned papers:* Karen Foster Design and Club Scrap; *Embossing paste:* Golden Medium; *Pen:* Pigma Micron and Gelly Roll, Sakura; *Acrylic paint:* Plaid Enterprises; *Other:* Shells.

Permission Slip

- ○ Play with whatever techniques strike your fancy.

- ○ Enjoy the creative process just as much (or more?) as you enjoy getting caught up on your scrapbooking.

- ○ Choose an artistic technique to enhance your photographs and add just one (such as a painted background) to your page. Your art can be as simple or as complex as you'd like it to be.

Words as a Starting Point

Words might be your starting point if:

- As a child, you scribbled countless stories in spiral-bound notebooks.

- Friends enjoy meeting you for lunch to hear your latest story about your life.

- Family members love receiving handwritten letters and e-mails from you.

- You love words and find writing an enjoyable experience.

- Your favorite *Creating Keepsakes* column is Sharing the Story.

- You read the journaling on every page in the magazine each month.

- When you look out the window, you're daydreaming about which words to use to describe the beauty of the day.

Tell your story with words.

Denise Levy says that "being creative is a great way to express myself." On this layout, she shares the positive changes she's seen in her creative life by writing three pages every morning.

Denise uses words to tell the story on her page. Here's what she did (you can, too):

1 Set up her journaling in columns and typed what she wanted to share.

2 Printed her journaling on a transparency so she could layer it over the apple image she drew freehand and painted with watercolors.

3 Selected a quote for her title and referred back to it at the end of her journaling block.

4 Referred to her daily handwritten notes for ideas to share.

5 Chose a significant aspect of her life to share with readers.

With an apple I will astonish Paris. —Paul Cézanne

In college I discovered that being creative was a great way for me to express myself. It was then that I began painting and making my own cards. I even ended up with a Bachelor of Fine Arts degree in Art History after thinking I would major in Accounting.

For years people have told me I should sell my handmade cards. However, over the years my belief in myself and my abilities slowly declined and this non-belief and negativity blocked my creative spirit. This past fall I decided that I needed to do something about it. In October I began reading The Artist's Way by Julia Cameron. This wonderful book is a 12 week program that helps you unblock you inner artist. The book is based on doing morning pages, where you write three pages every morning of whatever is on your mind. The program also involves doing artist's dates and other assignments aimed at helping you to unblock and create more. This book has helped me in every aspect of my life. I'm less anxious, I'm working out in the morning and I'm actually creating instead of procrastinating at the computer. Doing the morning pages has freed me by getting all of the worries down on paper and out of my system. The changes I've made in the past three months have put me on a path that not only is helping me create, but has made me healthier, both mentally and physically.

My main goal for 2005 is to persist with this wonderful program by continuing on with my morning pages, stopping the negative self-talk, and continuing to workout in the morning. I still have a long way to go. I still can get stuck at the computer spending way too much time on scrapbooking message boards, instead at my scrapbook desk creating. Every morning I want to sleep in and some days I feel anxious. But, I know I'm on the right path and a year from now I hope I'll be able to say, "I astonished Paris."

"With an Apple" by Denise Levy. **Supplies** *Watercolor paper:* Grumbacher; *Watercolor paint:* Cotman; *Computer fonts:* Arial Narrow, Microsoft Word; Hannibal Lecter NFI, downloaded from the Internet; *Decorative brad:* Making Memories; *Ribbon:* Fibers By The Yard; *Transparency:* Hammermill. *Idea to note:* Denise drew and painted the apple with watercolors.

Permission Slip

○ Take up as much space as desired for your words. If space permits, add a photograph or an embellishment or two. Instead of hiding any journaling, why not hide the photographs instead?

○ Embrace your personal writing style. Create a layout that spotlights a poem, story or narrative essay you've written. Your photos and page accents can help illustrate your writing.

○ Communicate in the way that makes you happiest, whether it's your handwriting, a computer font or a mix of both styles. You get to choose since there are no rules for your page! ♥

Shop at Home

Shopping for scrapbook supplies can comprise a good portion of our scrapbooking time. Although we enjoy our frequent jaunts to the local scrapbook store, sometimes we may wish to use that time to work on our pages instead. We may also find ourselves on a budget or looking to use resources we already have on hand. Whatever the case may be, consider the following shopping solution:

It's nighttime and you finally get to scrapbook! But what do you do when you can't find what you want in your stash and it's too late to run to the store? Why not use goods you already have on hand in different rooms of your house? Consider the following options:

In the bathroom:
• Bobby pins serve as clips, but with a fun, feminine touch.
• New make-up applicators work great for inking, chalking or painting.

In the kitchen:
• Soda tabs make cute ribbon buckles. Simply clean and sand the tabs, then coat them with embossing ink, then embossing powder in the color of your choice. Melt the powder with your heat gun. Apply two to three coats for a smooth and shiny finish.
• Twist ties add a sassy touch to tags or other accents.

In the office:
• Paper clips transform into colorful accents with solvent-based ink.
• Staples offer a casual or edgy way to fasten journaling blocks, title elements or accents to your page.

In the garage:
• Metal alphabet stamps can be used to imprint metal scrapbook accents or thin metal sheets.
• Flat metal washers make interesting embellishments when stamped with letters or images. Use a solvent-based ink for best results.

In the Sewing and Laundry Room:
• Fabric is a versatile alternative to paper—use it as a background, cut it into title letters or rip it into strips and use it like ribbon.
• Buttons make great page accents! Use them as is, tie them off with embroidery floss or place them over a punched flower.

—*Lori Fairbanks*

Got 15 Minutes?

Get a jump-start on scrapbooking goals by Faye Morrow Bell

Author Ernest Hemingway wrote, "Now is no time to think of what you do not have. Think of what you can do with what there is." Truer words were never spoken—especially when it comes to scrapbooking. Most of us don't have hours to devote each day to our hobby. Still, I'll bet you can find 15 minutes! The ideas here will keep you organized, playing and moving toward your goals. ▶ ▶ ▶

FLAG A MAGAZINE OR IDEA BOOK.

How often do you find yourself thumbing through books and magazines for that layout you saw "just last week"? Take 15 minutes and use Post-its or other repositionable notes to flag ideas for future reference. It's also a good idea to jot a note about what attracted you to the layout.

FIND A NEW USE FOR A PRODUCT.

Take a product you use often and experiment with new and innovative ways to use it. Here's an idea to try: Practice combining rub-on alphabets with other types of lettering (like your handwriting or label-tape strips).

PERUSE NON-SCRAPBOOKING MAGAZINES FOR IDEAS.

Fashion and home décor magazines are especially good. Here are a few suggestions to guide you through the pages:

- Note inviting color schemes.
- Look for title ideas.
- Sketch the layout of an ad that captures your attention.

JOURNAL A MEMORY.

You think you'll never forget the cute conversation you had with your daughter while grabbing a quick bite at McDonald's, but you will! Write down the memory while it's fresh and the details are clear.

SKETCH.

Many of us come up regularly with ideas for layouts. Don't lose these flashes of inspiration! Take 15 minutes to make sketches of the ideas.

EMBELLISH THE COVER OF YOUR SCRAPBOOK.

Cloth-like covers make this especially easy. I like to use metal accents, fabric paints, ribbons and rub-ons. Marian and Me (*www.marian-andme.com*) offers a line of pewter album ornaments that make embellishing a snap.

ESTABLISH A BLOG.

Weblogs, more commonly known as "blogs," are taking the Internet by storm. A blog is essentially an online journal—a place to collect, organize and share items of interest. Your blog can become a resource for future page ideas and journaling. A few blog sites to consider are *www.typepad.com, www.blogger.com* and *www.blogidentity.com.*

SCRAPLIFT AN ACCENT.

Sometimes I'm in the mood to create but am not in the mood to design. That's when I scraplift! Find a great accent or embellishment idea in your spare 15 minutes.

DOCUMENT YOUR DAY.

Holidays, vacations and special occasions represent only 5 percent of our lives. Make sure you capture the other 95 percent in your scrapbook. You'll be glad you did!

Take 15 minutes to document your day. What is your morning routine? Where do you shop for groceries? What do you prepare for dinner? These details can be added to a future "day in the life" page.

SHOP.

Take a quick inventory of your supplies and make a list for your next trip to the scrapbook store. There's nothing worse than spending $50 on a "latest and greatest" item, only to return home and discover that you have no adhesive! If you shop online, 15 minutes is all you need to place your next order.

PURGE A SUPPLY.

Select one type of supply—such as cardstock, stickers or metal accents—and get rid of items you know you won't use. Friends, schools and some charities will welcome your castoffs.

CROP PRINTED PHOTOS.

We've all got photos that could benefit from cropping. Use a few spare minutes to crop your photos with a paper trimmer, craft knife or computer program.

DOWNLOAD NEW FONTS.

You'll find terrific (and free!) font resources online at *www.dafont.com, www.scrapvillage.com* and *www.onescrappysite.com*. Or, uninstall fonts from your computer that you rarely use.

CLEAN YOUR DIGITAL CARD.

I'm guilty of not moving images from my camera's digital card as quickly as I should. Take 15 minutes to delete images you no longer need, then move the rest to permanent storage like your computer's hard drive or a CD.

PLAY IN AN ART JOURNAL.

Afraid you'll mess up a new technique you want to try? Spend a few minutes practicing the idea, whether it's foam stamping, painting, embossing or something else. Record the results in an art journal you can reference later.

PRACTICE YOUR HANDWRITING.

It's important to include it in your scrapbooks. Set aside a small journal or sketchbook for your handwriting, and play with different pencils and inks.

CLEAN YOUR SCRAP SURFACE.

Set a timer for 15 minutes, and clear away as much surface clutter as possible.

MAKE PAGE KITS.

Pull together photos, papers and embellishments. When time permits, you'll be ready to scrapbook.

☐ **CLEAN YOUR RUBBER STAMPS.**

I'm not always diligent about cleaning my rubber stamps after each use. Using your favorite rubber stamp cleaner, give your dirtiest stamps a good "once-over."

☐ **CLEAN THE OUTSIDE OF YOUR CAMERA.**

To remove dust from the lens and LCD screen (if your camera is digital), use a microfiber cloth or photographic blower brush. If you have neither of these, breathe on the lens and wipe it *lightly* with a soft, dry, dust-free cloth or lens-cleaning paper. Avoid touching the metal fittings.

Use a soft, dry cloth to dust the body. Avoid using solvents, chemicals or detergents to clean your camera. Replace or recharge batteries if needed.

☐ **ORDER OR PRINT PHOTOS.**

If you have a photo printer at home, take 15 minutes to print your last photo session. If you order prints online, you can place an order over the Internet.

Do you have your photos processed locally? You can edit and upload your photos to most local camera shops.

☐ **EDIT YOUR DIGITAL PHOTOS.**

If you use photo-editing software, take 15 minutes to clean and crop a few photos so they're ready for printing when needed.

☐ **CUT PHOTO MATS.**

Do you consistently use one color (for example, black or white) for your photo mats? Save time by cutting multiple mats at once.

☐ **SHARPEN YOUR CUTTING TOOLS.**

Gather supplies like scissors, paper trimmers and punches. Sharpen or change the blades so they're always in top cutting condition. *Tip:* Sharpen punches by punching them through aluminum foil.

☐ **SET UP A SYSTEM.**

Once you invest in the initial setup, you'll receive ongoing dividends of increased time and reduced frustration. Here are organization ideas you can establish in 15 minutes:

- Fill a binder with page protectors. Use the binder to organize all the ideas (color, layout and accent) you tear from magazines.
- Identify a blank book to use for sketching or as an art journal. Embellish the cover and attach a pencil.
- Buy a photo box and label the index tabs.
- Set up folders on your computer to manage your digital photo files. ♥

Light My Fire

50 WAYS TO FUEL YOUR CREATIVITY

BY
ALLISON
STRINE

I love the warm feeling of community in scrapbooking. Sharing albums with friends can be both inspiring and enlightening. Too often, though, I've seen one person look at another's work and comment, "Oh, I wish I could do something like that, but I'm just not creative." How can anyone say she's not creative? I firmly believe we were all born with gobs of creativity flowing through our souls. We just need to learn how to nurture it and set it free! Here are 50 ways to get your creative juices pumping.

1 We each have an inner critic. She squints over our shoulders and tells us our work isn't as good as someone else's. Tell that chick to buzz off!

2 Store torn magazine pages, color swatches, photographs and other inspirations in a creativity idea binder. It can be your greatest source of inspiration.

3 Remember all the things that make up you and your life. Kids, family and careers pull at you and your time. Sometimes you're just too tired to be creative. Accept the fact that some layouts won't be masterpieces. Or, gently give yourself a time-out from scrapping.

4 Creativity comes from keeping perspective. Twenty years from now, family members won't care which paper or button you used on your layout. They'll love that you took the time to record your fondest memories, so enjoy the process.

5 Don't feel like you can't take time for yourself unless your house is immaculate. The laundry doesn't have to be folded for you to create!

6 If you're in a scrapping funk, pull out your albums and just enjoy them. It may give you the inspiration you need to see how much you've already accomplished.

Creativity In Your Head

7 Walk away! When you're in the middle of a layout and something isn't working, leave the room for a few minutes. Go for a walk. Observe the world around you. When you come back the answer may be staring you in the face. Or, sleep on it, and in the morning your page will tell you what it needs, if anything. That's how this layout about my daughter, Olivia, came together.

8 Try a completely new-to-you craft project. Make a bookmark with polymer clay, sew a pillow or decorate a candle. The act of doing something different will fuel your creativity.

9 Remember, you're scrapbooking for yourself and your family. You don't have to keep up with the Joneses. Do what makes you happy, and your family will thank you for it.

Page by Allison Strine. **Supplies** *Patterned papers*: Allison's own designs; *Rubber stamps*: Hampton Art Stamps (lines) and Catslife Press (diamonds); *Stamping ink*: Ancient Page, Clearsnap; *Negative strip and beaded trim*: Creative Imaginations; *Acrylic paint*: DecoArt; *Computer font*: Courier New, Microsoft Word.

HoW To Make
a HaPPY FaMiLY #48

love

Go to the neighborhood egg hunt together.

Wall art by Allison Strine. **Supplies** *Patterned papers and epoxy stickers: Sandra Magsamen, Creative Imaginations.*

10 Whether you work on your dining room table, in a corner or even a closet, why not call it your studio? The word "studio" makes me think of artistic freedom, and that's what you want on your pages, right?

11 Try scrapbooking at different times of the day. Getting out of a rut may surprise you.

12 Your mother doesn't work at your desk. When you put down a coffee cup, a magazine or a pen, it will sit there until you put it away. Stuff on your desk interferes with your ability to create, so declutter your space!

13 There's no rule saying you have to keep every item you've ever purchased. Too many supplies can be overwhelming. Sort through your stuff and make a pile to give away or "fling." You'll bless someone else with supplies and grace your creative space with room to breathe. (Visit *www.flylady.net* for more ways to free yourself by flinging and blessing.

Your Creative Space

14 Fill your studio with art that makes you feel creative. Better yet, use your supplies to create wall art that makes you happy.

15 Different styles of music will affect you in various ways. To set the mood for a specific layout, try a unique flavor of music, such as classical, jazz or country.

16 Surround your workspace with inspirational quotes. Read them and believe in them. (I've listed some of my favorite quotes on page 37.)

17 Paint your room. In color therapy, orange is the color for creativity. Yellow promotes knowledge and learning. Purple represents inspiration and spirituality. (Don't miss the fun color-tool tip on page 116.)

18 Go to a card store and browse the cards for inspiration. Look at design elements, colors and textures. Remember, if your kid touches a card with gooey chocolate hands, even if it's a cat sympathy card you have to buy it! (Just a friendly reminder—I'm sure this would never happen in real life.)

19 Punch a 1" hole in the center of a 3" x 4" piece of cardboard. Take your new image finder on a walk. Looking through the hole forces you to lose context and lets you focus on small areas with a new eye for detail.

20 Watch TV commercials. Pay attention to font choices and color combinations. Jot down sketch ideas in your idea binder.

21 Look at clothing with an eye for color and pattern. Go to a fabric store and view the different fabric designs and patterns. Get samples!

22 Use your five senses to notice everything that's around you.

23 Analyze a professional garden, art gallery or museum for design, shape and color ideas.

Laurie Keller's *The Scrambled States of America* is a catchy example of how a book cover can inspire a clever title treatment.

24 Kids' books have a surplus of inspiration! Whether the book is a baby book with bold colors or a child's picture book, it can incite creativity for your scrapbooking.

25 Reduce scrapper's block by typing up a list of your supplies, then brainstorming techniques that can use those supplies. Cut the list into strips and put it into a creativity jar. Pull out a few strips at a time and use the ideas on a layout.

Quotable Inspiration

Awaken your creativity by posting inspiring quotes all over your house. Here are some of my favorites:

Be thankful for mistakes. They may lead you to solutions you never would have discovered before.
—*Marilyn Hughey Phillis*

All children are artists. The problem is how to remain an artist once he grows up.
—*Pablo Picasso*

There would be no universe without creativity and in my little world, it's a must.
—*Juanita Williams*

Imagination is more important than knowledge.
—*Albert Einstein*

Creativity requires the courage to let go of certainties.
—*Erich Fromm*

The best way to have a good idea is to have a lot of ideas.
—*Linus Pauling*

An avalanche begins with a snowflake.
—*Joseph Compton*

Shoot for the moon. Even if you miss it you will land among the stars.
—*Les Brown*

You will do foolish things, but do them with enthusiasm.
—*Colette*

There is nothing In a caterpillar that tells you it's going to be a butterfly.
—*Buckminster Fuller*

---

26 Join and participate in a scrapbooking web site. Don't just lurk! Include yourself in challenges and swaps. You'll make friends and unearth new techniques. You don't have to be "good" or "creative." Just do it!

27 Use Internet search engines to find other artistic souls. Look up "paper artists," "poets," "dancers" or "potters." Get lost in someone else's creative endeavors.

Creativity in the Community

28 For layout topic ideas and journaling helps, answer one of those surveys your friends send you via e-mail. (Or see page 46 for our fun list.)

29 Attend a group crop and sit next to a happy person.

30 Spark creativity by shopping! Look with a discerning eye at the products you love. Why do you like them? What inspires you about them?

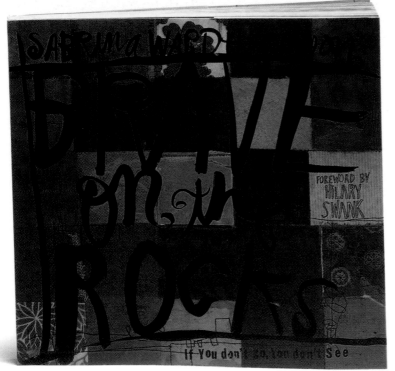

Go for a bold text presentation like that on *Brave on the Rocks* by Sabrina Ward Harrison.

31 Pull out your photos and write down your thoughts about them. Be guided by what your heart responds to in the photos. Don't worry about grammar or the person who might see what you've written. Just jot down the first feelings that come to your mind and write to your heart's content.

32 Sign up to receive a word of the day by e-mail. Who knows—you might find yourself using "forsooth" in your journaling! Check out *www.dictionary.com*, *www.wordsmith.org* and *www.m-w.com* for ideas.

33 Improve your journaling with a thesaurus. I like *www.thesaurus.com*.

In Your Words

34 For a fun way to wake up your brain, open a dictionary and write down the first word you find. Brainstorm 10 words that your word makes you think of.

35  For imaginative title ideas, visit *www.rhymezone.com*.

36 Play with your words. Quickly write down 20 random words. Do it again, then write your journaling. The results may surprise you.

37 Doodle like crazy! While one side of your brain is on the phone, let the other side doodle on a note pad.

Inspiring Literature

Immerse yourself in the creativity of other people and the muse will follow. Here's a list of some of my favorite creativity books:

The Artist's Way by Julia Cameron
True Colors by Somerset Studio Publication
Celebrate Your Creative Self by Mary Todd Beam
Living Out Loud by Keri Smith
Spilling Open by Sabrina Ward Harrison
Living Juicy: Daily Morsels for Your Creative Soul by Sark
Brave on the Rocks by Sabrina Ward Harrison
Artists' Journals & Sketchbooks by Lynne Perrella
Creative Sketches for Scrapbooking by Becky Higgins

Creativity on Your Layout

38 Take a class at your local scrapbook store. Or, take any kind of class, even if it's not scrap-related. Who cares if you'll never use stained glass on your page? Treat yourself to an education.

39 Use your supplies! We're all familiar with the "this is too cool to use" syndrome. Be brave and use that favorite item.

40 Create a card. You'll make someone else feel good, and you'll fire up those creative juices.

41 Play a game with yourself. Set a timer and force yourself to complete a page in the allotted time. Remember to have fun with the challenge!

42 Shake up the order in which you work. If you usually journal first, start with pictures.

43 Look at your past layouts. Which ones do you love and why? Part of your journey toward discovering your creative self is learning what you like about what you did before.

44 For your next layout, limit yourself to using just five supplies. See how quickly you can work when you're not bombarded with hordes of supplies.

45 Scraplift with authority! Look through your favorite issue of CK for ideas. Nothing spurs creativity like working from the balance, color choices and themes of a layout you admire.

46 Browse a favorite scrapbooking idea book, and choose one item from each of several layouts. Combine color schemes, photo placement, products and embellishments to make your own page.

Card by Allison Strine. **Supplies** *Patterned paper:* Wordsworth; *Rubber stamps:* Catslife Press (sentiment) and Stampa Rosa (heart); *Stamping ink:* Ancient Page, Clearsnap; *Polymer clay:* Premo! Sculpey, Polyform Products; *Acrylic paint:* DecoArt; *Metallic acrylic paint:* Lumiere, Jacquard Products.

Mini book by Allison Strine. **Supplies** Patterned papers and stickers: Wordsworth.

47 Give yourself a real kick start by scrapping for someone else. There's nothing like a gift album deadline to get those creative juices flowing.

48 Swap photos with another scrapbooker. Scrap her photos and see what a great job she does with yours.

49 Make a list of techniques you want to try. Create a layout (or card) with the top three things on the list.

50 To make more time for scrapping, set a timer and work on a page for 10 minutes at a time (you don't have to finish it!). You have 10 minutes, don't you? ♥

10 TEN DAYS to better JOURNALING

Take steps to improve your writing

I'm a visual person who has to make lists. In fact, I have a white board that covers a large portion of one wall in my office. It's filled with blue, black, red and green marks indicating things I need to do, people I need to call, places I need to go, deadlines I need to meet. You get the idea. As I finish each item, I get such a sense of satisfaction from erasing it from the board. →

BY TRACY WHITE

PHOTO © ANTHONY REDPATH / CORBIS

Our lives are busy. Whether you're a working mom, a doting grandma, or just starting out in a career, you have plenty of activities to fill your life. Journaling your scrapbook pages shouldn't be just another thing on your list of things to do. Rather, if you're like me, it should be something you look forward to—a way to escape your hectic, fast-paced life.

With that in mind, I've come up with 10 fun writing prompts to help you get those creative writing juices flowing. When you've got some time to scrap, sit down with this list of ideas and tell yourself, "Today, I'm going to have fun journaling my pages."

DAY 1: *Ask "Why am I scrapbooking this?"*
Every year, we scrap a lot of the same subjects—holidays, birthdays, back to school and more. Ask yourself what makes this year's events different from every other year. Write down your answers!

By taking inventory of why a particular subject or event is important, you'll journal much more purposefully.

DAY 2: *Really get to know someone.*
People come and go in our lives, but families are here to stay. Sit down with a family member and really get to know that person. Pay attention to body movements, emotions and tone. Use the following questions to help start your conversation. (For more interview ideas, see Day 8.)

• What's your favorite holiday memory?
• What's your earliest childhood remembrance?
• What is your most treasured possession?
• What do you want to be when you "grow up"? (Trust me, this question works for any age. I'm still trying to figure this one out!)

It must be hard to be the younger sibling, but since I do not have any older siblings, I cannot fully understand. But watching Claire stand so very still and quiet as Jackson learned to ride his new bike for the first time, I was in awe of this relationship. It seemed so sad that she was left behind and left only to watch as Jackson enjoyed his new toy... But when I looked closer I saw that he was watching her. Watching for his baby sister, making sure that she was paying attention, making sure that she knew that it was okay with him for her to continue

...to follow

Pages by Carrie Owens. **Supplies** *Textured cardstock:* Bazzill Basics Paper; *Pen:* Zig Millennium, EK Success.

Carrie journaled about her daughter's reaction to watching her older brother learn to ride a bike. When she started talking about the layout, however, Carrie shared the following (then later included it as hidden journaling on this layout):

"As I look at these photos of you, I can't help but see how much you've grown up. You're just over a year and a half old. So tall and grown up for your age, yet still so young. You look as if you should be headed off to school, not on a walk around the block. I love seeing you in that little coat, passed down to you from Jackson.

"Your little tights and clunky shoes remind me of being a girl. I hope that you will love wearing dresses and tights as much as I did when I was young. These photos are so much more to me than just pictures of you and Jack in the cold. I see your cheeks bright red from the crisp air, your wispy hair up in a ponytail that I'm surprised is still intact. I see that I opted not to put a hat on you . . . probably not the wisest choice in the snow. And I see my little girl, fresh into toddlerhood, already looking like a little girl."

DAY 3: *Pick up your pen and free write.*

Writer's block. It happens to all of us, doesn't it? When I'm stumped for the right words, I pick up my pen and just start writing about whatever comes to mind. It can be as zany or as serious as I feel. Try these journaling jump-starts and write as many details as you can. Just remember to tell *why* you answered the way you did.

• My scariest moment was . . .
• My goal in life is . . .
• I feel like a little kid again when I . . .
• If I were a color, I would be . . .
• I am inspired by . . .

DAY 4: *Record different perspectives.*

My sister and I can recall the same event very differently. Ask your loved ones about their perspectives of those shared events. What do loved ones have to say? Here are a few ideas for events you might ask about:

• A family wedding
• Birth of a child
• A memorable historical event, such as September 11, the day President Kennedy was assassinated or when the Challenger exploded.

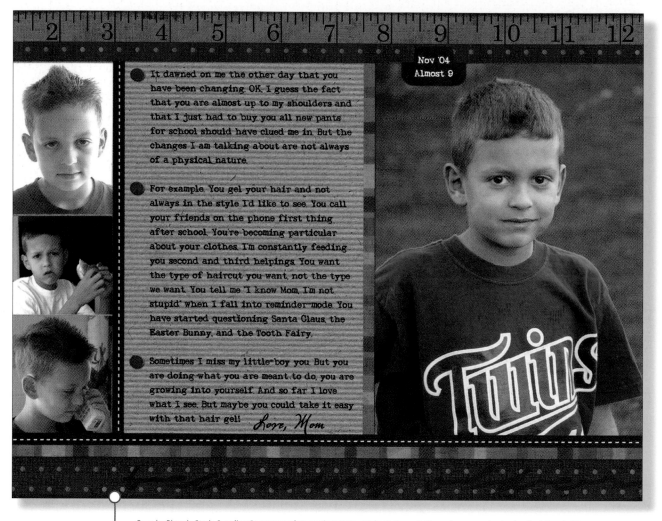

Page by Rhonda Stark. **Supplies** *Computer software:* Photoshop, Adobe Systems; *Patterned papers, ruler, brads, clip, ink and ribbon:* Gina Cabrera, *www.digitaldesignessentials.com; Computer fonts:* 2Peas Hot Chocolate, downloaded from the web site *www.twopeasinabucket.com;* CBX-Scriptorium, "Journaling Fonts" CD, Chatterbox; CK Maternal, "Heritage, Vintage & Retro Collection" CD, *Creating Keepsakes.*

Rhonda spent some time thinking about her son and the changes he's going through. She journaled her thoughts, then chose pictures to complement the journaling.

DAY 5: *Tell the "rest of the story."*

We create scrapbooks for other people to enjoy, right? Invite a friend over, pull out your albums and share them with her. Your goal is to keep talking. Yes, that's right—if you feel compelled to tell her more about a layout than what's written on the page, you've left something out of your journaling. Write down those thoughts and find a way to include them on your page. Or, slip the printed text into the sheet protector, behind your page.

DAY 6: *Read and analyze your journaling.*

OK, take a break from writing today. Instead, sit down with your scrapbooks and read your journaling. What does it say about you? Take inventory of what you like and don't like about your journaling style. Set a goal to work on one aspect.

Pages by Marie Hazzard. **Supplies** *Textured cardstock:* Bazzill Basics Paper; *Patterned paper:* BasicGrey; *Letter stickers:* Chatterbox and American Crafts; *Brads:* Happy Hammer; *Ribbon:* Making Memories; *Rub-ons:* Chatterbox and KI Memories; *Stencil numbers:* Ma Vinci's Reliquary; *Bookplate:* KI Memories; *Computer font:* AmerType, downloaded from the Internet.

Marie's mom died when Marie was just a little girl. She made a list of things she'd like to ask her mom, then scrapbooked this layout about a family phrase.

What was the biggest change in your lifetime?

What's your preference? Homemade dinner or fancy restaurant?

DAY 7: *Journal first, then add photos.*
We usually choose our pictures and then write about them. Instead of letting your photos tell most of the story on your page, make them work for your journaling. Write what your heart tells you to write, then choose and arrange your photos to support the journaling.

DAY 8: *Fill in the blanks.*
If you have an e-mail account, no doubt you've been sent lists of questions to answer and forward to your friends. (See our list on pages 46-47) From silly to serious, think about the reasons behind your answers, then write them down.

DAY 9: *K.I.S.S. and focus.*

Keep It Simple, Silly! We've talked about including the rest of the story. Now, let's reverse the process. Find one point about your layout that you want to talk about. For example, if you have park pictures, instead of talking about the slide *and* the swings *and* the climbing wall *and* the picnic *and* feeding the ducks, pick just one subject and focus your journaling on that one aspect.

DAY 10: *Dip into a journaling jar.*

Are there questions you wish you could ask a deceased relative, such as a great-grandmother or another significant person in your life? Write those questions on slips of paper, then store them in a jar.

When you're stumped for ideas, pull out a question and create a layout about yourself that answers the question. You'll ensure that your great-granddaughter knows the answers about you. Here are a few suggestions to get you started:

- What is your favorite recipe?
- What is your favorite family tradition?
- What appliance could you not live without? Or, what is your favorite invention that makes your day-to-day life easier?
- Who inspires you?
- What are your talents?

If you have an e-mail account, no doubt you've been sent lists of questions to answer and forward to your friends. From silly to serious, think about the reasons behind your answers, then write them down.

STATISTICS

- What is your full name as it appears on your birth certificate?
- How old are you today?
- What is your true hair color?
- Where were you born?
- What's your mother's maiden name?
- What is your eye color?
- Do you have a tattoo?
- Do you have scars? How did you get them?
- Do you have any nicknames?
- How many body piercings do you have?
- What are your children's names?
- If you could dye your hair any color, what color would it be?
- Were you named after anyone?
- What is your shoe size?
- How many wisdom teeth do you have?
- Do you wear contacts, glasses or neither?
- Do you have siblings? What are their names and ages?
- Where do you live?
- If you could have chosen your name, what would it have been?

SENSORY OVERLOAD

- What is your favorite smell?
- What are your favorite sounds?
- What do you do to vent anger?
- What smell do you consider the vilest?
- What makes you angry?
- What makes you happy?
- When was the last time you cried?
- What is the worst feeling in the world?
- What do you do to prevent anger?
- What kind of sense of humor do you have?
- If you were a crayon, what color would you be?
- What are you afraid of?
- Do you use sarcasm?

ON LOCATION

- How many states have you visited?
- How many countries have you visited?
- Where is your favorite relaxation destination?
- Where is your favorite place to relax?
- What is your favorite restaurant?
- Where is your least favorite place to be?
- If you could live anywhere in the world, where would it be?

- Where is your ideal vacation?
- Where would you like to retire?
- Do you prefer the beach, city or country?
- How many states have you lived in?
- How many cities have you lived in?
- How many countries have you lived in?
- Where's the place you've lived in the longest and how long was it?
- Where is your home away from home?

FOOD FANCIES
- What is your favorite drink?
- What is your favorite food?
- Do you prefer soup or salad?
- Do you prefer chocolate or vanilla?
- Do you prefer plain, buttered or salted popcorn?
- What is your favorite ice cream flavor?
- What is your favorite snack food?
- What is your favorite cookie?
- What are your favorite comfort foods?
- What is your favorite lunchmeat?
- What is your favorite sandwich?
- Do you prefer Coke or Pepsi?
- Do you prefer hamburgers or sushi?

MEDIA PLAY
- What is your favorite book?
- What is your favorite type of music?
- Who is your favorite Disney character?
- What is your favorite TV show?
- What is your favorite magazine?
- What is your favorite board game?
- What are your favorite children's books?
- What is your favorite cartoon?
- What is your favorite genre of book?
- If you were a Disney character, which one would you be?
- What is the last CD you bought?
- What book are you currently reading?
- What is the most embarrassing CD on your shelf?
- What is the last movie you watched at home? At the theater?
- Do you prefer scary movies or chick flicks?
- Do you prefer movies that make you think or ones with happy endings?

A FEW OF MY FAVORITE THINGS
- What is your favorite sport to play?
- What is your favorite sport to watch?
- What is your favorite car?
- What is your favorite flower?
- What is your favorite animal?
- What is your favorite word or phrase?
- What is your favorite restaurant?
- Do you prefer a car or an SUV?
- Are you a morning person or a night owl?
- Do you prefer gold or silver?
- What is your favorite fast food restaurant?
- What is your favorite brand of clothing?
- What is your favorite article of clothing?
- Where is your favorite place to be?
- Do you prefer cats or dogs?
- Do you prefer blue or black ink pens?

THE LITTLE THINGS IN LIFE
- What is most important in your life?
- How many keys do you have on your key ring?
- What time do you go to bed?
- Have you ever been in a car crash?
- What was your first car?
- What color is your bedroom carpet?
- What color is your bathroom?
- What do you do when you are most bored?
- What is the first thing you think of when you wake up in the morning?
- Do you have any bad habits?
- Are you a daredevil?
- Can you swim?
- Do you have a journal?
- Which laundry detergent do you use?
- Who would you hate to be stuck in a room with?
- Do you love your job?
- Have you ever been toilet papering?
- Do you sing in the shower?
- Do you sing in the car?
- What's your most embarrassing moment?
- If there was an emergency and you could rescue only one thing from your home, what would it be?

30 ways to INDULGE Your Scrapping PASSION

Give yourself the perfect gift this year *by Leslie Miller*

in the words of actress Sarah Jessica Parker, "Every once in a while, a girl has to indulge herself." I agree! And isn't that what scrapbooking does? It lets us indulge our creativity, our memories and our selves.

This year, don't forget that perfect gift to self— indulging in your passion. You deserve to be pampered, too! Here are 30 suggestions — you'll even see how much time to allot for them!

30 minutes

▶ Choose a subject and spend 30 minutes taking as many photos as you can. Keep that camera moving. Commit to scrapping only the three best photos.

▶ Spend 15 minutes looking through your favorite non-scrapbook-related magazine at ads and other design ideas. Take another 15 minutes to write down as many ideas as possible in your sketchbook. Include page topics, possible color combinations and composition ideas. The next time you sit down to scrap, all of your ideas will be ready for you.

▶ Scraplift a layout from your favorite scrapbook artist. Consider what makes you love his or her style.

▶ Make a list of all the things (techniques, products and more) you want to try on a scrapbook page.

▶ Call one of your scrapbooking friends and chat about recent "discoveries" you've made. Discuss new products, the current issue of *Creating Keepsakes* or your favorite layouts.

"I love soaking in a hot bath—with or without bubbles—with the latest magazine or idea book in hand. At other times I pull out older idea books and rediscover them."

—Wendy Sue Anderson, Frequent Contributor

"On occasion I grab my sketchbook, drop Tyler at school and head straight to Barnes & Noble. I look at the magazines first, then the design/architecture and children's books. The bright colors and bold graphics in children's books always inspire me. Last, I head to a favorite restaurant, request a quiet table or booth, and sketch and write to my heart's delight!"

—Faye Morrow Bell, CK Contributing Editor

2 hours

▶ Make accents without a thought of where you'll put them. Just play and have fun. File those accents away for use on future pages.

▶ Register for and take a class at your local scrapbook store.

▶ Shut the door and turn the music up—then scrap according to the mood the music puts you in. Don't worry about what you "should" be doing.

▶ Create a page without photos or a page without journaling (whichever strikes your fancy). See if you can tell your story effectively.

▶ Wander through your local shopping center, paying attention to only the things below eye level. Look for patterns, textures and colors.

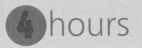

4 hours

- Make a "scrap date" with one of your kids. During that time together, scrap just photos of him or her. Listen to music and eat favorite snacks. Let your child tell stories about what he or she remembers from the photos or share what you remember from them.

- Take a field trip to your local botanical garden or park. Pay attention to color combinations and shapes that could inspire pages.

- Commit to sorting through your scrap supplies and making a "favorites" area in your scrap space.

- Buy an organizational tool (such as a file caddy) to keep better track of your scrapbook supplies. Spend a whole evening sorting and organizing. You might be surprised at the forgotten treasures you find.

- Hire a babysitter and lock yourself in your scrap room, away from the worries of the "outside world."

- Work on a mini album as a nice break from the full-sized projects you normally do.

"My one indulgence is to walk away and do something else, like quilt. Working with fabric helps relax my mind and gives me ideas for layouts or designs."

—Allison Kimball, 2004 Hall of Fame

8 hours

- Collect photos you love from magazines, ads or friends. Spend the afternoon doing a photo shoot to re-create one of your favorite pictures.

- Get messy! Try the cool techniques you've been avoiding because of the mess involved. Create scrapbook pages, cards and other paper crafts at the same time. It will all be worth the cleanup in the end!

- Organize a neighborhood party. Invite friends and neighbors to bring their favorite photos (and some supplies if they're scrapbookers). As the kids play together and the adults talk, share the stories of your favorite photos and scrap a layout together.

- Gather your scrapbooking friends for a crop/praise party. Look at and admire each other's work and get great new ideas!

- As a twist on the typical crop, meet with scrapbooking friends and "analyze" each other's styles. Point out scrapbooking strengths and what you admire on each page. Swap photos and scrapbook each other's pictures according to your own strengths.

 eekend

▶ Register for and attend a CKU session or other scrapbooking retreat.

▶ Organize your own scrap retreat with friends. Choose a local hotel or community center where you can reserve a room and leave your equipment out and set up for the entire time you're there.

▶ Send your family on a weekend "getaway," then scrap away. Order in your favorite foods, work in your pajamas and do whatever strikes your fancy.

▶ Dedicate two days to "remodeling" your scrap space. Organize your supplies. Paint your room a new and inspiring color. You'll be amazed at how refreshed you are when items are organized and your space is "new."

"Every once in a while, a girl has to indulge herself!"

—Sarah Jessica Parker, actress

"On occasion, my scrapping buddies and I go on a scrapbooking road trip. We pack an over- night bag and hit the road for Atlanta or New Orleans. We shop at unfamiliar stores and find new things along the way. The best part is spending time together, sharing laughter and catching up on each other's lives while the miles pass."

—Brenda Arnall, CK Contributing Editor ♥

"My favorite indulgence is a nap. Thinking as I drift off to sleep always results in great ideas."

—Jennifer McGuire,
2002 Hall of Fame

Collect and compile magazine clippings, quotes and notes that inspire you in your very own "idea book." Notice how Kelly altered a college viewbook and transformed it into an artful resource of design concepts.

Inspiration Book by Kelly Anderson. **Supplies** *Rub-ons:* Making Memories; *Letter stickers:* Sticker Studio; *Stickers:* Pebbles Inc.; *Bubble number and letter stickers:* Creative Imaginations; *Tag:* Avery; *Pens:* Gelly Roll, Sakura (white) and Zig Millennium, EK Success; *Computer font:* Garamouche, P22 Type Foundry; *Other:* College viewbook.

10 THINGS I'VE LEARNED ABOUT SCRAPBOOKING

Relax with these simple truths

Aren't "a-ha" moments priceless? The hair stands up on your neck, your heart beats a little faster and you *finally* get it! Just discovering the art of scrapbooking was a watershed moment for me. At last, all the hobbies and interests I'd developed over the years were aligned. Everything "fit."

As I've worked, played and experimented in my studio, I've had several "a-ha" moments as I've discovered one truth after another. Here's what I've learned about scrapbooking. →

BY FAYE MORROW BELL

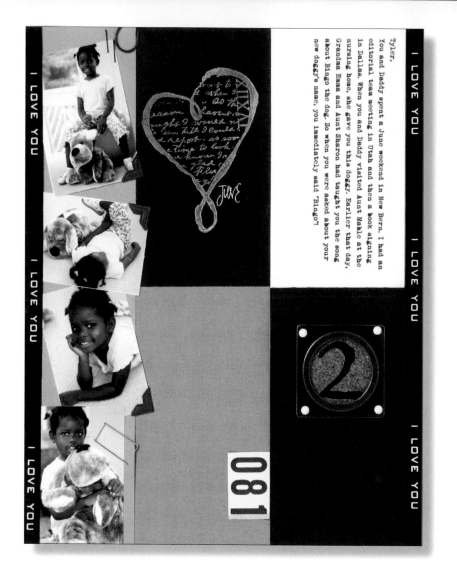

Page by Faye Morrow Bell. **Supplies**
Textured cardstock: Bazzill Basics Paper;
Word rub-ons and ribbon: Making
Memories; *Photo corner:* Canson; *Brads:*
Doodlebug Design; *Rubber stamp:* EK
Success; *Stamping ink:* Stampin' Up!;
Bookplate: Li'l Davis Designs; *Computer
font:* CK Typewriter, "Fresh Fonts" CD,
Creating Keepsakes; Other: Paper clip
and staples.

When I analyze my style, I
see that I use some of
these elements on almost
every layout:

- One or two photos
- Black-and-white photos
- Dimensional
  embellishments
- Patterned text paper
- Fonts and lettering
- Something green
- Rubber stamps
- Ribbon or twill
- Metal accents
- Muted colors
- Cardstock

1 We each have a scrapbooking style, whether we know it or not.

What do Audrey Hepburn, Ansel Adams or
Nancy Reagan have in common? They each have
a definitive style. Audrey helped make "the little
black dress" popular, while Ansel became famous
for his black-and-white photography of natural
landscapes. Nancy Reagan? She's known for her
love of the color red.

Style is not a mysterious phenomenon. It's
about originality and consistency. Think about a
scrapbook artist whose style you admire. If you
look closely, you'll notice that what you admire
most is his or her repeated, consistent use of certain design elements.

To "excavate" your own scrapbooking style:
- Invite over a few friends. (They can be scrapbookers or not—the latter could be preferable!)
- On a table, spread out six layouts you've
completed in the past three months.
- Ask your friends what elements they see repeated in your work. Take notes!

The elements and techniques you use consistently represent your core scrapbooking style.
You repeat them because you like them and are
comfortable using them. Experiment with combining these elements and techniques to create a
scrapbooking style that is uniquely your own.

June 10, 2002
You did the cutest thing this afternoon! As we were sitting at a traffic light, a couple of birds were flying and circling just over the car. When you saw their flapping wings, you started to laugh and wave your hand "bye-bye" because you thought they were waving at you!

You also learned that you can reach the doorknobs if you really, really, really stretch. We have plantation shutters throughout the house. We also have them on the french doors in the family room. Well today you pulled yourself up to standing by holding on to the shutters on the french doors and you got on your tippy toes and tried to turn the knob! You were really proud of yourself!

Tuesday
June 11, 2002
You ate cheese for the first time. We have a block of Land O'lakes Mild cheddar. I cut a few small pieces for you which you enjoyed.

Grandma Morrow had a toy phone for you. It's a cellular type phone with realistic ringing sounds. And when you push the buttons, they beep like a real phone. Everytime your phone would "ring", you would put it against my ear so that I could answer it!

Daddy received his first Father's Day card today from Aunt Dorothy.

Wednesday
June 12, 2002
FINALLY!!! Today felt like your first full "normal" day (in terms of waking, napping, eating, temperment, etc.) in about than 3 weeks! I think you've finally recovered from Nicky's visit, getting your finger fractured, traveling to New Bern and Emerald Isle and then dealing with the 3-finger splint!

We grilled hamburgers this evening, so you had an opportunity to sit on the deck. You are so content to sit on our laps and look and point and babble about the airplanes overhead, the birds flying by and twittering in the trees, and the leaves moving on all of the trees.

I've been meaning to note that you now say "fish". It's usually just "sh" or sometimes "ish", but we know what you're saying!!

Thursday
June 13, 2002
Daddy tried to put you in the grass for the first time today. You were OK with standing on the grass, but when he tried to sit you down, you weren't quite so sure!

Your bedtime routine has become a special time for us. You're such a brave and independent little girl, that you've never been big on snuggling and cuddling during the day. You'd much rather observe and explore. But bedtime is different. I take you upstairs and we sit in the rocker where you like to cuddle and kiss/lick my face. Then I undress you (in the rocker). I put you on the changing table to change your diaper and put on your sleeper. Typically you're fairly sleepy, so I just put kiss you goodnight and put you down for the evening. Occasionally, I'll rock you a little more to help get you drowsy

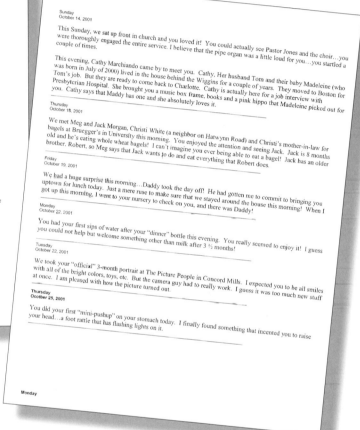

Sunday
October 14, 2001
This Sunday, we sat up front in church and you loved it! You could actually see Pastor Jones and the choir...you were thoroughly engaged the entire service. I believe that the pipe organ was a little loud for you...you startled a couple of times.

This evening, Cathy Marchiando came by to meet you. Cathy, Her husband Tom and their baby Madeleine (who was born in July of 2000) lived in the house behind the Wiggins for a couple of years. They moved to Boston for Tom's job. But they are ready to come back to Charlotte. Cathy is actually here for a job interview with Presbyterian Hospital. She brought you a music box frame, books and a pink hippo that Madeleine picked out for you. Cathy says that Maddy has one and she absolutely loves it.

Thursday
October 18, 2001
We met Meg and Jack Morgan, Christi White (a neighbor on Hatwynn Road) and Christi's mother-in-law for bagels at Bruegger's in University this morning. You enjoyed the attention and seeing Jack. Jack is 8 months old and he's eating whole wheat bagels! I can't imagine you ever being able to eat a bagel! Jack has an older brother, Robert, so Meg says that Jack wants to do and eat everything that Robert does.

Friday
October 19, 2001
We had a huge surprise this morning...Daddy took the day off! He had gotten me to commit to bringing you uptown for lunch today. Just a mere ruse to make sure that we stayed around the house this morning! When I got up this morning, I went to your nursery to check on you, and there was Daddy!

Monday
October 22, 2001
You had your first sips of water after your "dinner" bottle this evening. You really seemed to enjoy it! I guess you could not help but welcome something other than milk after 3 ½ months!

Tuesday
October 22, 2001
We took your "official" 3-month portrait at The Picture People in Concord Mills. I expected you to be all smiles with all of the bright colors, toys, etc. But the camera guy had to really work. I guess it was too much new stuff at once. I am pleased with how the picture turned out.

Thursday
Occtber 25, 2001
You did your first "mini-pushup" on your stomach today. I finally found something that incented you to raise your head...a foot rattle that has flashing lights on it.

Monday

Keep a simple text file with notations of date and event.

2 If we spent as much time organizing our journaling as we do our photos and supplies, we would never be at a loss for words.

I'll never forget my daughter Tyler's response when I asked about her first day of school. "We had cookies, Mommy," she cheerily replied. You might think I'd never forget Tyler's words because they were sweet, but I'll never forget them because *I recorded the words in my online journal.*

Most of us have systems for storing our photos, supplies and design ideas. But how about a system for storing our journaling? Our written memories are certainly worth it! Because I spend a fair amount of time at my computer, I organize my journaling in a Microsoft Word text file. I simply enter the date and an account of the event I want to recall later. Your system can be as simple as a $.99 composition book or an index-card system.

Here are pages from a June 2002 journal and an October 2002 journal. While I haven't scrapbooked all of the events referenced, the beauty is that I can include any or all of these memories in my scrapbook if and when I choose.

TOGETHER

December 2003

We had such a wonderful holiday in New Bern this Christmas season. We were excited that my mother joined us. Last year was the first that she went with us to New Bern. It was also the first time in lots of years that George and I BOTH saw our mothers on Christmas day.

George and I are so fortunate to both have such great mothers. When we got married, we never expected that our mothers would become friends and develop a relationship separate from us! Although it was really strange at first to learn about things happening in New Bern

through my mother who had talked to George's mother! But we wouldn't change a thing. And I can't begin to write how excited Tyler is when she has both of her Grandma's together. We hope my mother joining us in New Bern is the beginning of a tradition.

Page by Faye Morrow Bell. **Supplies** *Textured cardstock:* Bazzill Basics Paper; *Computer fonts:* Arial, Microsoft Word; Plastique, downloaded from the Internet; *Other:* Ribbon.

3 Not every layout has to be a masterpiece.

As much as I love designing layouts, the thought of "original design schemes," "extreme art techniques" and "extensive, heartfelt journaling" can be daunting! Some days I'd rather *create* a layout than *design* one. That's when I turn to my "standard format" layouts. I can add custom touches but avoid the pressure of design decisions.

The page here is adapted from an interior design magazine. Following my standard format, I kept the same basic structure but varied the elements. In the title, for example, I changed the font to match the mood of the layout. Although I've used this format for other layouts, the title is always in the same position.

The break between the top and bottom of the page is perfect for a simple embellishment. Sometimes I use ribbon or label tape. Other times I use a row of buttons or bookplates.

"'So me day' is here... ...your Prince has come." 06.07.03

... Ken whispered in my ear minutes after being married...

Jennifer McGuire uses a standard format page for her favorite photos. Says Jennifer, "Whenever I have a favorite horizontal or vertical photo, I enlarge it to 11" x 14" and crop one side to 12". After placing the photo on my page, I add interest by varying the technique along the photo's edge. Here, I layered lots of ribbons."

Page by Jennifer McGuire. **Supplies** *Computer font:* AL Singsong, downloaded from the Internet; *Other:* Ribbon and fibers.

two (tōō), n. 1. a cardinal number, 1 plus 1. 2. a symbol for this number, as 2 or II. 3. a set of this many persons or things. 4. a playing card, die face, or half of a domino face with two pips. 5. in two, into two separate parts as halves. 6. amounting to two in number.

O F f 2 School

Brecken and Chanelle have been peas in a pod since they met. The girls were so excited about their first day of school this fall. And how could they not be? Armed with new backpacks, fresh ponytails, and hearts full of joy and wonder, this year promises to be their best ever!

Pages by Faye Morrow Bell. **Supplies** *Canvas letters and metal accent:* Li'l Davis Designs; *Ribbon, jump ring and foam stamp:* Making Memories; *Rickrack:* me & my BIG ideas; *Rubber stamps:* Postmodern Design; *Stamping ink:* VersaColor, Tsukineko; *Computer fonts:* Times New Roman, Microsoft Word; Bondi, downloaded from the Internet; *Other:* Brads.

4 Color doesn't have to be complicated. Who among us doesn't own a priceless photo with clashing colors? You know—the one with a child dressed in pink and purple sharing secrets with a friend who's dressed in green and orange. Well, I've learned a few tricks that can help you scrapbook these photos:

◆ *Visually "ground" colorful photos on a neutral background.* When Lisa Bearnson asked me to scrapbook a photo of her daughter and her daughter's best friend, pink papers were the obvious choice. Instead, the bright-colored papers proved a distraction. I opted for neutral colors to save design time and help direct people's eyes to the photos.

5 There are no rules for knowing when your layout is finished.

Scrapbooking is art, and like most artistic endeavors, there are no rules. Here are three ways I check what I've just created:

◆ I leave the layout out on my design island overnight. When I walk into my studio the next morning, I get a quick impression of my layout.

Sometimes the impression's good and sometimes it's bad, but I'm able to see my work with new clarity.

◆ I hold my layout at arm's length and squint. I'm always surprised at how this technique highlights imbalances or overly prominent elements.

◆ I take a digital photo for an objective and critical perspective. I can immediately see which areas need more work on my layouts.

Erin Lincoln used a similar approach to scrapbook photos of her family. Erin grounded the photos with a neutral color, then added color back with pink and orange accents.

◆ *Change the photos to black and white.* If the colors aren't an integral part of the mood and message, change them to black and white. I no longer sacrifice precious design time because Tyler's shirt clashes with her shorts!

Pages by Erin Lincoln. **Supplies** *Patterned paper:* Karen Foster Design; *Rub-ons:* Doodlebug Design; *Stamps:* Making Memories; *Stamping ink:* Stampin' Up!; *Stitching template:* Li'l Davis Designs; *Computer font:* 2Peas Tubby, downloaded from *www.two-peasinabucket.com; Other:* Floss and page tabs.

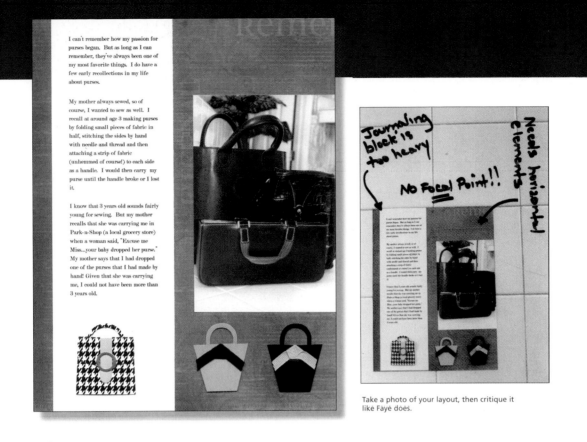

Take a photo of your layout, then critique it like Faye does.

6 Inspiration is everywhere.

Since I started scrapbooking, I literally see physical things differently. Are you ready to do the same? Watch for interesting colors, shapes, textures and sounds. Note how Rebecca VanDerGoot incorporated the metallic look of her father's lunchbox on the layout here.

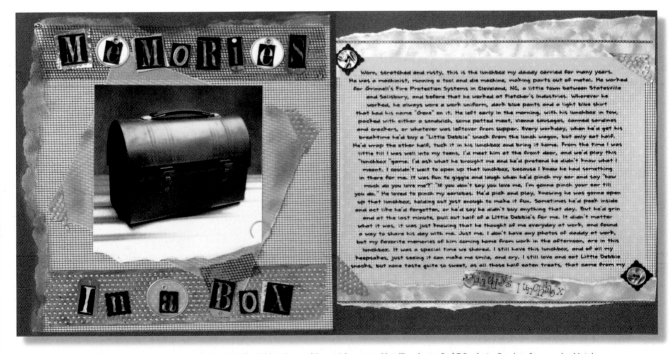

Pages by Rebecca VanDerGoot. **Supplies** *Patterned papers:* The Robin's Nest and Paper Adventures; *Metallic rub-ons:* Craf-T Products; *Conchos:* Scrapworks; *Metal-rimmed tags:* Making Memories and Office Depot; *Metal sheeting:* EK Success; *Drywall tape:* Home Depot; *Acrylic paint:* Delta Technical Coatings; *Border stickers:* me & my BIG ideas; *Letter stickers:* Provo Craft; *Metal plant tag:* Jest Charming; *Brads and eyelets:* Making Memories; *Silver leafing pen:* Krylon; *Computer fonts:* 2Peas Gift (title), downloaded from *www.twopeasinabucket.com*; LD Notepad (journaling), "Lettering Delights" CD, Inspire Graphics; *Other:* Vellum, nailheads, key ring, square fluted punches, metal buttons and heart brad.

Pages by Pam Kopka. **Supplies** *Watercolor paper:* Canson; *Beads:* Jewelry and Craft; *Foam stamps:* Making Memories; *Paint and silver pen:* American Craft; *Other:* Rhinestones and feathers.

7 Not every layout needs a photograph.

Too often we hear that a memory is only valid and page-worthy if a photo accompanies it. Not true! Here are three ways to scrapbook those "precious yet photo-less" memories:

◆ Use mixed-media techniques. Pam Kopka incorporated paint, a picture from a magazine, glitter and feathers.

◆ Include a *related* photo. For example, my friend Pansy helped me shop for my wedding gown. While I don't have pictures of our shopping experience, I can journal about the shopping and include a photo of my gown or a photo of Pansy and me taken at another time. *Note:* When scrapbooking this way, be sure to indicate the date of the photo and the date of the journaling.

◆ Use copyright-free collage clips and ephemera to embellish your layout.

8 Flowers, plaids and stripes can co-exist on one layout.

It's no secret that I love patterned text papers. But I also love them with bold stripes, hound's-tooth check prints and diamond patterns. The fun gets even better when I combine multiple patterns!

For the layout on page 63, Mellette Berezoski combined floral, stripe and "argyle" patterns. She used patterned papers with similar color values to add a cohesive feel. To keep her layout from feeling static, Mellette varied the size of the designs and the amounts of paper used.

To work successfully with multiple patterns:
◆ Use coordinated papers from one manufacturer to simplify the selection process.
◆ Vary the amount of each patterned paper. For example, use a "tablespoon" of one pattern, a

MAKE A DATE!

Want to discover and maintain your creativity? Use my favorite tool—the artist date—from the book *The Artist's Way* by Julia Cameron. Julia describes it this way:

"An artist date is a block of time, perhaps two hours weekly, especially set aside and committed to nurturing your creative consciousness, your inner artist. In its most primary form, the artist date is an excursion, a play date that you pre-plan and defend against all interlopers. You do not take anyone on this artist date but you and your inner artist, a.k.a. your creative child."

This is the time to nurture your creative self—to give it the undivided attention you afford other relationships. Here are six suggestions for play dates:

◆ Go for a walk in the park.
◆ Spend $10 in an art supply store.
◆ Attend a chamber music concert.
◆ Learn to play the harmonica.
◆ Play with paper dolls.
◆ Go ice-skating.

My dates have ranged from buying perfume to scouring magazines for inspiring images. The only rule is to listen to your inner artist and play. Your scrapbooks will thank you.

Now that you are a teenager, remember that

the **ATTITUDE** you carry will determine the

direction your life will take. Believe in

yourself, trust your instincts, and take

responsibility for every decision you make.

Maysie – at 13 · October 2004

Attitude is the palette
by which our lives
are painted.

happiness

Page by Mellette Berezoski. **Supplies** *Textured cardstock:* Bazzill Basics Paper; *Patterned papers:* Making Memories (stripes), KI Memories (plaid) and Bo-Bunny Press (floral); *Metal word tile, leather photo corner, paint, floss, brads, staples and metal rim tag:* Making Memories; *Embroidered letter:* Joy S.A. Inc.; *Quote:* KI Memories; *Ribbon:* Making Memories, Rusty Pickle and May Arts; *Ribbon charm:* Maya Road; *Flower pebble:* Pressed Petals; *Computer font:* Times New Roman, Microsoft Word; *Other:* Silk flowers and buttons.

"teaspoon" of a second and a "pinch" of a third.

◆ Limit the range of colors and vary the size of the patterns. If you use all large patterns, you may overwhelm your photos. If you use all small patterns, the layout may appear flat.

◆ Look for interesting pattern combinations in home design magazines. Note how interior designers always work with a minimum of three colors in a room.

◆ Play with your patterned papers, putting different styles and colors together to find the most pleasing combinations.

PRACTICE.

Practice. I know that's the only way to improve my handwriting! I just never seem to make the time. So, I'm caught in this circle of "I should include my handwriting" BUT "I don't care for my handwriting" so "I should practice" BUT IN THE MEANTIME "I should include my handwriting".... well, this layout is a start. Perhaps with a photo and a few embellishments it won't be so bad!

Page by Faye Morrow Bell, photo by Donna Downey. **Supplies** *Patterned papers:* BasicGrey, Making Memories, 7gypsies and Rusty Pickle; *Pen:* Zig Writer, EK Success; *Letters:* Making Memories; *Acrylic paint:* Delta Technical Coatings; *Wings:* ArtChix Studio; *Circular embellishment:* 7gypsies.

9 Even if I dislike it, my handwriting belongs in my scrapbooks.

I am not fond of my handwriting, yet I try to include it because I believe handwriting offers an interesting glimpse into people's personalities. Is the handwriting even and precise, or loopy and artistic? Either way, it's reflective of you and later generations will care more about it being authentic than perfect.

Here are three pain-free ways I'm including

a chill in the air

Comers Farm

FIELD

trip

Page by Jenni Bowlin. **Supplies** *Patterned paper, label sticker, wood letters, bingo letter and canvas frame:* Li'l Davis Designs; *Rub-on phrase and paint:* Making Memories; *Other:* Vintage label, staples and twill tape.

handwriting in my scrapbooks:

◆ I designed a layout about my handwriting and incorporated it.

◆ I often include my handwritten initials and the date on my layouts. After all, layouts are works of art. Why not sign and date them like the great artists do!

◆ I like to incorporate a few handwritten words. In the example here, Jenni Bowlin hand-wrote descriptive words on labels for her layout.

10 Playing keeps my creative energies flowing.

As a child, I loved to color—to focus, create and feel free. Guess what? I still make time to color, and it still brings me untold joy! You may find me on the floor alongside Tyler and her Dora coloring book, or in my studio with my watercolor pencils and my Matisse or Chagall coloring book by Dover Publications.

What activities did you enjoy as a child? What makes you smile? Make a list of 20 activities, then do one each day for a week. You'll love the creative boost you get!

from our FOUNDER

I saw Faye Morrow Bell's article "10 Things I've Learned about Scrapbooking" (page 55). I was so inspired and motivated, I came up with my own list! Here are 10 of the top things I've learned about scrapbooking:

1. Spend more time *making* memories than scrapbooking them. Both are valuable, but the hours spent with family and friends are what will enrich everyone's lives the most.

2. Experiences are more important than things. Spend your money on trips and other incredible memories rather than expensive houses and cars. I wasn't raised in a fancy house with fancy cars, but my parents always saved their money to take us on a fun trip every summer. I cherish these memories of times spent with my family.

3. Events you scrapbook will be better remembered than those you don't. I always think I'll remember details forever, but I've found that the older I get, the more I forget the big details (and the small ones, too). Write down the specifics!

4. Scrapbook products will change—so will your style. Remember, scrapbooking is an evolving craft.

5. There's truly no wrong way to put together a scrapbook as long as you have the right tools.

6. Film is cheap (digital is even cheaper). Take lots of pictures. The photos you keep will be worth the ones you toss.

7. Great photos make even a ho-hum page look great. Invest in a good camera and study photography.

8. Look for inspiration everywhere (such as billboards, magazine ads and children's books). You never know when you'll need inspiration for a page.

9. After creating a layout, clean up your mess! You'll enjoy the creative process a lot more if you start with a tidy work surface.

10. Buy cheap sunglasses! I recently looked at all my photos from the past year and noticed that whenever I'm wearing sunglasses, they're new pairs.

What are the top 10 things *you've* learned about scrapbooking? Compile a personal list to see how you've grown with this hobby! ♥

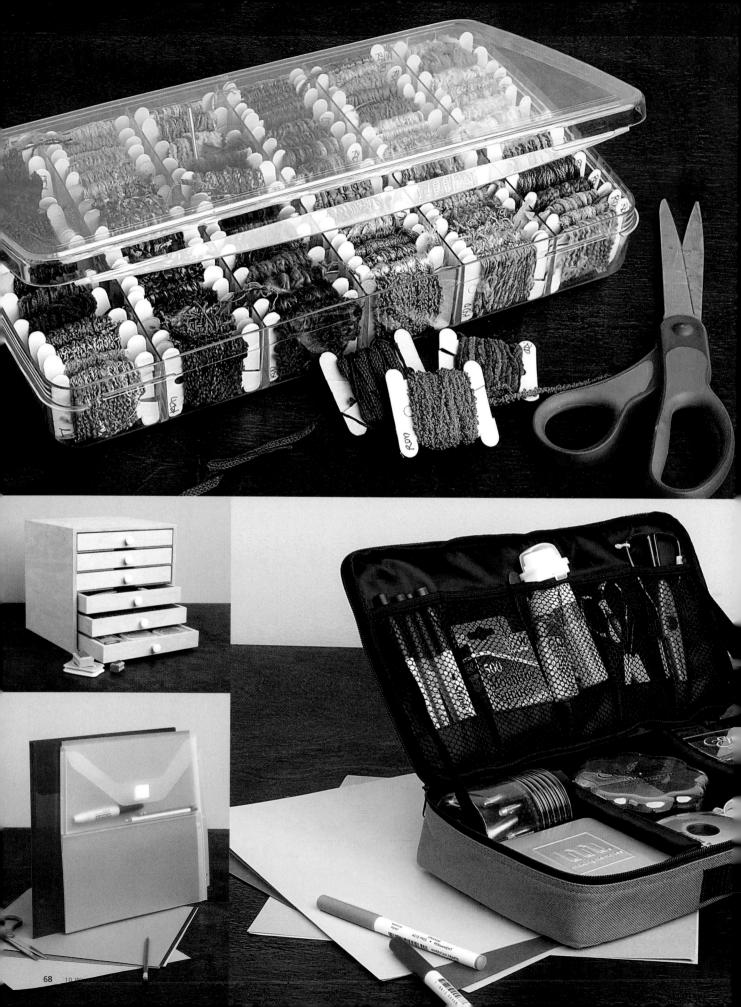

10

WAYS TO ORGANIZE YOUR SCRAP SPACE

Top tips to achieve your ideal scrap room

Whether you have a dedicated scrap room with custom built-in shelves, cabinets and drawers or a niche to hold just a few containers, organization is the key to decreasing clutter. It's also the key to increasing productivity, because you can't work with your materials unless you know where they are! Want a dream (and clean) scrap room? Here are the top 10 tips I've found for maintaining my ideal workspace when I scrap. →

BY DENISE PAULEY

GETTING YOUR ROOM READY

Walk into your work area and assess what you have. Then:

Figure 1. When stacking containers like these Stack-N-File units from Caren's Crafts, layer them no more than two high. You'll find them easier to access, which will save you time when you're looking for paper.

1 Decide what you need. Consider your ideal work flow and your supply stash, then devise an arrangement to help you quickly remember, find and use what you've got. Study other scrappers' systems and choose what is practical for your design process.

Remember, a friend's paper rack or stamp caddy might look cool, but that doesn't mean the items will be practical for *your* creative process. Setting up a scrap space isn't about "keeping up with the Joneses"—it's about designing one that fosters your creativity.

2 Designate maximum capacity. Purchase all of the containers that can fill and function well in your workspace. Once those containers are full, vow to either use or purge existing supplies before purchasing new ones. By refusing to buy additional containers, you'll keep your stash manageable.

3 Keep it together. Store like items in the same area—cardstock near patterned paper and embellishments clustered by type, for example. When creating a layout, make one pass from zone to zone, pulling any materials that might work well on your layout.

By compiling possible page elements on your desk, you can better "preplan" your design. You'll also eliminate numerous trips around your scrap space or repeated searches for paper and accents, which can halt your productivity.

4 Think shallow. I live by the "two layer" rule: Place top-loading containers and crates no more than two high (Figure 1). I'm amazed by the time I save not having to unstack, search and restack each time I retrieve something. If you want to store vertically, use columns with shallow drawer units instead.

5 Label. Determine a place for everything (and keep everything in its place), then label your areas. File new supplies immediately—you'll be less likely to end up with random piles that multiply quickly before you use items or put them away.

6 **Decorate . . . functionally.** Use empty wall space to hang dowels for storing ribbon spools, hooks for embellishments, or corkboards for showcasing sketches, cards, accents and ads with inspiring designs or color schemes. Or, use empty wall space as a mini gallery for your favorite creations.

7 **Play favorites.** Keep quests for basic supplies from interrupting your scrapbooking by keeping them nearby. Consider purchasing a storage unit specifically for the "basics." For example, my tool caddy holds adhesives, scissors, alphabet stamps, ink pads, pens, tools and a button box filled with fasteners, small tags and other embellishments (Figure 2).

8 **What's on deck?** To save time, I pull paper, cardstock and accents for several layouts at once, then pile the "page kits" (Figure 3) in a large basket. Whenever I have a minute, I can scrap immediately without having to hem and haw over what's right for my color scheme or embellishments.

9 **Update your idea banks.** Magazines and idea books are a great source of inspiration—if you can remember where you saw what and if it still suits your style. Sort routinely through your older publications, removing helpful articles and favorite layouts, and store them in a binder according to subject, theme or style. Place the binders, along with newer and timeless publications, in a magazine holder near your desk for quick inspiration.

10 **Prevent clutter.** I used to want *every* scrapbooking product on the market, but I now realize that more supplies to sift through means less time to scrapbook. So, what's my anti-clutter secret? Never let items that don't suit my style become part of my stash. I send them straight to a "Donate" box where they won't take up valuable storage space or pile up in a corner.

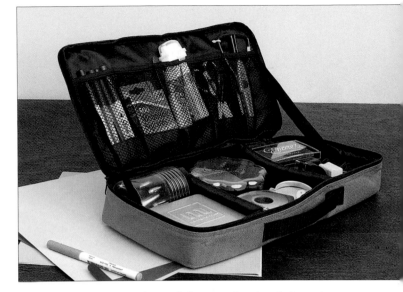

Figure 2. A Cropper Hopper Flat Pack stores all of my commonly used supplies in one place.

Figure 3. Find a storage envelope to fit your layout needs. Croppin' Companion folders let you securely stack numerous dimensional layouts without the threat of them tipping. If most of your pages are flat, the Storage Envelopes from Smead Retrospect may suit your style.

SETTING UP YOUR SUPPLIES

Once your niche is settled, it's time to sort each container, drawer and file to maximize space and provide quick access to every supply. Here's what works for me:

Figure 4. Organize your photos as soon as you get them. Group and store them together, such as in this 12" x 12" Photo Supply Case from Cropper Hopper. You'll love having your photos ready when you have a spare moment to scrap.

1 Photos. Although they're not really considered "supplies," photos should always be scrap ready. As soon as I get a batch of photos, I sort them into three categories. "Unusable" shots are tossed, "eh" pictures are moved to spare photo boxes (one for each child) and "keepers" are separated for future layouts. I group the "keepers" (noting their dates and pertinent facts), then place them in a box with dividers for each of my current albums (Figure 4).

2 Paper. I organize patterned paper and cardstock according to color, with 12" x 12" cardstock standing upright (Figure 5), 8½" x 11" sheets in three-drawer Sterlite units, and patterned paper in clear folders. When I'm creating a page, I simply pull the stacks of coordinating colors, then mix and match them to fit my layout.

3 Small accents. Find containers that don't take up much space but hold numerous embellishments within customizable compartments (Figure 6). Plano double-decker tackle boxes are my favorite for storing fasteners, charms and other little embellishments—I have one for each supply type. Tiny items, like beads, are kept in button boxes or plastic bags.

Figure 5. Upright containers, like the Paper Holders in this Home Storage Cube from Cropper Hopper, allow you to see your cardstock and paper colors at a glance.

4 Big accents. I keep items such as frames, slide mounts, silk flowers and acrylic tiles separated in plastic desk drawer dividers (with compartments for paper clips, pencils and such) within shallow drawer units. Then, I loosely organize my drawers by material type, such as metals and acrylics.

5 Alphabets. Tired of discovering that I'd already used the "good" letters in my alphabet sets, I now store all of my letters (metal, twill, acrylic and wood) together, categorized by letter. Using bead boxes with 32 compartments, I can easily see which letters are available in what styles (Figure 7).

6 Flat supplies. I house all of my "flat" supplies (stickers, templates, fabric, ephemera, scraps, etc.) in file folders within metal mesh crates. I sort the items into the most specific categories possible, such as "black letters," "word epoxy" or "gauzy fabric." Then, I can pull out a single folder to find what I need.

7 Ribbon. I have so much ribbon and fiber that color coding is essential. After purchasing a multicolored pack of fibers, I remove everything from the packaging, wind individual lengths on floss cards, and store them in ArtBin boxes grouped by color (Figure 8). Then, I just grab one box when matching a specific shade.

8 Writing utensils. While I store black pens in my "often-used" tool caddy, I house other markers horizontally in EK Success containers for long-term storage (it keeps the ink flowing smoothly). Colored, watercolor and pastel pencils are simply kept in buckets—where my kids can access them, too!

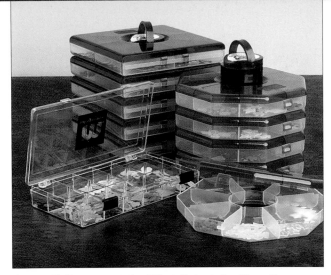

Figure 6. With 40 compartments, these Ultimate Stackers by Sweet Scrapsations are a great option for vertical storage. If you need flatter storage units, consider the clear 18-compartment Sortables from Making Memories.

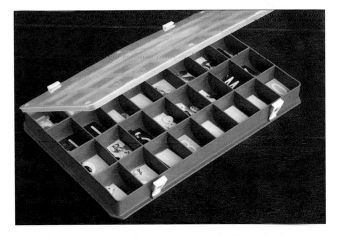

Figure 7. Storage units with more than 24 compartments, like this Bead Tray from CraftStor, are ideal for storing letters. I use the extra slots to store my numbers as well.

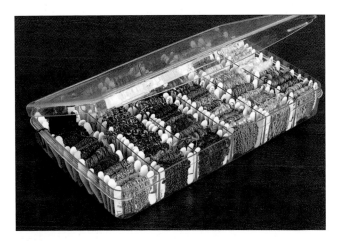

Figure 8. Wrap your fibers on floss cards and store them together where you can quickly see which styles you have. I store mine in this Prism Box from ArtBin.

Figure 9. Shallow drawer units provide a nice system for storing stamps and inks. With Cubits from ScrapNcube, you can select the number and size of the drawers to fit your needs.

9 Stamps and inks. I use shallow drawers to hold wood-mounted stamps and inks in single or sometimes double layers (Figure 9). I group the stamps by theme, such as sentiments, ornamental, nature, events and textures, and inks according to type, such as dye, chalk, pigment and solvent. I keep unmounted and foam alphabet stamps in plastic bags (grouped by font) within baskets.

10 Anything messy. Though I try to confine my supplies to one area, I do keep paints, embossing supplies and other mediums in large Rubbermaid bins, organized by type, in the kitchen pantry. When I want to paint, for example, I pull the paint container and head to the kitchen counter, where it's easiest to create and clean up.

{No Room? No Problem!}

How I and others scrap in small spaces

I LOVE MY SCRAP SPACE. I can eat and entertain in it…in fact, I often do. It's my dining room! Although I'll have a beautifully decorated studio *someday*, I refuse to let my lack of "real estate" interfere with my scrapbooking *today*. If you're frustrated by your limited area—or budget—read on to find scrap space solutions for the rest of us!

by **Denise Pauley**

{overlooked Anything?}

You can create anywhere . . . on the floor, the kitchen table, a bed tray. The key to being productive, however, is storing most of your supplies near your favorite workplace. Every room has space for scrap storage—you just need to know where to look.

Beautiful built-in cabinets . . .

. . . conceal supplies in a space-efficient way.

Family and living rooms
- Empty corners
- Open areas near the base of floor lamps
- The floor beside your couch
- Built-ins under stairwells
- Space beneath end tables
- A shelf in your TV stand
- Bookshelves

The kitchen
- A cabinet
- A shelf in your cupboard
- One side of your walk-in pantry
- The open area beneath a butcher block
- Shelves on a baker's rack
- Junk drawers

The dining room
- Space along a wall or the least-used side of the table
- Drawers beneath your china cabinet
- The area beneath your dining-room table

The bedroom
- A closet or under your bed (try lifting it on risers for even more space)
- Along the wall on your side of the bed
- A dresser and nightstand drawers
- Wall space (swap pictures for shelves above your desk or dresser)
- A footlocker

{ Try a New Twist }

Practical Project

If you can't find a spot for new storage, commandeer a piece of furniture to hold supplies instead!

When our old entertainment center was relegated to the dining room, its only practical purpose was to hold the stereo. Now, the compartment that used to house a TV hides four three-drawer units and several acrylic embellishment boxes.

Bead boxes filled with fasteners and alphabets are on the shelf below, and the other cubbyholes contain tools and vertical storage for cardstock and patterned paper. Books from the shelf were moved up top and replaced with canvas bins that stow fabric, tags, pencils and more. When I'm not working, I close the doors and visitors are none the wiser!

When closed, this looks like a regular entertainment center . . .

. . . but open, you can see it holds scrapbooking supplies.

{Adapt an Item}

Can't find a scrap-specific item? Adapt a handy item from a kitchen or home improvement store!

Practical Project

Organizers don't have to be used as intended. Consider clever applications or space-saving ideas.

Consider:

- Revolving spice racks for acrylic paints, pens or small tools. Or, empty the jars and fill them with beads, eyelets or other accents.

- DVD shelving for 6" x 6" cardstock, sticker sheets, envelopes or small embellishment boxes

- Hanging cap racks with clips for lengths of ribbon, bags of embellishments, die cuts or inspirational ideas

- Stair-step spice organizers for stamps (they'll stand upright for easy visibility)

- Hanging canvas shoe holders for bead boxes, stamps or ribbon cards

- Fold-out jewelry and toiletry bags for accents, lengths of ribbon or stamps

- Hairdryer holsters for embossing guns or other large tools

- Under-shelf cup hooks for baggies of ribbon or accents hung with metal rings

- Platter racks for vertical cardstock storage

- Sliding baskets for paints, mediums or stamping supplies

The Kamenstein magnetic spice rack, available online at Target or Amazon, can sit on a desk or hang on a wall. Simply turn the lids to sprinkle or pour contents like embossing powder, eyelets or larger accents.

Use an expandable plate rack to hold large and mini spools of ribbon.

The plate rack here and organizer shown on facing page are by Lipper International Inc. For prices and links to sites carrying these products, visit www.froogle.com.

{Camouflage}

Have you found space but now find your family objecting to supplies "cluttering" the living areas? Employ camouflage tactics or storage that can double as décor, such as:

• Canisters, bread boxes and cookie jars

• Lined baskets and straw tote bags

• Canvas-covered bins, photo boxes, magazine holders and drawer units

• Fabric "skirts" that can cover a table and conceal what's beneath it

• A piece of thick glass custom cut to fit your work surface. (Work on a layout, then place the glass over it when your family wants to use the table.)

Can you find Irma's scrap supplies? Neither can her guests!

Practical Project

Scour flea markets, auction sites and garage sales for gorgeous furniture that can also serve as cool containers.

Irma Gabbard has filled her living and dining room with scrap supplies . . . but you wouldn't know it. Her creative storage finds include an antique library card file she purchased from eBay. Using chipboard, she converted the drawers into 48 usable compartments that hold wood letters, bookplates, alphabets and more. She also acquired a "fake wine box" file drawer to hold memorabilia!

{Build Up, Not Out}

Make the most of your scrapbook nook by maximizing capacity without wasting floor space.

• To take advantage of wall space and the nine-foot ceilings in her "studio closet," Teri Fode installed wire shelving all the way up. The small space now holds the bulk of her supplies in drawers, horizontal paper trays and wood boxes purchased at Target and painted to match. Teri stores the least-used supplies up top while the rest is within reach.

• The area beneath tables is perfect for tote bags, bins or rolling carts, such as the new unit by Cropper Hopper designed to hold 10 of their vertical paper holders.

• Drawer units are ideal (regardless of their height, everything is instantly accessible). My favorite piece of furniture is an 11-drawer wood chest *(shown below)* from the Home Decorators catalog. Tucked into a corner, it conveniently holds most of my stamps, inks, ribbon and small embellishments (organized within plastic desk drawer dividers).

Like Teri, Karen Russell is a "closet scrapper," housing supplies and a work surface in the walk-in closet of her bedroom. To make the walls fun and functional, she created a magnetic molding strip to hang layouts, photos and supplies.

Karen purchased molding from a home improvement store, cut it to size, then used Liquid Nails adhesive to attach a strip of galvanized metal to the center. After coating it with white paint and acrylic sealer, she tacked the molding to the wall with drywall screws. She uses magnetic bulldog clips (which cling to the galvanized metal) to hang items from the strip.

{function and flow}

It's vital that your new system help—not hinder—your creative process. Follow these hints from small-space strategists:

- If you store in multiple rooms, group like items together. Keep all of your patterned paper and cardstock in one place and your embellishments in another.

- Keep a work-in-progress "out in the open," even if it's just on a tray stashed atop a bookshelf. This will allow you to complete small steps whenever you get a minute, without the discouraging thought of having to find and unpack what you need.

- Give yourself room to work. Dece Gherardini—who scraps at a small table in her family room with supplies tucked beneath—says, "I use all available space and furniture to keep my supplies at arm's length. I've even been known to pull the coffee table and chairs over while I'm scrapping."

Each holder fits approximately 250–300 sheets of paper (smaller sizes can be staggered). If a slot isn't stuffed full, Kristi adds a small piece of cardboard to help the paper stand up straight.

Practical Project

What do we have a lot of? Wall space! In addition to shelving, find ways to make it work to your advantage.

Because she keeps supplies along the wall between her living room and kitchen, Kristi Baumgarten's floor space is at a premium. To conserve it, she turned paper holders into cool hanging storage for her patterned paper. The three-tiered mesh containers—purchased at Target and designed to sit vertically on the desktop—feature a wide base and lots of room. Kristi simply drilled through the backs and attached them to the wall with screws.

{ Step It Up! }

Too often, "out of sight" means out of mind. Instead, display supplies like rubber stamps on a step-shelf organizer. Not only can you see them at a glance, their designs will add a touch of artistry to your work area!

View rubber stamps with ease on a step-shelf organizer.

{ Label and Relax }

Jamie Harper—who stows her supplies in a corner of her bedroom and opens a folding table to scrap—uses Cropper Hopper paper holders labeled "done," "in progress" and "getting started" to group ongoing projects and to eliminate the need to unpack when she's in the mood to scrap. "As I choose to work on things I can pull the folder I need. The contents for each layout are kept in page protectors, so when a page is done I can slip it into my album," Jamie says. ❤

Practical Project

To save time and stay motivated, pull materials for several layouts at once, creating individual page kits. With the photos, paper and embellishments ready to go, you'll be able to scrap at a moment's notice.

{ Hold It! }

Search your kitchen, estate sales, thrift and hardware stores for containers that can become inventive scrapbook storage.

1 clear out the cupboard.

Need an inexpensive way to keep small accents separated and within reach? Try Kim Kesti's muffin-tin storage. Not only is it ideal for items like buttons, clips, tabs and tiles, you get a funky vintage touch for your scrap space as well. *Tip:* This idea will work with colorful plastic or metal ice cube trays, too!

2 find lovely at low cost.
While browsing at Ikea, Michaela Young-Mitchell spotted these old-fashioned glass candy jars (only $3 for a set of four). They immediately became sweet storage for her silk, paper and ribbon flower collection! The containers would also be great for metal embellishments, ribbon, acrylic shapes and more.

3 scour hardware stores.
When Laurie Newton spotted the InterDesign Inc. toilet-paper holders at Ace Hardware, she knew they'd be the perfect way to see and store her ribbon collection. Using one holder for each color, Laurie places ribbon into the container, threads the ends out the top, closes the lid, then simply pulls and cuts what she needs!

10

ROOMS,

10 TOP SCRAPBOOKERS

Get a sneak peek at what works for them

A peek into someone else's house, room, closet, life—just can't resist, can you? (Neither can the millions of people who watch reality TV shows.) It's fun seeing where other people live and work.

Ever wondered where Ali Edwards creates her pages? How about Lisa Brown Caveney or Lisa Bearnson? We'll show you—plus give you a glimpse into the incredible scrap spaces of seven other top-notch scrapbookers! →

BY MARIANNE MADSEN

ALI EDWARDS

One of my favorite rooms in our home is my studio. With French doors into the room and out to the patio (so I can conveniently keep an eye on Simon while he plays in the backyard), my room is my happy place where I nurture creativity.

The item I love most in my studio is my kitchen-island table. Originally purchased as a changing table for my son, it was transformed into my scrapbook table when the time was right. The table is the perfect height for me.

The shelves in Ali's kitchen-island table hold scrap paper, a basket of mini albums, and recent magazines. The drawers hold her cutting tools and adhesives.

KELLY ANDERSON

I don't tend to use items when I can't see them, so I try to keep everything in clear view and easily accessible. I like to keep random odds and ends hanging on bulletin boards and wire mattress spring organizers. I love that I can just tuck little items (like postcards, photos or ephemera) into the wire springs for display.

I really like the easy organization system that keeps my room clean and contained. I use bins, baskets, boxes, buckets—anything I can throw items into and yet keep organized.

I also use small metal bins shelved inside a shoe rack to contain smaller supplies, such as inkpads, tags and accents.

A metal grid system set up along one wall holds diverse containers (such as glass jars, cargo boxes, metal bins and wire baskets) for Kelly.

FAYE MORROW BELL

My husband, George, actually gave me the design footprint for my studio. We were reading the Sunday morning paper when he saw an ad for California Closets. He said, "This is exactly what you need."

I like to stand while I scrap, so the feature I love most in my work area is the counter-height design island. It's 5 feet long and 2½ feet deep, providing lots of great workspace. Three drawers across the front hold all my essentials (adhesives, trimmers, scissors and more) so they're always within reach when I need them.

A newspaper ad served as inspiration for this room.

Faye scraps standing at her design island.

Lisa loves how she can store more paper in the same amount of space with vertical paper storage. Finding the right colors and styles is simpler as well.

LISA BEARNSON

I usually scrapbook standing up so it's easier to access all the supplies I need. Because of this, I made my workstation counter higher than my other counters so I wouldn't have to bend over too far. (This is much easier on my back.)

My best tip for setting up a workspace? Label EVERYTHING! If you've assigned a place to every item and put it in a labeled container, you'll be able to find anything easily.

After trimming paper and photos, Lisa drops unwanted pieces into a "hole in the counter" garbage can.

HEIDI SWAPP

Although my scrapbook room is not clean and tidy (ever), I know where pretty much everything is. I love to have stuff hanging on the wall. When I get done with a layout, it always goes up on the wall before it makes it into an album. I also like to hang photos that I love, or that I'm getting ready to work on.

I'm a stand-up scrapbooker, so I'm usually working at my island. All my supplies and tools are in drawers and cupboards in the island and behind me. The walk-in closet is a bonus—but it needs to be three times larger.

JENNI BOWLIN

My scrapbooking style is very eclectic. I love using items with a history (such as ledger paper or old trims and buttons). I generally work at my desk, but just the other day I realized I'd been standing for over an hour. Maybe I'm evolving!

My room is small, but filled with things I love—things that make me happy and inspire me. My two tables are old farm tables with peeling paint—perfect for me! The benches hold items close without taking up the space I need to work. I also collect small glass, silver or ironstone pieces from flea markets to hold my tiny embellishments.

Jenni keeps her rubber stamps organized with shelves made by her father-in-law from plywood and bead board.

JENNIFER MCGUIRE

I'm very organized, so I spent a lot of time planning my scrapbook room before diving in and spending a lot of money.

I arranged to have my plastic drawers out in the open so I could move them around easily. I made sure the room contained a lot of space for my kids to play and for me to "spread out." Ken and I got a countertop that would handle ink stains since I'm a stamper.

I also have two countertops that stick out from the wall and are back to back. When I work, I'm not facing a wall but another counter where my daughters or friends can work and play along with me. I love it!

Jennifer bought tall cabinets from Home Depot and added spice racks to each shelf to keep her rubber stamps organized.

LISA BROWN CAVENEY

I'm not very organized when I scrapbook. I pull out all sorts of things, and I don't tidy up until I'm done with my page. I like to sit, sometimes at my desk but usually on the floor so I can really spread things out.

When I saw this little room, I knew it would make the perfect scrapbook haven. The tall ceiling, hardwood floor and abundance of windows make it bright and homey. Since I can't paint the white walls (I live in an apartment), I decided to decorate the room with reds and oranges to liven it up.

To organize her scraps, Lisa purchased a red canvas toy-storage unit and mounted it to her wall for easy access.

Rebecca uses antique pieces (such as an old office cabinet, post office boxes or oak library shelves) to store scrapbook supplies.

REBECCA SOWER

I've seen neat, organized studios with a place for everything—that's not my studio. On an average day it's chaotic at best. While I call it creative chaos, my husband calls it "that big mess." Doesn't matter, I love the room where I create, design and am inspired.

My studio is a big, finished attic space where I keep most items within sight, in glass jars or hung from pegs. Several of my storage items are pieces of furniture I've found at antiques shops. As you know, I love anything from the past and these pieces bring a lot of comfort and inspiration to me as I work. I think that's what most important—evolving your creative space into what feels right and comforting for you.

KEEP IT SIMPLE

Becky loves her closet "nook" where almost everything is at her fingertips.

BECKY HIGGINS

Our attic is my scrapbook room/office. It's a quirky but cool space with built-in shelves and (almost) enough room to store everything. I painted the walls Asparagus and Scotland Isle and hung pictures everywhere.

I don't have a single dedicated scrap space. Instead, I work in different places depending on whether I need to be close to my computer, want to spread out my items, or need easy access to my sewing machine.

I have a closet with a long table that has several organizing bins, drawers and containers. This is where my most-used supplies are housed, as well as my trusty sewing machine. I put a mirror on the wall to visually "open up" the closed-in space (not to check my hair while I'm scrapbooking!).

embrace your space

the little things | by DENISE PAULEY

A SCRAP SPACE isn't just a place to store your supplies—it's also a spot to relax, to be motivated, to create. By infusing your niche with meaningful and functional touches, you can boost the pleasure and productivity of each scrapbooking session.

These five scrapbookers discovered that one small change to a studio can affect something as big as inspiration, storage space or work flow. Let their ideas encourage you to find the "minor" change that will have a major impact on the way you work and play. ➤

1

2

3

1 **personality.** Pam Kopka sprinkles her room with meaningful, hand-crafted touches like these knobs, magnets and monograms. Using Easy Cast epoxy and molds, Pam added family photos to the elements to give her whimsical magnet board added significance. Decorating with favorite images can fuel your desire to scrapbook!

2 **work surface.** After becoming a "stand-up scrapbooker," April Peterson devised a simple solution that didn't require a new work surface. "Bed risers" ($8) at Target fit the legs of her desk, lifting it to the perfect height, while an anti-fatigue light helps during long scrapbooking sessions. How can you make your workspace more comfortable?

3 **storage.** The jewel of Christine Traversa's scrap space is her wall of stamps. Her husband purchased Armstrong suspended ceiling brackets at Home Depot, then used long wall screws to install the plastic pieces above her workspace. Open storage like this can turn your collection into functional décor and help you locate designs quickly.

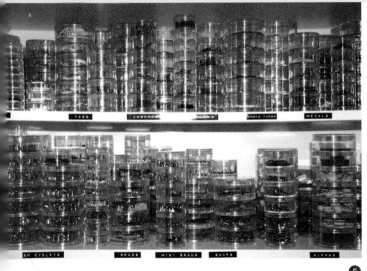

4 inspiration. Take motivational word décor a step further by altering letters with favorite supplies and techniques. Michelle Urteaga purchased cardboard letters at Recollections and turned them into colorful décor with patterned paper, stickers and other embellishments. They not only inspire her to create, but showcase her style as well!

5 organization. Don't let tiny supplies take up massive space. Julie Scattaregia tames her stash with clear, stackable, screw-top canisters. The Darice containers maximize space while allowing Julie to instantly recognize and reach the contents. For even more compact storage, look for flat boxes—like these tins from Boxer Industries—that can be consolidated in decorative baskets or bins.

trading spaces

by DENISE PAULEY

FOR YEARS, Julie Turner's family begged her to "do something" with her growing stash of scrapbook supplies. At last, a kitchen remodel gave Julie the perfect opportunity to turn the breakfast nook into a multi-functional scrap space!

If you hope to convert a common living area into a studio, read Julie's tips for using existing pieces and adding inspirational touches.   >

"To keep supplies from invading every room of the house, create a niche to keep them together for more pleasant and productive scrap sessions."

—Julie Turner

1 **be economical.** Rather than purchasing new furniture, Julie works on the kitchen table and has lined her walls with bookcases moved in from other rooms. New or old, the units keep all of her supplies within easy reach by surrounding her workspace.

2 **make it yours.** Although she works in a common room, Julie finds ways to personalize the space. She uses label holders on her tool caddy to frame motivational quotes (the Pottery Barn Kids caddy was a "splurge" at $45), displays photos with decorative clips, and even enlists the refrigerator as an inspiration board for artwork and ideas.

3 **expand where you can.** Julie makes her space seem larger by taking advantage of the floor plan—allowing supplies to seep into the kitchen. With open shelving, the kitchen island becomes the perfect "hiding spot" for clear boxes of small embellishments. She can access them quickly, but most visitors don't even notice they're there!

4 **containerize to accessorize.** Clear, colorful and eye-catching storage pieces make Julie's space a charming retreat. By clustering tools, mediums and embellishments within clear jars and boxes, wood cubicles and metal bins, Julie creates a space that's pretty *and* convenient.

Show off your work! Find a cute stand to display your latest layout, or fill a basket with fun mini albums.

under cover | by DENISE PAULEY

DON'T THINK YOU HAVE ROOM for a scrap space? See what Jennifer Stewart has nestled in the corner of her kitchen and you'll change your mind.

When closed, Jennifer's pine armoire blends right into the room. Once open, it's a space saver's dream, holding all of her supplies without hogging floor space. Discover how you can turn a single piece of furniture into a fully functional and organized space topped with plenty of decorative touches! ›

Don't let a lack of room foil your plans for a productive scrap space. A desk, dresser or well-appointed armoire like this can keep your supplies compact, organized and accessible.

1 find a sweet spot. When planning your space, select an area with a pre-existing work surface. Not only is Jennifer's kitchen "in the middle of the action," it also has a large table that lets her spread out and keep containers of frequently used supplies within arm's reach while working.

2 don't waste space. After organizing (and reorganizing) her armoire, Jennifer has devised ways to use every nook and cranny. Spice racks on the typically plain doors add storage for cans, jars, bottles and flip-top containers full of embellishments. Pockets on the doors hold long envelopes and accents. Bulky punches even find an out-of-the-way home, hung on long nails along the inside wall!

3 give it up. The key to making a small area super efficient? Keeping it organized. This may mean sacrificing a cool container for a system that saves valuable space. Although Jennifer loved storing ribbon in jars, she realized she could stash a lot more in less space by using compact, stackable floss boxes instead. She now winds individual lengths around floss "bobbins" for easy visibility and access.

4 add personality. Remember, "small" doesn't equal "boring." Being the only female in the household, Jennifer wanted to include lots of pink and "girly" touches in her space. Creative storage pieces help make her mark—a pink framed area showcases cards, photos and a calendar, while a charming pitcher, printer's tray and lace perfume box reveal her love of vintage decor.

have it your way | by DENISE PAULEY

We scrapbookers are a picky bunch—always striving for a space that's incredibly fun as well as functional, constantly searching for storage to keep our supplies handy *and* keep us motivated to create.

Loni Stevens discovered a way to obtain her ideal studio— recruiting her father to build storage units that suit her exact specifications. Let the results of their five-month project serve as inspiration if you hope to create and construct your own dream room. ❯

A good custom design creates an attractive, convenient home for everything. Keep oft-used items within reach and other items in easily accessible containers.

"I love to incorporate inspiring words throughout my room where I can see them every day."

1 **turn your vision** into reality by sketching your ideas first, then creating detailed "blueprints" with exact dimensions for your builder. Consider making cardboard models to be sure the measurements, design and fit are accurate, especially if you're working with tight spaces.

2 **although** you shouldn't risk mistakes by rushing, you can still find time-savers throughout the construction process. For example, Loni built with Melamine, a pressed wood with a white finish that eliminates the need to paint. She also suggests consulting an in-store expert to ensure you purchase the correct materials the first time.

3 **don't have time** to construct large pieces? Start small! Loni's first project was the modular unit on her desk that features drawers, shelves and a magnet-board cabinet. Designed to resemble miniature furniture, useful storage like this can be integrated into a studio of any size.

4 **easy-to-make** magnet boards can display recent purchases, oft-used tools and inspirational items. Loni cut and mounted inexpensive metal sheets to her paper storage units and walls. Surrounding the pieces with frames turned them into decorative displays as well.

10
10
+
10

Tim's Top
Tips to Try

Create "wow" looks in minutes

I love to spend hours playing with scrapbooking supplies. Mixing a little of this, inking a little of that—all to come up with innovative techniques for my projects. But I also have a secret. Some of my all-time favorites are those that look difficult but require only a few steps. You know, the ones I can sit down and create in minutes. What are they? I'll let you in on my secrets if you promise not to tell anyone how easy they are!

BY TIM HOLTZ

Pretty in Pink by Tim Holtz. **Supplies** *Textured cardstock:* Bazzill Basics Paper; *Patterned paper, safety pins, snaps, brads and bookplate:* Junkitz; *Rub-ons:* Creative Imaginations; *Die-cut letters:* QuicKutz; *Chipboard letter:* Making Memories; *Paper flowers:* Prima; *Rubber stamps:* Hero Arts; *Stamping ink and embossing powder:* Ranger Industries; *Other:* Staples and thread.

RIBBON STAMPS
AND CARDSTOCK

With ribbon stamps, you can incorporate any color of "ribbon" by simply changing the color of the cardstock or ink. While you can stamp directly onto your layouts, the images will appear more realistic if you stamp them onto a separate sheet of cardstock and cut them out. You get a dimensional look without the bulk of real ribbons and fiber. My favorite aspect of this technique? Its simplicity.

Creating Cardstock Ribbons

A. Ink a ribbon stamp and transfer it to cardstock.

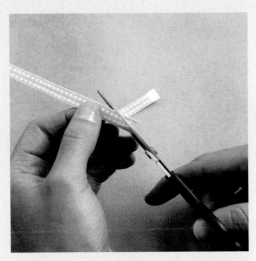

B. Cut out stamped image, leaving a thin border. Cut a decorative notch from each end.

Tim's Tips

❶ For an eclectic look, attach paper ribbons with an assortment of safety pins, snaps, brads or staples.

❷ Add texture by embossing page elements (such as chipboard letters) with powders that match your ink colors.

❸ Use a variety of rub-ons to turn simple cardstock into an eye-catching border or background.

❹ Ink paper flowers and other paper accents to coordinate with your layout.   >>

Blue Eyes *by Tim Holtz.* **Supplies** *Textured cardstock:* Bazzill Basics Paper; *Patterned papers:* Design Originals; *Tile letters:* Li'l Davis Designs; *Tag and envelope:* American Tag; *Suspender clasp, button, brads, epoxy stickers and fabric swatches:* Junkitz; *Rubber stamp:* Stampers Anonymous; *Stamping ink:* Ranger Industries; *Label tape:* Dymo; *Other:* Twine, staples, letter charm and safety pin.

ANTIQUE BURNT EDGE

No more running to the sink to put out a burning accent gone bad! By simply applying layers of ink to a tag, you can create faux burnt edging without setting off your fire alarm. This technique is my distressing favorite, and it's also popular with students in my classes.

Adding Faux Burnt Edging with Ink

A. Ink edges of tag with a light-brown ink and blend into center of tag.

B. Apply walnut ink to tag edges only.

C. Apply black ink directly to edges of tag with an inkpad. Blend inked edge into center of tag with an applicator to create a "burnt" edge look.

Tim's Tips

⑤ Ink the edges of fabric scraps and ribbon to "age" them.

⑥ Rip and tear apart envelopes to create pockets for your layouts.

⑦ Use this technique on photo mats, background papers and accent strips for added depth. >>

Cooper *by Tim Holtz.* **Supplies** *Textured cardstock:* Bazzill Basics Paper; *Rub-ons:* Rusty Pickle; *Flourish die cut (used beneath foil tape):* QuicKutz; *Metal twig:* Global Solutions, Erico; *Rickrack:* Making Memories; *Acrylic tabs, metal frame, safety pins, epoxy sticker and jump rings:* Junkitz; *Foil tape:* Nashua; *Other:* Acrylic paint.

YOUR OWN
METAL-RIMMED ACCENTS

Heading to the hardware store? Pick up foil tape and you'll be rolling out custom, embossed metal in no time. You'll need a rubber brayer and a dimensional design, which can be die cut or hand cut from cardstock. Or, use premade cardstock stickers.

Brayer Embossing Metal

A. Cut shapes from scrap cardstock. (I used a die-cutting machine for this project.) Adhere to cardstock strip. *Note:* Use your scraps for both the shapes and the strip—none of the cardstock will show!

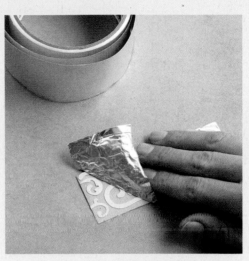

B. Wrap foil tape around the decorated strip.

C. Roll a soft brayer directly over the foil to emboss the metal and reveal your design.

Tim's Tips

8 Try coloring the foil tape with ink or paint.

9 Cut out freehand cardstock designs. Or, use a stencil to draw a design on other paper before cutting it out.

10 Instead of adding cardstock images to your strip, create patterns from string or hot glue for a funky embossed design. >>

Paris Postale *by Tim Holtz.* **Supplies** *Tag:* American Tag; *Hat pin:* EK Success; *Metal edges, safety pins, jump rings, brads, binder ring, epoxy sticker and book-plate:* Junkitz; *Rubber stamp:* Stampers Anonymous; *Stamping ink and dimensional adhesive:* Ranger Industries; *Other:* Ribbon, bobby pin and staples.

UNIQUE METAL-RIMMED TAGS

Want to create a custom metal-rimmed tag but can't find the correct punch size for the insert? No problem! Glue a metal rim *over* paper, a photo or a sticker, then cut around the rim after it's dry. You'll get a perfect fit every time.

Customizing Metal Tags

A. Adhere metal rim over desired paper or photo section. Let dry.

B. Cut out metal tag using detail scissors for a clean edge.

C. Punch hole with hole punch and add a jump ring. Hang on your layout or attach with a brad or eyelet.

Tim's Tips

⓫ Place a clear epoxy sticker over the finished tag for glossy dimension. Or, achieve a similar look by covering the center with clear dimensional liquid adhesive.

⓬ Use mini pictures from contact sheets to create metal-rimmed photo tags that showcase your family, friends and pets.

⓭ Instead of placing a jump ring through the end of your tag, adhere it over a bobby pin for a fun accent. Check out my "p" monogram pin on page 110.   >>

Generations *by Tim Holtz.* **Supplies** *Textured cardstock:* Bazzill Basics Paper; *Patterned papers, slide mounts and metal clips:* Design Originals; *Mica tiles:* USArtQuest; *Label tape:* Dymo; *Foam tape:* Venture Tape; *Stamping ink:* Ranger Industries; *Other:* Memorabilia, snaps, photo corners and brads.

HAND-TINTING A PHOTO

A hand-tinted photo evokes the feeling of timeless nostalgia. To achieve this effect, pull out your stamping inks and get ready to play! (Use inks that are formulated to work directly on glossy photo papers.) Practice on a spare photo first.

Tim's Tips

14 When tinting, less is more. Stick with a simple accent, such as the lips on this picture.

15 To enhance the distressed look on your photo, scratch it lightly with sandpaper. >>

Photo Tinting with Ink

A. Print a black-and-white photo onto glossy photo paper. *Note:* The photo can be a laser photocopy, printed on an inkjet or with toner. Test your ink on the paper before proceeding to make sure it will stay.

B. Apply ink to part of your photo, using a small nib or cotton swab for precise detail. I tinted the lips red on this image.

C. Cover the entire photo with a linen-colored ink; you can transfer directly with the inkpad. Immediately remove excess ink with a sponge applicator.

D. Ink edges of photo with a darker ink color to add a shadow.

We all have special mementos tucked away in trunks, boxes and jars. Start showing them off on your scrapbook pages! You can create enclosed areas with simple slide mounts and incorporate dimensional objects you thought were off-limits to your scrapbooks.

Making Slide Mount Shadow Boxes

A. Remove inserts from a slide mount set. Sand edges of slide mounts, then ink for an antique look.

B. Apply adhesive to all edges of back side of slide mount. Secure a mica tile on one side of slide mount.

C. Fold slide mount closed to "sandwich" mica tile. Cut off excess mica.

D. Apply dimensional adhesive to back of slide mount window, then adhere slide mount to your layout.

Tim's Tips

16 Use transparencies or acetate in place of the mica tiles.

17 Adhere a patterned paper below your slide mount to help set it apart. I used a different patterned paper for each of the shadow boxes on my page.

18 Apply additional layers of dimensional adhesive as needed to hold especially thick memorabilia.

19 Clip large memorabilia, such as photos, to your layout with a "clothesline" made from twine and metal clips.

20 This technique is perfect for making mini book covers as well as clever keepsake cards! ♥

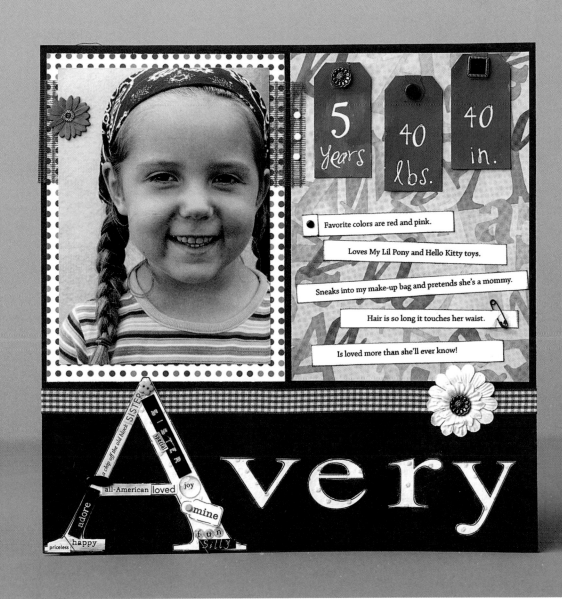

cool, clever tips

Embellished Monogram

When my daughter turned five, I wanted a quick way to record her size and what she likes right now. Monograms are all the rage, so I decided to highlight the "A" yet still use Avery's whole name. I cut her name from textured, handmade paper, then embellished the first letter with little words or sentiments that describe her. It's a great way to use up leftover stickers, rub-ons and tags while creating a fun page element. ➤

—*Shannon Watt, Newhall, CA*

Decorate the first letter of your child's name for a sharp monogrammed look. *Page by Shannon Watt.* **Supplies** *Patterned paper:* Deluxe Designs and KI Memories; *Handmade paper:* Artistic Scrapper, Creative Imaginations; *Mesh paper:* Maruyama, Magenta; *Flowers:* K & Company and Making Memories; *Brads, tags, rub-on letters and numbers:* Making Memories; *Stickers:* Making Memories and Pebbles Inc.; *Acrylic paint:* Delta Technical Coatings; *Computer font:* Times New Roman, Microsoft Word; *Other:* Ribbon, safety pin and staples. *Idea to note:* Shannon painted the tags pink to match her layout.

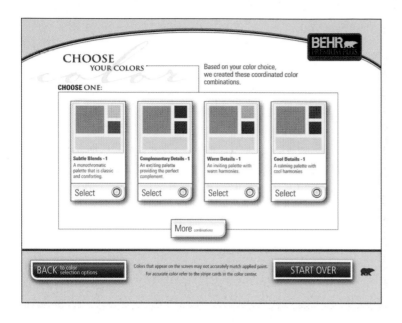

Decide which color combination will work best with your photos, desired tones, preferences and paper.

Free Color Tool

Knowing which colors to combine while scrapbooking can be tricky, so I was delighted to discover the amazing ColorSmart tool at www.behr.com. Here's how to use it:

① After accessing the web site, click on the Explore Color tab.

② Select Interior or Exterior from the Browse Colors section in the middle. Behr's proprietary ColorSmart tool will begin loading.

③ Choose a starting color from the Color Range bar.

④ Select Fine Tune and adjust the color if none of the preselected color combinations works with your photos. This sure beats having to pull out reams of paper! Click on Coordinate.

⑤ Specify whether the color you're exploring is a Main or Accent color. Four coordinated color combinations will appear (see example here). Click on More Combinations to see four new options. Choose Select, and you can print off the combinations and take them to your nearest scrapbook store. Or, do a little experimenting for your next paint project!

The Behr site is so helpful that I have it bookmarked and refer to it often. Its features, combined with interesting articles about color and design (don't miss the Inspiration section), help keep me on the leading edge of what's hip!

—Sandy Walker, Shawnigan Lake, BC, Canada

Note: We asked designer Pam Black to put the Behr color tool to the test. Note the fabulous results at right.

WARNING: This site is addicting. Not only can your scrapbook pages benefit, but your home décor as well. View your color combination in a room setting—you simply tell which colors to apply to ceiling, walls, accents and trim. Supply your room measurements, and the site tells how many gallons of paint you'll need for your project. Remodeling should be this easy!

Sketches Rolodex

I enjoy using Becky Higgins' sketches! I organize them in a Rolodex card file according to the number of photos on each sketch. When I decide to use a particular sketch, I pull the card out while I work on my layout, then replace it when I'm done. I sketch my own layout ideas on blank cards and file them as well.

A really neat thing I've discovered while pasting these sketches to Rolodex cards? By turning and flipping the sketches in different directions, I actually get more—20 sketches suddenly become 80. I love how versatile these sketches are!

—Pam Steinke, Las Vegas, NV

Journaling Notes

I now use digital photography exclusively, and I like to record my memories with the downloaded pictures. To catalog my photos and scrapbook ideas on my computer, I group the pictures by date in a folder. I add a text file to that folder for journaling thoughts, layout ideas and any other information about the set of photos. When I'm ready to scrap a particular event, I have all the information I need in one handy spot.

—Shari Shaw, Kingston, ON, Canada

Use the Behr color tool at left to suggest stunning color combinations for a page. *Page by Pam Black.* **Supplies** *Textured cardstock:* Route 66, Dark Scarlet, Dark Rosey, Battenberg and Fern, all by Bazzill Basics Paper; *Patterned papers and tags:* BasicGrey; *Rubber stamps, black brads and staples:* Making Memories; *Stamping ink:* Ranger Industries; *Black safety pin:* Jo-Ann Crafts; *Antique mini brads:* Lost Art Treasures; *Acrylic paint:* Delta Technical Coatings; *Ribbons:* May Arts; *Computer fonts:* 2Peas Inside Out, downloaded from www.twopeasinabucket.com; Times New Roman, Microsoft Word; *Word charm:* All My Memories.

Straighten Ribbon

To get "dents" and bends out of ribbon and some twines and fibers, use a curling iron. Clamp the ribbon like you would a strand of hair and quickly pull the curling iron down the ribbon. This works like a charm!

—*Shannon Lowe, Holladay, UT*

Editor's note: This technique may melt some ribbons. Test a small section at the end of the ribbon before trying this technique.

Removing Rub-On Letters

I enjoy the ease of using rub-on letters while scrapbooking, but I've discovered you can make mistakes with them. After making a mistake, I feared I'd have to redo my entire layout but thought I'd try using un-du Adhesive Remover first. I put a dab of the solution on my fingertip and lightly rubbed it over my mistake. The adhesive remover removed the errant rub-on without damaging my layout.

—*Carolyn Donoghue, Hemlock, MI*

Scan clothing to create accents that match your photos perfectly. *Page by Lisa Soares.* **Supplies** *Textured cardstock:* Bazzill Basics Paper; *Green vellum:* DMD, Inc.; *Circle tag:* Making Memories; *Rubber stamps:* Wordsworth (title), All Night Media, Plaid Enterprises (circle tag) and Hero Arts (corners); *Stamping ink:* StazOn, Tsukineko; *Eyelet:* The Stamp Doctor; *Computer font:* 2Peas Dragonfly, downloaded from *www.twopeasinabucket.com*; *Other:* Heart button, ribbon, embroidery floss and chalk.

Perfect Coordinated Paper

Before creating this page, I wanted to find a perfect color match for the outfit I'm wearing in the photo. I tried several options, but none of the colors were quite right. I realized I could create my own coordinated paper by scanning my jacket.

To scan my jacket, I simply laid the fabric on my scanner, previewed the scan area, and selected a section without seams that best showed off the clothing pattern. Next, I scanned my original photo into a separate file for comparison, then I adjusted the fabric scan until the colors and saturation matched the photo. Finally, I printed the image onto photo paper and cut out a tag shape.

Variation: You can also save the image as a JPG file and import it into a word-processing or desktop publishing program Layer a clear text box over the image to type your title or journaling.

—*Lisa Soares, Aliso Viejo, CA*

Photo Test Image

If you print your photos at home, you've probably printed large photos only to discover that the colors look wrong and you've wasted ink and photo paper. Here's a tip I use religiously with every large photo I print to prevent this problem.

Once you get the look you want using your photo-editing software, resize the photo to a thumbnail and print a test image. If it looks right, go ahead and print your large photo. If the colors are off, make some adjustments and print another thumbnail.

You can use the little image on your layout as an accent or save it to use in a mini album.

—*Allison Strine, Roswell, GA*

fun, fab ideas

Faux Ribbon

I'm addicted to ribbon! I love the color and interest it adds to my scrapbook pages. However, I sometimes have trouble finding the right ribbon color or I don't want to use up too much of my stash. I started creating "faux ribbon" by simply cutting strips of patterned paper. When they're mixed in with real ribbons, you can't tell them apart. ➤

—*Jennifer McGuire, Cincinnati, OH*

Create the illusion of ribbon with strips of patterned paper. *Page by Jennifer McGuire.* **Supplies** *Letter beads:* Hobby Lobby; *Pins:* Prym-Dritz; *Patterned papers:* Anna Griffin, Colors By Design, EK Success, Making Memories and The Scrapbook Wizard; *Other:* Ribbon.

computer tip

Family Vacation *by Amy Tanabe.* **Supplies** *Photo-editing software:* Photoshop Elements 3.0, Adobe Systems; *Digital kit:* Peas in a Pod, created by Michelle Underwood and downloaded from *www.acherryontop.com; Inked edges effect:* Downloaded from *www.atomiccupcake.com; Alpha stamp brush:* Created by Nancie Rowe Janitz and downloaded from *www.scrapartist.com; Computer fonts:* Satisfaction, downloaded from the Internet; CK Sassy, "Fresh Fonts" CD, *Creating Keepsakes.*

Add Oomph with Brackets and Ink

Next time you want to emphasize a photo or page element, consider adding brackets or ink digitally. It's fun *and* easy!

BRACKETS. For the page above, I selected brackets from a digital kit (they were included as an element). I electronically erased the lines between the brackets since I didn't need them for journaling.

Next, I selected the opacity option from the Layers palette in Photoshop Elements and set the opacity at 75% so the brackets would look stamped. I then enlarged them to frame the photo.

Want to make your own brackets or doodles? Draw them directly on your page with a Wacom tablet. Simply open a new layer above the piece you want to draw on, choose your brush size and color, then draw! Erase sections and change the opacity for a stamped look. To distress your image, choose the Eraser tool, select a grunge-style brush, and "erase" small portions.

DIGITAL INKING. Get the look in one of three ways:

• **Option 1.** Download the related effect or action from a website such as www.atomiccupcake.com. Select the item you want inked and click on an icon. If you use Photoshop or Photoshop Elements, the program will do the inking for you!

• **Option 2.** Choose the paper you want "inked," select the color desired, then "brush" the edges of the paper with a grunge-style brush. To achieve a worn look, brush along the edges only.

• **Option 3.** Set an overlay (offered by digital scrapbooking designers) on top of the paper or item to be "inked" or "distressed." Change the overlay's color, or make it white for a sanded look.

—Amy Tanabe, La Junta, CO

Icy Accents

For this hockey layout, I made embellishments that looked like ice for my title and page accents. Here's how:

① Punch several squares from white cardstock. Rub white and blue metallic rub-ons randomly over the squares. Dab a little of the pewter metallic rub-ons on the edges.

② Place the squares on a piece of wax paper. Squiggle clear dimensional adhesive on the squares and let them dry for a few hours.

③ Stamp your title letters on the squares with a solvent-based stamping ink like StazOn. For a more dimensional look, stamp while the glaze looks clear but is still slightly tacky.

—Allison Landy, Phoenix, AZ

Add a wintry touch to your layouts with icy accents. *Page by Allison Landy.* **Supplies** *Metallic rub-ons:* Craf-T Products; *Dimensional adhesive:* Diamond Glaze, JudiKins; *Letter stamps:* Ma Vinci's Reliquary; *Stamping ink:* StazOn, Tsukineko; *Pen:* Jimnie Gel, Zebra; *Brads:* Lost Art Treasures; *Eyelet numbers:* Making Memories; *Waxed linen:* Scrapworks.

Color Help

I love finding new color combinations for layouts and cards, and I recently discovered a great resource: clothing catalogs that come in the mail. Before I recycle them, I cut out the pictures that contain color combos I like. I glue each picture to a 3" x 5" card, punch a hole in the top, and add it to a binding ring. Now, when I need color ideas I just flip through the cards.

—Teri Anderson, Idaho Falls, ID

computer tip

Our love is not measured in time.

There was no beginning

There will be no end.

It has existed always.

And it always will be.

Forever, my daughter.

Forever, your mom.

Create a Cool Brushed Effect

I designed this computer-generated page a few months after I brought my adopted daughters home from Russia. Even though they'd only been with me for a short time, I don't remember a day I didn't think about them or pray for them, even before I'd met them. When I saw this photo, the words "Forever Eternal" came to mind and I used them for my title.

To create the brushed look here, I selected the Pin Light Layer Mode feature in Adobe Photoshop. I placed the photo layer over a skin-colored background, then used numerous electronic brushes to delete and add texture behind. I used the Levels feature to intensify contrasts in the photo. I didn't do any recoloring—the colors are the results of other effects I added.

—*Veronica Ponce, Miami, FL*

Page by Veronica Ponce. **Supplies** *Computer software:* Adobe Photoshop CS; *Computer fonts:* Crack Babies and High Tower Text, both downloaded from the Internet.

tips to try today

Embellished Journaling Blocks

I originally wrote my journaling in one large block, but it seemed lengthy and hard to work with, so I cut it into separate pieces. I combined stamped letters with my handwriting for a fun and spontaneous look. For additional visual variety, I chose an accent color to make certain letters pop. ➤

—Kelly Anderson, Tempe, AZ

Embellish handwritten journaling with random stamped letters. *Pages by Kelly Anderson.* **Supplies** *Textured cardstock:* Paper Garden; *Leaf accent:* EK Success; *Patterned paper:* Li'l Davis Designs; *Mini gold frame, photo turn and buckle:* 7gypsies; *Alphabet stamps:* Hero Arts and PSX Design; *Stamping ink:* Brilliance and VersaColor, Tsukineko; *Typewriter stickers:* All My Memories; *Pen:* Zig Millennium, EK Success; *Date stamp:* OfficeMax; *Ribbon:* Midori; *Label tape:* Dymo; *Other:* Charms, buttons and Concordia College ephemera.

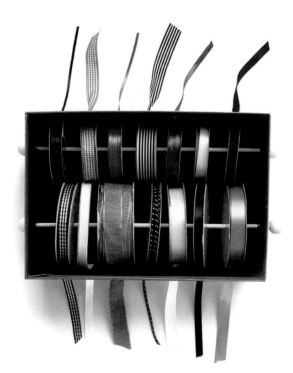

Make Your Own Ribbon Box with Faye

I love ribbon and buy it regularly, which means I need an efficient way to keep it organized. While a friend got me two great ribbon boxes at a fabric store, I couldn't find more once I'd filled them. My solution? I fashioned a fun ribbon box out of a photo box! It was easy *and* economical, and the supplies were all available at my local craft store. Here's how to create a similar box of your own.

Ribbon is usually sold in either a 3¼" spool or a 4⅛" spool. A standard photo box will hold a row of each size!

Before you get out that ribbon, gather a few supplies and tools as noted here.

Supplies

☐ Photo box with lid (a box *without* a label holder on the end works best)
☐ Two 12" wooden dowels that are ³⁄₁₆" in diameter
☐ Four 20mm unfinished wooden beads
☐ ¼" silver eyelets with a setter tool
☐ White acrylic paint

Note: I got my oversized eyelets in kits that sell at craft and fabric stores for approximately $2.50 and include the setter tool. If you have wide ribbons, consider including some ½" or 1" eyelets.

Tools

☐ 6" ruler or protractor
☐ Ribbon on a 4⅛" round card
☐ Ribbon on a 3¼" round card
☐ White pencil for markings
☐ Large hole punch or craft knife
☐ Foam paintbrush

steps

To make your ribbon box:

1 Paint the wooden dowels and beads with the white paint, then set them aside to dry.
Tip: Need a third hand to steady each bead as you paint? Attach the bead to the end of an extra wooden dowel. Now you can easily turn the bead with one hand while you paint with the other! ∨

2 Mark where the dowels will enter the ends of the box. The large spools will go on one dowel and the small spools on the other.

Markings for dowel with large spools
Place a large spool of ribbon on the inside of the photo box at front right. Use the white pencil to make a mark in the center of the spool's opening. ∨

Place the spool of ribbon at the back right of the box. Use the white pencil to make a mark in the center of the spool's opening. ∨

Markings for dowel with small spools
Place a small spool of ribbon on the inside of the photo box at front left. Use the white pencil to make a mark in the center of the spool's opening. ∨

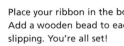 >

Place the spool of ribbon at the back left of the box. Use the white pencil to make a mark in the center of the spool's opening. ∨

Note that the markings for the small spools are lower than the markings for the large spools. Raise the marking about ½" so the markings are at the same level. The dowels will now extend from the box at the same height. *See diagram below.* ∨

Back left of box · Back right of box
Marking for small spools raised to height of large spools
Marking for large spools
Original marking for small spools

3 Use a ruler or protractor to mark the placement of the eyelets along the insides of the box. *Note:* I placed seven eyelets on each side of my box. You can include more eyelets if you have more spools of ribbon.

4 Follow your markings from steps 2 and 3 to make holes in the ends of the box and on the sides. Use either a very large hole punch or a craft knife to make the holes.

5 Use the setter tool to set eyelets in the ends of the box and along the sides.

6 Place your ribbon in the box and insert the dowels. Add a wooden bead to each dowel end to keep it from slipping. You're all set!
—*Faye Morrow Bell, CK Contributing Editor*

Get more use from your letter stencils by using the letter outline. *Pages by Heidi Swapp.* **Supplies** *Brads:* Bazzill Basics Paper; *Chipboard alphabet and photo corners:* Heidi Swapp; *Colored pencils:* Prismacolor, Sanford; *Pens:* Zig Millennium and Zig Writer, EK Success; Slick Writer, American Crafts.

More Stencil Looks

Stencil and chipboard alphabets are so much fun to use as word embellishments. Something cool I've discovered? After you use the letter, you're left with a very useable matrix (the portion left after the letter is removed). Try these two methods:

• Cut out portions of the negative letter space and use it as a letter embellishment (see the "Favorite" title).

• Use the matrix to trace the letter, then color it in with colored pencils (see the "Colton" title). You'll get quick, easy—and inexpensive—results.

—Heidi Swapp, Mesa, AZ

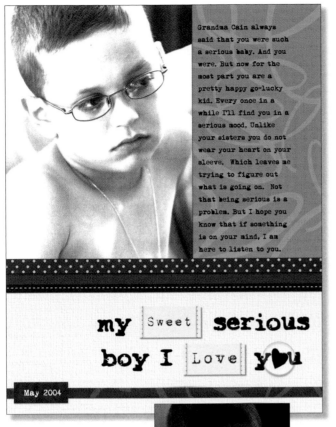

Grandma Cain always said that you were such a serious baby. And you were. But now for the most part you are a pretty happy go-lucky kid. Every once in a while I'll find you in a serious mood. Unlike your sisters you do not wear your heart on your sleeve. Which leaves me trying to figure out what is going on. Not that being serious is a problem. But I hope you know that if something is on your mind, I am here to listen to you.

my Sweet serious boy I Love you

May 2004

Page and photo by Rhonda Stark. **Supplies** *Software:* Photoshop, Adobe Systems; *Computer fonts:* Mom's Typewriter, downloaded from www.scrapvillage.com; Smash, downloaded from the Internet; *Elements:* Papers, Ribbons, Stitched Word Labels, Black Tag and Heart Pebble, downloaded from www.DigitalDesignEssentials.com.

YOUR EYES AMAZE ME. I TRY TO CAPTURE JUST HOW BLUE THEY ARE IN A PHOTO. BUT THE CAMERA CANNOT DO THEM JUSTICE. FOR JUST LIKE YOU THEY MUST BE EXPERIENCED FIRSTHAND TO BE APPRECIATED.

June 2004

blue HEAVEN

Page and photo by Rhonda Stark. **Supplies** *Software:* Photoshop, Adobe Systems; *Computer fonts:* Texas Hero, downloaded from www.scrapvillage.com; 2Peas Task List, downloaded from www.twopeasinabucket.com; *Elements:* Letter Pebbles, downloaded from www.DigitalDesignEssentials.com; *Stamp:* Made from a brush downloaded from http://veredgf.fredfarm.com/vbrush/main.html.

Improve Your Photos

To electronically tweak my photos to perfection, I regularly use the Levels dialog box in Photoshop. One day, while trying to rescue a very dark photo, I discovered some pretty cool effects when adjusting settings.

The Levels dialog box provides a histogram of your image's range of tones. While a darker image (underexposed) will have the map bunched to the left-hand side, a lighter image (overexposed) will have the map bunched to the right-hand side. A properly exposed image will have an even distribution of the map from left to right.

Changing your image is as simple as moving the sliders to the position you want. As you move the sliders, your image will be adjusted accordingly.

For the page about my son, I converted my image to black and white. I then "corrected" the photo by moving the highlights to the left where the map first started going up. Because this image was shot with higher ISO, it contains more grain, but I love how this contributes to the photo's moody feel. You can expect a grainier look from very dark images or images shot with higher-speed film.

I took the photo of my daughter while sitting across from her. I remember how blue her eyes seemed. Still, when I got the results, I was unhappy. I knew the picture was underexposed and needed a little lightening, so I adjusted the tones electronically. I overcompensated and overexposed the shot. To my delight, the tweaking made my daughter's eyes "pop" more visually and gave the photo an artistic feel. I decided to scrapbook it that way.

—Rhonda Stark, Plymouth, MN ♥

Flattened Bottle Cap Accents

When flattened, a bottle cap's fluted edge rolls up to create a neat-looking ruffle—perfect for mini frames! To flatten the bottle cap evenly, follow these steps:

1 Place the bottle cap right side up on a hard surface. Pound it a couple times with a rubber mallet.

2 Flip the bottle cap over and give it one hard pound to create a perfect small frame.

3 Place mini photos, stickers, alphabet letters and more in the center, then attach the cap to your page. Variation: Punch a small hole in the rim and thread it with wire or ribbon before attaching it to your page.

—Barbara Burnett, Design Originals

Flatten bottle caps to create cute circle charms. *Page by Bonnie Lotz.* **Supplies** *Patterned papers:* Chatterbox (orange) and KI Memories (blue); *Textured paper:* Provo Craft; *Initial paper clip:* Scrapworks; *Ribbon:* May Arts; *Bottle caps and stickers:* Design Originals; *Foam stamps:* Making Memories; *Embroidery floss:* DMC; *Acrylic paint:* Delta Technical Coatings; *Computer font:* Battlelines, downloaded from the Internet.

try a
new take

Resist Tag

Love the stamped "resist" look? Try it on the glossy side of a merchandise tag, available at office supply stores. To create the look:

① Stamp an image with VersaMark ink on the glossy side of the tag. Let the image air-dry completely (or use a heat gun for faster drying).

② Rub colored stamping dye generously over the tag with a make-up applicator. The inked image will resist the dye.

—*Jennifer McGuire, Cincinnati, OH*

Create cool tags with a resist technique and stamping inks. *Page by Jennifer McGuire.* **Supplies** *Rubber stamps:* Hero Arts; *Stamping inks:* VersaMark, Tsukineko; Dye Cube, Hero Arts; *Tags:* Office Depot; *Heart:* Making Memories; *Rub-ons:* Autumn Leaves; *Other:* Ribbon.

Mat photos in style with ribbon strips. *Pages by Erin Roe.* **Supplies** *Textured cardstock:* Bazzill Basics Paper; *Ribbon:* May Arts; *Alphabet pogs:* Autumn Leaves; *Rub-ons:* Craf-T Products; *Brads:* Making Memories; *Computer font:* 2Peas Hot Chocolate, downloaded from *www.twopeasinabucket.com.*

Ribbon Photo Mats

I've accumulated a huge ribbon stash and am always coming up with new ways to use it. For this layout, I added double ribbon mats around each photo. I placed strips of ribbon along the top and bottom of the photo/journaling strip, then fastened the ribbon in place with brads. I love the texture and bright color that ribbon can add to a page!

—*Erin Roe, Hampton, VA*

Curly Fabric Flowers

To add dimension to the edge of your cut fabric pieces, simply hold the edge of the fabric and try to tear it. You'll end up with a curled edge. I really love the added texture created by this easy technique!

—*Jennifer McGuire, Cincinnati, OH*

Create a curled edge for easy dimension. *Card by Jennifer McGuire.* **Supplies** *Button:* Hero Arts; *Computer font:* 2Peas Weathervane, downloaded from *www.twopeasinabucket.com;* *Other:* Fabric, thread and faux flowers.

BEACH

getaway

Create a stylish accent by placing an acrylic tag over a stamped image. *Page by Patricia Anderson.* **Supplies** *Textured cardstock:* Prism Papers; *Patterned paper and circle tag:* Rusty Pickle; *Acrylic tag:* Heidi Grace Designs; *Rubber stamp:* Stampa Rosa; *Stamping ink:* StazOn, Tsukineko; *Rub-ons:* Provo Craft; *Mini tag:* Making Memories; *Computer font:* HMK Pegsanna, "Hallmark Card Studio" CD, Hallmark; *Other:* Deco art and transparency.

Just a family weekend getaway – and it was exactly what we needed! Even though the weather was cold (we expected that), and the water was contaminated, (we didn't expect that), we had a good trip to the Oregon Coast. I had wanted to go to the beach all summer and finally, in October, we went. Christian built sand castles, dug for treasure, and played chase with Craig and Ethan. The second Ethan stepped foot on the beach he took off running! He was in compete awe at the lack of boundaries around him. Craig followed him along the coast until his little exhausted legs gave out. This trip made me realize we need to have more family getaways!
October 2004

seascape

Layered Sticker Accents

To get cool dimensional looks, place stickers on both the top and bottom of clear acrylic accents. The "Love" tag here has a small open square, perfect for adding another embellishment. Get this dimensional look with rubber stamps as well!

—Patricia Anderson, Selah, WA

Layer flower stickers under an acrylic frame. *Accent by Patricia Anderson.* **Supplies** *Acrylic frame:* Heidi Grace Designs; *Flower stickers:* EK Success; *Definition sticker and mini brad:* Making Memories; *Concho:* Magic Scraps; *Ribbon:* Michaels (striped) and Morex (stitched).

computer tips

Create a "Contact Sheet"

As a digital photographer, I take a lot of pictures. Recently I took over 50 hoping to capture an "instant classic" of my son. I did—and couldn't wait to show it on a layout. I also wanted to include the "outtakes" I took trying to get the perfect shot.

Since I print my own photos from home, I didn't have easy access to a contact sheet. I considered printing one from my computer, but I couldn't find a template that would work with 53 photos (horizontal and vertical). I turned to Adobe Photoshop for help. Here's how to create this multi-photo look in Photoshop:

① Open a new document (8½" x 11").

② Determine what size your photos should be. I did some quick math and determined that each horizontal photo should be 1½" x 1" and each vertical photo should be 1" x 1½". Not great at math? Sketch your desired format on paper, then measure.

③ Create guidelines for correct spacing between pictures (mine are ¼" apart on all sides). Go to View and select New Guide. Choose to add either a vertical or horizontal guideline, then type how far over you want it to be. I added my first guideline at ¼", then I returned to New Guide and created my second guideline at 1¾". I did this until I had guidelines spaced correctly across my page. I then went down the page and made my horizontal guidelines.

④ Open each digital photo and crop it to the right size. Use the Move tool to easily drag and drop the photo into place.

⑤ After completing the first row, clear the guidelines and create new ones as needed to accommodate the rows that follow. "Stagger" a few rows and add variety by inserting a few vertical blocks as space fillers. You can even decorate them with ribbon, brads or other decorative elements!

—Jocelyne Hayes, Ladera Ranch, CA

Create a "contact sheet" look with computer software. *Pages by Jocelyne Hayes.* **Supplies** *Photo-editing software:* Adobe Photoshop; *Ribbon:* May Arts; *Vellum:* Accent Designs; *Rub-ons for title:* Making Memories; *Stamping ink:* ColorBox, Clearsnap; *Computer font:* Esat Hoxha NRML, downloaded from the Internet.

New Guide

Orientation
○ Horizontal
● Vertical

OK
Cancel

Position: 0 in

Want a faster "outtake" look?

See Angie Cramer's variation at right.

Cut and piece index prints to get the look you want. *Pages by Angie Cramer.* **Supplies** *Circle punch:* Marvy Uchida; *Computer fonts:* Bookman Old Style, Courier New and Times New Roman, Microsoft Word. *Idea to note:* Angie used a circle punch directly on the index print.

Index Strip Shortcut

I love the look of mini photos but don't always have time to place digital images separately. Instead, I create a similar look with index strips. For this layout, I cut index prints apart and pieced them together for a long border strip. I didn't have enough images to work with, so I made a color copy of the original index print and integrated the duplicate images.

—*Angie Cramer, Redcliff, AB, Canada*

Digital Time-saver

Upon switching to a digital camera, I found it harder to organize my photos. I couldn't just place them in a file box until I was ready to scrap them! Thank goodness I came up with a great alternative.

When I download pictures from my camera, I put them in an electronic file folder with the date on them. I then create another folder titled "To Be Scrapped." I go through the pictures I've downloaded and copy those I want to scrap to my "To Be Scrapped" folder. After the photos are scrapbooked, I simply delete them from the folder.

This has ended up being a big time-saver. I can find the "right photo" quickly and know when it was taken. Just as nice, the photos I love best don't get forgotten in a pile!

—*Tracey Odachowski, Newport News, VA*

There's no funner place to immerse yourself in American History than Williamsburg. Everyone had their favorites from the ghost tours to eating "Wild Game Pie," it made for tons of fun memories for the entire family.

Fake a stitched look with a serrated tracing wheel. *Page by Sande Krieger.* **Supplies** *Patterned paper and button:* K&Company; *Brads:* Making Memories (small) and Creative Impressions (large); *Ribbon:* C.M. Offray & Son (solid) and May Arts (gingham); *Stamping ink:* Ranger Industries; *Rubber stamp and paper clips:* Making Memories; *Tracing wheel:* Dritz; *Linen thread and circle tag:* OfficeMax; *Twill:* Scenic Route Paper Co.; *Computer font:* Book Antigua, Microsoft Word; Gunplay, downloaded from *www.dafont.com.*

Faux Stitching

Love the sewn look but prefer to mimic it without a sewing machine or thread? Just run a serrated tracing wheel (available at fabric and craft stores) along the edge of your paper to create an impression.

For added color, run the wheel through an inkpad before beginning or rub the serrated paper with chalk or an inkpad. To keep a straight line, I use a ruler and run the tracing wheel along the edge.

For a shabby chic look, run the tracing wheel back and forth several times to create overlapping lines. For a darker look, run the wheel across an inkpad before each pass.

—*Sande Krieger, Salt Lake City, UT*

fun, fast solutions

Quilted Accent

Make a hand-stitched "quilt" on your scrapbook page with patterned paper and felt. Here's how:

① Cut your shapes from coordinating patterned paper and felt.

② Cut the shapes down the middle, then mix your patterns and felt shapes. Adhere them together and sew along the seams with embroidery floss.

③ Assemble your design. I created a flower here, but this technique would also look great as a page border, a photo mat or various other page accents.

—*Danielle Thompson, Tucker, GA*

Use patterned paper to create a warm, quilted look. *Page by Danielle Thompson.*
Supplies *Textured cardstock:* Bazzill Basics Paper; *Patterned paper:* DieCuts with a View; *Letter stickers:* BasicGrey; *Embroidery floss:* DMC; *Buttons:* Junkitz; *Circle and oval cutters:* Creative Memories; *Adhesive dots:* Zots, Therm O Web; *Photo-editing software:* Adobe Photoshop; *Computer font:* Futura, downloaded from the Internet; *Other:* Felt. *Idea to note:* Danielle altered the colors in her photo electronically for a soft, duotone look.

my two favorite people in the world

gO, sIMon **go**
Go, dOG, gO!

Simons favorite read right now is Go, Dog. Go! Last night it was requested while we were eating at the dinner table (we are still trying to stick to our dinner table routine, trying is the operative word) Our main issue at dinner time (besides staying at the table) is getting Simon to eat something other than fruit So, if he wants to sit on Chris' lap and read Go, Dog. Go! and eat his chicken and brown rice then we are all for it! And he did And he asked for 'more chicken' And we were happy Small steps right?

And, almost even cooler...he is saying 'Go, Dog, Go!'

Maybe we should change it to 'Go, Simon Go!'

Round Pages

Circles are hot, so I created a page shaped like one! One of the coolest things about scrapbooking is the chance to try new things, to step outside your normal creative comfort zone and play.

I use circles on many of my layouts, mostly to break up the hard lines of my photos. Here, I created a page in the shape of a circle. Even though it has elements that go off the edge of the page (see the initial accents stapled at top left), the layout still fits into a 12" x 12" page protector.

—Ali Edwards, Creswell, OR

Create a page using a circle format. *Page by Ali Edwards.* **Supplies** *Textured cardstock:* Bazzill Basics Paper; *Patterned papers:* BasicGrey and Flair Designs (smiley face accent); *Letter stickers:* Chatterbox (small) and American Crafts (large); *Rub-on letters:* Making Memories; *Initial accents:* Autumn Leaves; *Pen:* American Crafts; *Corner rounder:* Marvy Uchida; *Stamping ink:* VersaColor, Tsukineko; *Computer font:* 2Peas Hot Chocolate, downloaded from *www.twopeasinabucket.com.*

Idea to note: To cut a perfect circle from a 12" x 12" sheet of cardstock, Ali traced the edge of a large bowl, then cut the circle out with scissors.

Bobbin Time-saver

I do a lot of sewing on my pages and have found that switching bobbins whenever I want to use a new thread color can be a bit time-consuming. To avoid this problem, I now use a product called "invisible thread," available at most mass-merchandising stores in the sewing section.

The clear thread is like monofilament (fishing line), and I use it on my bobbin for a perfect match to any thread color I happen to be using. No more switching bobbins! The clear thread is also great for any kind of "invisible sewing" you might need to do.

—Melissa Kelley, Pueblo, CO

computer tip

Create a custom title against a dark background with a computer font and acrylic paint. *Page by Olga Waywood-Joyce.* **Supplies** *Computer fonts:* Amazone (title) and Times New Roman (journaling), Microsoft Word; *Flower stamp and staples:* Making Memories; *Textured cardstock:* Bazzill Basics Paper; *Ribbon:* Masterstroke Canada.

White on Dark

Interested in showing a white computer font on dark cardstock? You can—simply trace the font with acrylic paint. Here's how to use the font of your choice in any color on cardstock:

1. Choose a word processing or graphics application (such as WordArt in Microsoft Word) that lets you print an outlined version of your font (see example).

2. Select your font, size and title.

3. Output the text to your selected paper or cardstock.

4. Select the desired color of acrylic paint, then paint over the title with a small paintbrush. This works great if you want certain colors that your printer doesn't have.

—*Olga Waywood-Joyce, Winnepeg, MB, Canada*

Acrylic Photo Accents

To create darling accents with small photos and clear, domino-shaped acrylic tiles:

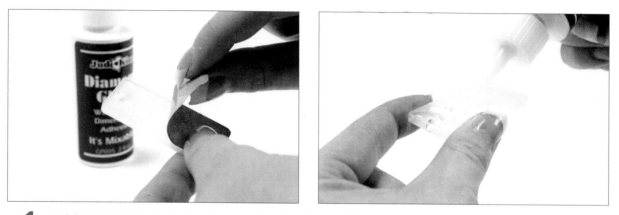

1 Peel the paper backing off a tile. Cover the rough side with a thin layer of Diamond Glaze.

2 Trim your photo to size and place it face-down in the glaze. Sprinkle tiny colored beads in the glaze.

3 Cover the same side of the tile with one more coat of Diamond Glaze. Let it dry.

4 Thread ribbon or fiber through the hole to finish the tile, then adhere it to your page.

Variations: In place of a photo, try this technique with patterned paper or stickers. For a polished look, ink the sides of the tile with a Slick Writer pen from American Crafts or StazOn ink from Tsukineko.

—Julie Geiger, Gold Canyon, AZ

Enhance acrylic accents with mini photos. *Page by Julie Geiger.* **Supplies** *Patterned paper:* Art Warehouse, Creative Imaginations; *Textured cardstock:* Bazzill Basics Paper; *Clear domino tiles:* Krystal Kraft, Sunday International; *Bottle cap:* Li'l Davis Designs; *Ribbon, rub-on letters, eyelets and staple:* Making Memories; *Number sticker:* Pebbles Inc.; *Stamping ink:* Stewart Superior Corporation; *Dimensional adhesive:* Diamond Glaze, JudiKins.

Ribbon Storage

I have a small scrapbooking space, so I'm always looking for ways to keep my supplies neatly hidden. I loved Faye Morrow Bell's ribbon storage box (page 124), but I needed a solution that would hold even more ribbon in less space.

I decorated a 7" x 8" x 8" paper maché box and cut chipboard cards to fit inside it. I wrap the ribbon around the cards and secure the ribbon ends with tiny pins, much like the fabric stores do for their trims. Some of the cards hold up to 25 yards of ribbon! This is a great space-saving solution for my limited space.

—Linda Albrecht, St. Peter, MN

Store ribbon by wrapping it around chipboard cards. *Ribbon box by Linda Albrecht.* **Supplies** *Patterned paper and brads:* Chatterbox; *Other:* Ribbon and paper maché box.

Vacation Photos Solution

Unfortunately, vacation photos don't always turn out the way we hoped. Maybe we couldn't zoom in close enough, we left our favorite camera at home and took a point-and-shoot or disposable camera instead, or maybe we just missed a shot. A great solution is to crop your photos small and mix them with small images cut from memorabilia items like postcards, playbills, brochures, or even small magnets like the one I included here.

—*Kelly Anderson, Tempe, AZ*

Supplement your vacation photos with cropped postcards and other memorabilia. *Pages by Kelly Anderson.* **Supplies** *Foam stamps and acrylic paint:* Making Memories; *Stickers:* Pebbles Inc.; *Other:* Souvenir magnet, playbill and postcards.

Postage Accents

I wanted fast, unique accents for the tags I often create for my pages. My solution? Cute stamps from the post office! I photographed them with my digital camera, then sized them as needed with photo-editing software. The "Happy Birthday" stamp is a must-have item!

—*Tammy Young, St. Peters, MO*

Add an easy graphic touch with a postage stamp. *Examples by Tammy Young.* **Supplies** *Rubber stamps:* Close To My Heart; *Stamping ink:* Close To My Heart and Stampin' Up!; *Fiber:* Fun Fur, Lion Brand; *Star punch:* EK Success; *Glitter:* Stickles; *Mulberry paper:* DieCuts with a View; *Background torn paper:* Michaels; *Other:* Postage stamps, patterned paper, button and more fiber.

Get a rich, soft look by printing scanned patterned paper onto velvet paper. *Page by Lynette Anderson for SEI.* **Supplies** *Patterned paper, velvet paper and ribbon:* SEI; *Pen:* Zig Writer, EK Success; *Stamping ink:* ColorBox, Clearsnap; *Foam stamps and acrylic paint:* Making Memories.

Velvet Patterned Paper

It's easy to add luxurious texture to your favorite patterned paper by simply photocopying or scanning and printing it onto velvet papers. Patterned paper copies best onto white or light-colored velvet.

Variation: Create a custom-text design on your computer, then print it out on darker-colored velvet papers.

—*Lynette Anderson, SEI*

Personalized Ribbon

Ribbon is a popular accent that can be used for many themes. Want to add extra punch? Consider ordering personalized ribbon. It comes in several colors, and you can choose ink color, edge style and whatever phrase or words you want on the ribbon.

Ribbon can be ordered cut (called hanger ribbon), or as continuous ribbon in 50-yard rolls. If you order continuous ribbon, be aware that it will last a while! Choose phrases that can be used on several projects. I ordered "Lovely Emma" and "Unmistakably Karl." Another idea is to choose generic phrases like "I Love You," "Family Memories" or "That Darn Cat!" and split the order with one or several friends.

—Karen Burniston, Colorado Springs, CO

Accent your pages with custom-printed ribbon. *Page by Karen Burniston.* **Supplies** *Patterned paper and rub-on images:* Christine Adolph, Creative Imaginations; *Brads and brad rub-ons:* Scrapperware; Creative Imaginations; *Personalized ribbon:* Mrbucks.com; *Paper crimper:* Fiskars; *Other:* Metal-rimmed tag, eyelet and gold thread.

Ideas to note: To make the flower accents, Karen cut petal shapes from patterned paper, matted them with cardstock, and put them through a paper crimper. She placed a pop dot underneath the bent petals for dimension and a rub-on embellished brad in the center. The sky picture at the top of the page is actually two photos—Karen hid the seam under the flower accent.

Then
AND
Now
1997
2004
Me & You
8 Years
I love looking at the old picture of us from the Marine Ball in 1997. We had been dating just over two months, and we were falling fast! It was one year earlier (exactly) that we met for the first time (of course we both know how that went!) Now here we are, eight years later! Who would have thought on that November night eight years ago that someday we would be married, with two beautiful children, and home in Yakima (no way – not Yakima!). It's so wonderful being with you Craig! I love you so much! I wonder what the next eight years will bring. Hopefully more of the same! December, 2004

ideas with sizzle

Puffy Quilted Accents

A touch of fabric gives a layout a rich feel and texture. By pulling the fabric through a cut-out design, you can create a unique look and add dimension without much bulk. Here's how:

① Draw your shape, then cut it out with an X-acto knife. Experiment with a variety of shapes, such as hearts, stars and abstract designs. Trace stencils for even more shape options!

② Place sheer fabric behind the cut-out shape and gently pull the fabric through until it puckers. >

Pull sheer fabric through a cut-out shape. *Page by Patricia Anderson.* **Supplies** *Textured cardstock:* Prism Papers; *Patterned paper, letter stickers and postage letters:* Mustard Moon; *Chipboard frame:* Rusty Pickle; *Decorative brads:* Making Memories; *Stamping ink:* Ranger Industries; *Computer fonts:* 1942 Report, downloaded from the Internet; Times New Roman, Microsoft Word; *Stitching guide (border design):* Lasting Impressions for Paper; *Other:* Sheer fabric and thread.

Puffy Quilted Accents cont.

③ Hand-stitch the fabric into place.

④ If the fabric is sheer, place a different color of cardstock behind it as the paper will show through.

Variation: Try this look with printed fabric, too! For added dimension, stuff small pieces of a cotton ball behind the fabric. Back it with a piece of cardstock to hold it in place.

—*Patricia Anderson, Selah, WA*

To emphasize your fabric accent, stuff it with pieces of a cotton ball. *Tag by Patricia Anderson.* **Supplies** *Textured cardstock:* Prism Papers; *Rubber stamp:* Rubber Stampede; *Button:* Junkitz; *Ribbon:* Textured Trios; *Stamping ink:* Stewart Superior Corporation and Ranger Industries; *Computer font:* American Classic, downloaded from the Internet; *Acrylic paint:* DecoArt; *Other:* Fabric.

Stencil Storage

I love using cardboard stencils on my layouts. Not only do I use the outside portions of the stencils, I often save the inside pieces for later use. I've found an easy way to organize the small pieces. Simply place repositionable tape on the back of the punched-out stencils and attach them to a piece of cardstock in their original configuration. When you need a letter, go to your stencil sheet and pull off the letter you want to use.

—*Dana Smith, Eden Prairie, MN*

Tidy Basket Solution

For me, the worst part of scrapbooking is tidying up odds and ends. Often I'll take out materials that I think will work on a page and not use half of them. Or, I'll have scraps left over that need to be sorted into my various scrap files.

As a solution, I've placed two baskets on my shelf: one for garbage and one for items that need to be put away. When I have a small item left over, I decide which basket to place it in. At the end of a session, my desk is clean and organized. Once every couple of weeks, I dump the garbage basket and put away the items in the filing basket. This saves me time and makes me feel like a very organized scrapper.

—*Lisa Lucchese, Courtice, ON, Canada*

Brush color washes over textured cardstock for a lovely watercolor effect. *Page and samples by Shannon Taylor.* **Supplies** *Textured cardstock:* Bazzill Basics Paper; *Color wash:* 7gypsies; *Printed transparency:* Artistic Expressions; *Heart frame:* Scrapworks; *Netting:* Naturally Pulsar; *Ribbon:* Anima Designs (green) and C.M. Offray & Son (orange); *Letter stamps:* PSX Design; *Spiral clip:* Clipiola; *Acrylic paint:* Making Memories; *Other:* Heart charm.

Idea to note: To highlight a portion of the text, Shannon brushed light-orange paint on the reverse side of the printed transparency.

Watercolor Texture

I've always loved watercolor paintings and wanted to use the cool canvas texture and brushstroke patterns on a scrapbook page. I found an easy way to get this look using 7gypsies' color wash on textured cardstock.

First, I use the dropper to fill a paintbrush. I then swish the color wash back and forth on the cardstock, letting portions of the cardstock peek through.

My favorite part is using the washes on different colors of cardstock. On the layout above, I used the red wash on light-orange cardstock. I've also had success with other color combinations like green on blue cardstock and red on lavender cardstock.

You can also use the color washes on specialty papers and fabrics. On the tag at right, I applied a blue wash to silk photo fabric (also available in canvas, twill and poplin). After it dried, I printed my picture on the fabric. I applied the same wash to the ribbon on the tag.

—*Shannon Taylor, Bristol, TN*

- Green on blue cardstock
- Blue on yellow cardstock
- Red on lavender cardstock

Supplies *Silk photo fabric:* Blumenthal Craft; *Word stickers:* American Crafts; *Buttons and buckle:* Junkitz; *Ribbon:* EK Success.

computer tip

During the summer, we enjoyed seeing a new resident out on the lake. Normally, the main birds we see are ordinary mallards, a few other grey-black ducks, and the occasional Canadian goose. This year, we noticed a snow-white duck (oddly reminiscent of the Aflac Insurance duck on TV) on the lake. She was very easy to spot, and we always kept an eye out for her. I say "she" because she was often in the company of a particular male mallard, and well...I'm sure it's apparent by the one photo that they certainly got together for more than just paddling around in the water! Before too long, there were about six downy ducklings following them around. Dev had a blast feeding the mama & papa duck out on the dock. And we'll likely feed them again next summer, too. I just hope that Snow White remembers that neither the plastic bread bag *nor* my fingers are edible...silly goose! ...I mean, silly duck! ;)

...duck.. duck..
Summer 2004

Add a Curve

I love the fluid, different touch a curved-edge photo adds to a layout. To create the curved edge here:

1. Insert a square shape onto the canvas and enlarge it as needed.

2. With the shape selected, click on "Distort" from the Effects menu. (I used the "Vertical Wave 1" effect.) Adjust the depth of the wave. Not deep enough? Simply distort it again. Stretching or condensing the length and width of the shape will further affect its curve.

3. If the wave is too wide but you still want to keep the shape intact, use the Marquee selection tool to slice out of portion of the middle (top to bottom). Combine the two halves by "flattening" them.

   If the wave is too thin, use the Marquee tool to cut the shape in half, insert a shape (square/rectangle) of the same length with the extra width desired, then combine (flatten) the three pieces together.

4. To create an hourglass shape, use the Marquee tool to cut the distorted shape in half top to bottom, then flip one half vertically. Flatten the two pieces together.

5. To "insert" the photos into the shapes, go to the Effects menu and select "Fill With Texture or Color." Choose "Picture," then select an image from your computer. Adjust the size and position of the image within the shape, then click "Done." Add a drop-shadow for definition.

   Note: I used the same distorted piece for all four photos—slicing, flattening and flipping vertically or horizontally as necessary. For the end photos, I flattened rounded corners to the shapes prior to adding the images.
   —*by Shannon Freeman, Bellingham, WA*

"Throw a curve" for a fun, custom touch. *Pages by Shannon Freeman.* **Supplies** *Photo-editing software:* Digital Image Pro 9; *Flowers:* Altered image from DIP9 stamp gallery; *Computer fonts:* Carpenter, downloaded from the Internet; Century Gothic, Microsoft Word.

faux and fabulous

Wallet Mini Book

I don't carry photos of my children in my wallet—in fact, I've had an empty photo sleeve in my purse for years! To remedy this situation, I turned the photo sleeve into a mini album that showcases my kids' recent photos. I love the results and can't wait to use this idea to create a quick yet terrific grandparents gift.

—Allison Kimball, Centerville, UT

Create a mini album from a wallet's photo sleeves. *Album by Allison Kimball.*
Supplies *Patterned paper and photo corners:* Chatterbox; *Rub-on letters:* Autumn Leaves, Chatterbox and Déjà Views, The C-Thru Ruler Co.; *Index tabs:* Avery; *Photos:* Jessi Stringham Photography.

Send duplicate photos to family members with a photo pocket card. *Card by Laura O'Donnell.* **Supplies** *Patterned paper, rub-on letters, metal-rimmed vellum tag and brad:* Making Memories; *Circle punch:* Marvy Uchida.

Card by Laura O'Donnell. **Supplies** *Metal sign accent:* Making Memories; *Letter stamps:* PSX Design; *Circle punch:* Marvy Uchida.

Card by Laura O'Donnell. **Supplies** *Woven label:* me & my BIG ideas; *Letter stamps:* Ma Vinci's Reliquary; *Stamping ink:* Stampin' Up!; *Circle punch:* Marvy Uchida.

Photo Pocket Card

As a scrapbooker, I take photos all the time. I like to send copies to friends and family after our get-togethers, and I try to send the photos out right away. The longer they stay with me, the more likely they are to get lost under a stack of magazines!

To create a handy pocket card like those shown here, I take two 5" x 7" pieces of cardstock and sew up three sides. (You can also take a 7" x 10" piece of cardstock, fold it in half, then sew up two sides.) I create a notch in the top with a circle punch.

The result is a pocket that's perfect for holding 4" x 6" photos. It's faster than creating a mini book, and it can be mailed out in a standard 5" x 7" envelope. Prefer not to stitch the edges of your pocket card? Attach them with staples or baby brads instead!

—Laura O'Donnell, West Chester, PA

Use an embossing stylus to apply small dots of paint around page elements. *Page by Lisa Le-Ray.* **Supplies** *Textured cardstock:* Bazzill Basics Paper; *Patterned papers:* Rusty Pickle and Paper Pizazz; *Printed elastic band:* 7gypsies; *Circle die cuts:* The Paper Loft; *Photo corners:* Making Memories; *Stamping ink:* Ranger Industries and Stamp It; *Acrylic paint:* Jo Sonja's; *Computer font:* Typewriter, downloaded from the Internet; *Other:* Buttons, ribbon, gold and silver thread.

Apply paint dots around flower images cut from patterned paper. *Card by Lisa Le-Ray.* **Supplies** *Patterned paper:* Urban Lily; *Stamping ink:* Distress Ink, Ranger Industries; *Acrylic paints:* Jo Sonja's; *Woven label:* Making Memories; *Other:* Jewel accents.

Dot Technique

Use small dots of acrylic paint to create a lovely, ornate look on your page! Although extensive dotting requires a steady hand and substantial patience, the technique is easy. Create the dots by dipping the round point of an embossing stylus into paint, then touching it lightly on the page. You should be able to get three dots every time you dip your stylus in the paint. Dot one layer at a time and remember to wipe the stylus clean each time you change colors.

A couple of quick tips? Make sure your paint is fresh and the consistency is good—it shouldn't be runny. To get the best effect with the dotting technique, choose simple shapes and ensure they're spaced so the pattern can flow around certain elements.

A fun variation? Try dotting around stickers or designs cut from patterned paper as well!

—*Lisa Le-Ray, Mawson Lakes,*
Adelaide, South Australia

Faux Animal Textures

While working with animal photos, I experimented with ways to re-create the texture of animal skins and furs. Here's how to use air-dry clay and a crackle stamp to create the look of deeply creased skin:

(1) Flatten your clay to about ⅛" thick with a rolling pin.

(2) Dust your crackle-pattern rubber stamp with cornstarch, place it on your rolled-out clay, and press very hard. If you want more creases, offset and rotate your stamp, then stamp it again until you like the look. (I stamped into the clay once for the elephant skin, twice for the rhino skin.)

(3) Use clay cutters to shape your clay into a round tag, a slide holder or another shape. Embed an animal button into the cut clay and follow package directions for drying instructions.

Tip: If you use clay that requires baking, avoid embedding objects that could melt. Wait until the clay has baked and cooled, then adhere the meltable objects with glue dots.

(4) After the clay is dry, paint your shape with brown and gray chalk. Add one or two drops of water directly onto your chalks. Mix it lightly with your brush, then paint. (You may need to do this several times. A little water won't damage your chalks—they'll be back to normal after they dry.) Let some chalk-water pool into the crevices of the animal "skin," then set it aside to dry.

Variations: To capture other textures, stamp the clay with a large stamp of the animal, then use clay cutters to cut out the texture you want. To get the texture of the lion's mane for my slide holder, I used a 4" x 5" stamp of a lion's head, then positioned my cutters over the mane. In place of chalk, I used two color washes with golden yellow and brown paint. I mixed one drop of acrylic paint to three drops of water.

—*Heidi Stepanova, Centralia, IL*

Fashion cool clay accents with animal-inspired textures. *Samples by Heidi Stepanova.* **Supplies** *Rubber stamps:* Embossing Arts (lion and leopard) and Rollagraph, Clearsnap (elephant and rhino); *Chalk:* Craf-T Products; *Acrylic paint:* Delta Technical Coatings; *Clay and clay cutters:* Makin's Clay, Walnut Hollow; *Tag:* DMD, Inc.; *Other:* Buttons.

Faux Epoxy Finish

For an inexpensive way to get the look of epoxy embellishments, apply a clear glass finish. Here's how to get this look with stencil letters:

1. Punch out the stencil middles and place them flat on a piece of wax paper. The wax paper will keep your embellishment from sticking to your work surface as it dries. Tip: To keep the wax paper in place as you work, splatter a couple of drops of water on your work surface before putting the paper down.

2. Apply at least three coats of acrylic paint to your stencil letters with a sponge brush. Allow each coat of paint to dry completely before applying the next one. Remember, you can mix your paints to get the perfect color for your layout!

3. Place your painted letters on a new sheet of wax paper and generously apply the clear glass finish. The liquid will appear cloudy as you apply it and

seem sticky as it begins to dry. This is normal—the finish will turn completely clear and smooth after it dries.

4. After your letters are completely dry, affix them to your page with adhesive dots.

Interested in a fun variation? Create the look on cardstock stickers! Simply:

1. Adhere the sticker to a white scrap of cardstock and trim away the excess.

2. Place the paper-backed sticker on wax paper and apply the glass finish. Let it dry fully.

3. Affix the accent to your layout with adhesive dots.
—*Donna Marie Bryant Durand*
North Attleboro, MA

Apply a clear, glossy medium to chipboard letters to create a faux-epoxy finish. *Page by Donna Marie Bryant Durand.* **Supplies** *Textured cardstock:* Bazzill Basics Paper; *Patterned paper and stickers:* Flair Designs; *Acrylic paint:* Making Memories; *Dimensional adhesive:* FolkArt Papier, Plaid Enterprises; *Stamping ink:* VersaColor, Tsukineko; *Slide mount:* Little Black Dress Designs; *Chipboard letters:* Making Memories; *Rub-on letters:* Li'l Davis Designs; *Computer font:* CK Sassy, "Fresh Fonts" CD, *Creating Keepsakes; Button:* EK Success; *Other:* Ribbon and mini brads.

Beribboned Chipboard Accents

Ribbons, ribbons, ribbons! I have so many and just keep collecting more. To use up some of my growing pile, I embellish chipboard shapes. To create colorful accents like these:

① Cut a piece of double-sided, high-tack tape to fit and adhere it to your chipboard shape.

② Peel away the tape's top layer and begin adhering strips of ribbon onto the shape. Alternate the sizes and patterns of ribbon and trim. Include fabric swatches if desired.

③ Once your design is layered onto the chipboard, turn the shape over and use it as a guide to trim off any excess ribbon.

—Allison Landy, Phoenix, AZ

Trim strips of ribbon to fit chipboard accents. *Page by Allison Landy.* **Supplies** *Patterned paper:* Déjà Views, The C-Thru Ruler Co.; *Letter stickers:* American Crafts; *Chipboard squares:* Bazzill Basics Paper; *Ribbon:* Carolace, C. M. Offray & Son and May Arts.

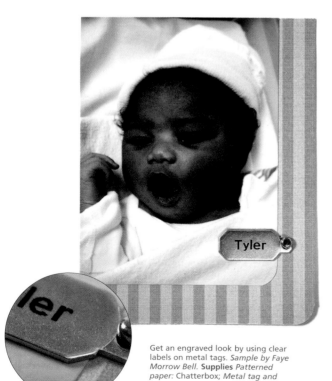

Get an engraved look by using clear labels on metal tags. *Sample by Faye Morrow Bell.* **Supplies** *Patterned paper:* Chatterbox; *Metal tag and brad:* Nunn Design.

Faux Engraved Tag

I love the look of machine-engraved metal tags but find them costly for scrapbooking. Here's how to get the look for less:

① Select a small, flat metal tag or photo stay.

② Print your text using a labeler and clear label tape. The example here by Faye Morrow Bell uses the LetraTAG QX50 labeler and clear plastic tape by Dymo.

③ Adhere the printed label tape to the tag.

④ Use sharp scissors or an X-acto knife to trim the label to fit the tag.

If you don't have a label maker or would like to make a larger tag, try these variations:

• Design your text using small alphabet stamps on clear labels or clear shelf-liner paper. Use permanent, solvent-based ink like Tsukineko's StazOn to prevent smearing.

• Create your text in a word processing program and print it on clear label stock (available at office supply stores). When purchasing clear label stock, be sure it's compatible with your printer (inkjet or laser) and completely transparent. Some labels advertise "transparent" but actually look translucent when applied to the tag.

—Becky Nunn, Nunn Design

Cover too large or small? Simply resize
it in your software program!

*Albums by
Lisa Winzeler.*
Supplies *Albums:*
Colorbök and Mrs. Grossman's.

Personalized Covers

I love creating custom 8" x 8" albums (they make great gifts and keepsakes!),
and I've come up with a fun way to personalize them. All it takes is photo-editing
software, photo paper, a Xyron machine and adhesive tabs. Here's how to create
a similar look:

1. Gather the supplies required, then open a new document in a photo-editing
   program like Photoshop, PaintShop or Digital Image Pro.

2. Size your document about 2" smaller than your album size.

3. Open up each photo in your photo-editing software, then drag it onto a new
   "layer" and resize it if necessary.

4. Arrange your photos how you'd like them to appear on your cover. (I like a collage approach.)

5. Add your text and graphics. While I make my own graphics, you can download
   numerous kits and elements online at places like www.scrapbook-bytes.com or
   www.twopeasinabucket. Be sure to add your text and graphics as new layers
   should you need to edit them later.

6. Save your arrangement as a working copy, with layers intact.

7. Make a copy of your document. Flatten the layers by going into the layers feature
   and selecting "flatten image," then save the results as a JPG or PSD file.

8. Select the best output quality available for your printer, then print your image on
   high-quality photo paper. Cardstock will also work, but you'll lose a little clarity.
   Canvas is another option; however, the results will not be as crisp as the other two.

9. After the image is dry, crop it if interested, laminate it with a Xyron machine, trim
   off any excess, then adhere the image to your album cover with Hermafix tabs.
   —*Lisa Winzeler, West Unity, OH*

Scrap Therapy

Sometimes even a mom needs a "timeout." When I
find myself getting overly stressed, I head to my scrap
room for "scrap therapy." I spend a little time sorting
things out—that is, my supplies as well as my
thoughts and emotions.

Somewhere along the way, I find the heaviness slipping away and the creativity starting to bubble up.
Works every time! When I'm ready to scrapbook, I
have an organized space where I can truly be creative.

—*Kelly Lautenbach, Bennington, NE*

computer tips

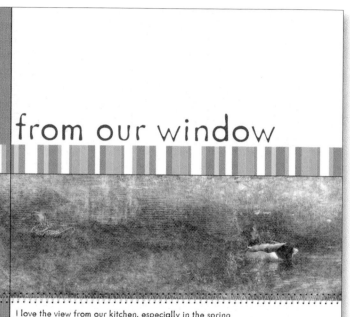

from our window

I love the view from our kitchen, especially in the spring and summer. I will just stand in the kitchen and watch the egret as it slowly goes around the perimeter of the pond, hunting for fish. Or I will watch the ducks as they swim along stopping every once in a while to duck their heads underwater eating their fill. I love having the windows open and hearing the chirping of the birds and the sounds of the crickets. But then sooner or later I am forced back to the reality of what I m doing in the kitchen in the first place, feeding you three animals!

June 1994

Packing-Tape Transfer, Digital Style

I love creating traditional scrapbooking looks on my digital pages. One of my favorites is a photo packing-tape transfer—without the tape. It's easy to mimic with photo-editing software and a "grunge" look electronic brush (create your own or do a search and download one for free from the Internet). I created the grunge brush here from a photo of a mica lampshade.

Once you've created or downloaded your brush:

1. Open a duplicate copy of your photo. In Adobe Photoshop, for example, click on the Eraser Tool in the Toolbox and select a brush from the Brush Palette. Reduce the Opacity to somewhere between 25% and 50%, depending on the look you want. Remember: The higher the opacity, the greater the amount of the photo that will be erased.

2. Click on the areas you wish to erase, either by single clicking or using more of a brush stroke. Continue erasing until you achieve the look you want. Position the photo on your digital page or print it out for use on a traditional page.

—Rhonda Stark, Plymouth, MN

Create a subdued, serene effect with a digital "packing-tape transfer." *Pages by Rhonda Stark.* **Supplies** *Photo-editing software:* Adobe Photoshop; *Digital papers and elements:* Gina Cabrera, Digital Design Essentials; *Computer fonts:* AL Gettysburg and AL Uncle Charles, "Essential" CD, Autumn Leaves.

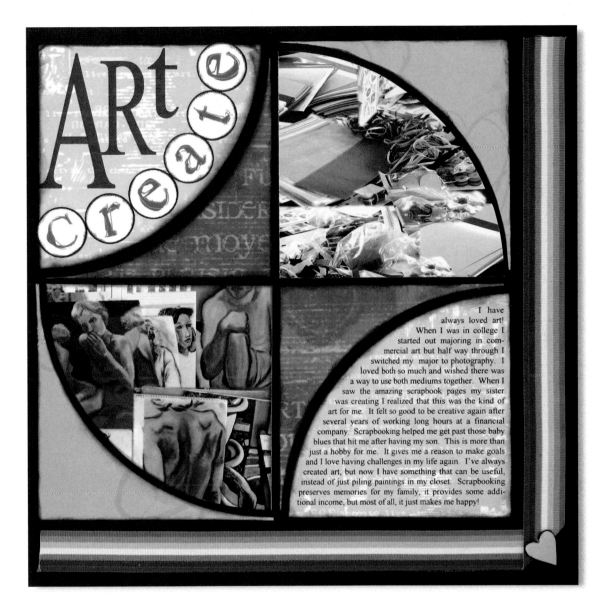

I have always loved art! When I was in college I started out majoring in commercial art but half way through I switched my major to photography. I loved both so much and wished there was a way to use both mediums together. When I saw the amazing scrapbook pages my sister was creating I realized that this was the kind of art for me. It felt so good to be creative again after several years of working long hours at a financial company. Scrapbooking helped me get past those baby blues that hit me after having my son. This is more than just a hobby for me. It gives me a reason to make goals and I love having challenges in my life again. I've always created art, but now I have something that can be useful, instead of just piling paintings in my closet. Scrapbooking preserves memories for my family, it provides some additional income, but most of all, it just makes me happy!

Do a Digital "Divide"

Want to create a distinctive look with squares, circles and lines that separate parts of a page? Simply create the shapes in Adobe Photoshop or another photo-editing program. Here's how:

1. Open a blank document in Photoshop. Choose Layers—New Layer from the Select menu.

2. Using the rectangle marquee tool, create a large square. Apply color with the fill tool by choosing Edit—Fill from the Select menu.

3. Create a second layer. Next, using the circle marquee tool, create a large circle within the square. (Tip: To make perfect squares and circles, hold down the Shift key as you drag the marquee to size.) Next, fill the circle with a different color.

4. Use the ruler guides to cut the square/circle grouping into four equal parts with the rectangle marquee tool (use cut and paste from the Select menu). Reverse some of the outer sections with the inner sections for a more dramatic effect.

5. After printing the resulting template, lay it over your photos and papers to use as a guide for cutting. The dark "lines" on the finished layout will come from the negative space when you adhere the spaced pieces to a dark cardstock background. You can also crop the photos into shapes directly in Photoshop, then print them out.

—*Erin Roe, Hampton, VA* ♥

Divide a page with the help of computer software. *Page by Erin Roe.* **Supplies** *Photo-editing software:* Adobe Photoshop; *Patterned papers:* Autumn Leaves, KI Memories and Creative Imaginations; *Textured cardstock:* Bazzill Basics Paper; *Computer fonts:* AL Scratched, "Vintage Fonts" CD, Autumn Leaves; Times New Roman, Microsoft Word; *Ribbon:* Les Bon Ribbon; *Charm and acrylic paint:* Making Memories.

Use magnets to help move interactive elements. *Page by Erin Lincoln.* **Supplies** *Patterned papers:* Paperfever, Making Memories and KI Memories; *Buttons:* American Crafts; *Chipboard letters:* Li'l Davis Designs; *Eyelets:* Creative Imaginations and Impress Rubber Stamps; *Rub-ons, metal tags, bookplate, sticker and ribbon:* Making Memories; *Laminator:* Xyron; *Computer fonts:* 2Peas Roxie, downloaded from *www.two-peasinabucket.com*; Times New Roman, Microsoft Word; *Other:* Magnetic strips.

Magnetic Solution

While driving to work, I had an epiphany about how to work around a page protector without cutting into it. My solution? Place thin magnet strips on the back of an interactive element and the corresponding area of a layout. The layout can be inside the page protector while an interactive element is held in place by magnets on the outside of the page protector.

Print out journaling, then cut it to fit over the magnetic strips on your layout. Adhere the journaling. It will help keep the magnetic strips hidden when the mini book is removed.

To protect the interactive element from dirt or small hands, place it inside the protector. The position isn't permanent—you can go back and forth as much as you like.

An idea to note? My mini book is actually a flipbook. My husband snapped a quick sequence of eight shots while I was juggling, and now when you flip through the book you "see" me juggle! If you repeat this technique, be sure to laminate your pages.

—Erin Lincoln, Frederick, MD

Handy Paint Trays

I love to use acrylic paints, but I hate cleaning up traditional paint trays. Instead, I use the plastic packaging from scrapbook embellishments. Many of the packages come with small compartments I can use to keep the colors from bleeding together. When I'm done painting, I simply throw the packaging away!

—Laura McKinley, Westport, CT

The layout includes journaling: "Baseball – America's favorite pastime. Somehow I thought you really didn't have the patience for the game. But once again you surprised me with your 'go get them' always-hustling attitude." with "PLAY BALL" letters and "T IS FOR TIGERS" accent.

savvy
tips

Faux Embroidered Monogram

Looking for an easy way to step up your die-cut letters? Set your sewing machine on a wide zigzag stitch and sew the letter in place.

Use thread that matches your cardstock for a clean look reminiscent of an embroidered monogram. Or, use a contrasting thread color for an edgy look. For this layout, I wanted to create an accent to resemble the embroidered "T" monogram on my son's baseball cap. I love the result!

—*Summer Fullerton, Tigard, OR*

Zigzag stitch a letter die cut to create an easy embroidered monogram accent. *Page by Summer Fullerton.* **Supplies** *Patterned paper:* Flair Designs; *Textured cardstock:* Bazzill Basics Paper (green) and The Paper Company (brown); *Rub-on letters:* Memories Complete; *Stamping ink:* ColorBox (black), Clearsnap; Distress Ink (brown), Ranger Industries; *Eyelets:* Stamp Studio; *Computer font:* Century Gothic, Microsoft Word; *Other:* Ribbon and twill.

Maximize Letter Stamps

Wouldn't it be great if you could embellish your favorite letter stamps with a variety of textures or designs? You can! (See page by Loni Stevens.) In stamping circles, this technique is called "kissing." Here's how to get this versatile effect:

1 Apply ink liberally to your texture stamp.

2 Press a clean, un-inked letter stamp directly to the inked texture stamp. The ink will transfer to the letter stamp in the pattern of the texture stamp.

3 Stamp your title with your textured letter stamp.

Tips for Success

- Make sure you generously ink your texture stamp. Pigment ink works best as it is wetter than dye- or solvent-based inks.

- Use a steady hand. If you rub the letter stamp against the texture instead of directly pressing or "kissing" it, you'll smudge the ink and your pattern won't be crisp.

- Ink the texture stamp first and "kiss" it with the letter stamp. This is more effective than inking the letter stamp and "kissing off" the ink with the texture stamp.

—Lisa VanderVeen for Leave Memories

Transfer ink from a texture stamp to a letter stamp. *Page by Loni Stevens.*
Supplies *Textured cardstock:* Chatterbox; *Patterned paper and circle sticker:* Scrapworks; *Vellum:* Paper Adventures; *Letter and texture stamps:* Leave Memories; *Photo corners:* Kolo; *Mini flower:* Savvy Stamps; *Rub-on circle and dashed lines:* KI Memories; *Dictionary tab, rub-on numbers and letters:* Autumn Leaves; *Printed transparencies:* Creative Imaginations (white text diamonds) and Li'l Davis Designs (tan leaves); *Rub-on numbers and words, staple, mini brad and photo anchor:* Making Memories; *Computer fonts:* AL Uncle Charles, "Essential" CD, Autumn Leaves; Lane Narrow, downloaded from the Internet.

Organize Small Items

Looking for a cute, inexpensive way to organize small embellishments? Decorate your leftover Tic Tac boxes and place small items inside. The boxes are compact, with easy-to-use lids that let you tap out what you need.

I wanted my Tic Tac boxes to look like little knick-knacks or decorations, so I covered them with patterned papers that would match the color scheme in my scrap room. Here are the dimensions:
- 3½" wide (1½" for front, 1½" for back, ½" for spine)
- 2¼" deep

—*Wendy Sue Anderson, Heber City, UT*

Store small embellishments in decorated Tic Tac containers. *Samples by Wendy Sue Anderson.*
Supplies *Patterned papers:* Chatterbox and 7gypsies; *Ribbon:* May Arts; *Stamping ink:* Stewart Superior Corporation; *Decoupage medium:* Mod Podge, Plaid Enterprises; *Tags:* Avery; *Pen:* American Crafts; *Other:* Hemp and Tic Tac boxes with the labels removed.

computer tip

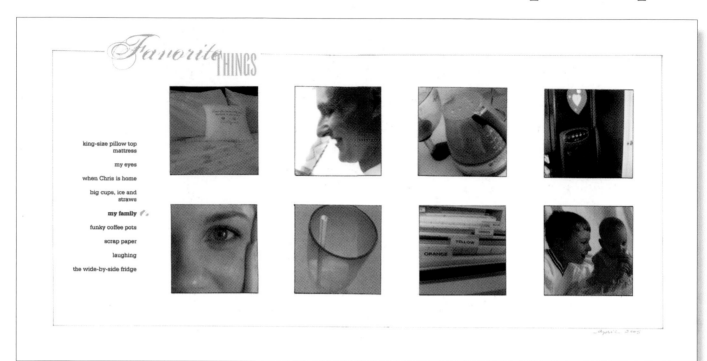

Go Online for Inspiration

Next time you need design ideas, go online and look at web-site designs! The inspiration for my "Favorite Things" layout came from a web-site template and a web-site design.

Anytime I'm looking for new design possibilities, I search Google Images (www.google.com) for "graphic design" or "graphic ads."

When I see a design I like (see two quick examples below), I right-click on it and save the image to an "Inspiration" folder I created on my computer. Whenever I need creative help, I just peek in the folder!

—*Tracey Odachowski, Newport News, VA*

Create a layout based on a web-site design you like. *Pages by Tracey Odachowski.* **Supplies** *Computer fonts:* Porcelain ("Favorite") and Runic MT Condensed ("Things"), downloaded from the Internet; Serifa BT (journaling), Microsoft Word; *Dingbat:* Designer Stuff; *Pens:* Stampin' Up!. *Idea to note:* Tracey drew borders around her photos with a fine-tipped pen. ❤

Samples from Google Images:

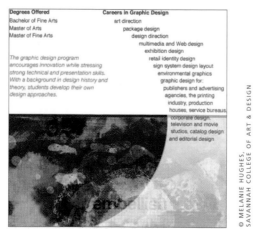

© MELANIE HUGHES, SAVANNAH COLLEGE OF ART & DESIGN

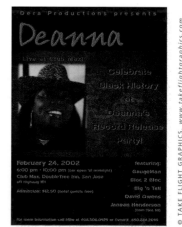

© TAKE FLIGHT GRAPHICS, www.takeflightgraphics.com

surefire solutions

Make It a Charm

Hate pulling out a hammer and eyelet setter every time you want to use an eyelet? Love decorative eyelets but wish you could use them more ways? Convert them into charms! You won't even need a hammer.

Simply pull off the back of an eyelet with pliers and file down any rough edges. Paint the eyelet if desired, add a jump ring and attach the resulting charm to your page. No hole for a jump ring? Adhere the eyelet with an adhesive dot.

—Amber Ries, Putzbrunn, Germany

Turn your decorative eyelets into darling charms. *Card by Amber Ries.*
Supplies *Patterned papers:* 7gypsies and The Paper Loft; *Acrylic paint:* Plaid Enterprises; *Decorative eyelet:* Dolphin Enterprises; *Computer fonts:* Binner Gothic, Hootie and Old Script, downloaded from the Internet.

Altered Window Pages

I love using precut window pages to complete wonderful layouts faster. All I have to do is choose some photos, adhere them to the back of the window pages, then embellish the results a bit.

The precut window pages can be trimmed down to create beautiful page frames. This window page originally had six openings—I cut out one connecting strip to make a larger opening for the bigger photo. Don't be afraid to cut and alter these precut window pages so they work for your photos. I like to sand the inner edges of the window openings to add a lovely distressed touch.

—Stacy Yoder, Yucaipa, CA

Cut precut window pages into page frames. *Page by Stacy Yoder.* **Supplies** *Textured cardstock:* Bazzill Basics Paper; *Cardstock page frame, leather frame accent and acrylic paint:* Making Memories; *Patterned paper:* Sweetwater; *Woven label:* me & my BIG ideas; *Label holders:* 7gypsies; *Computer fonts:* CAC Leslie, Primer Print (journaling) and Tintinabulation ("N"), downloaded from the Internet; Trebuchet, Microsoft Word; *Other:* Ribbon.

Create flowers and other cool shapes with anywhere hole punches. *Card by Rachel Ludwig.* **Supplies** *Textured cardstock:* Bazzill Basics Paper; *Patterned paper (used as a guide for the flower design):* KI Memories; *Letter stamps:* Fontwerks; *Stamping ink:* Nick Bantock, Ranger Industries; *Buckle:* Junkitz; *Other:* Ribbon.

Use anywhere hole punches to create a delightful page title. *Page by Rachel Ludwig, photo by Jill Beamer.* **Supplies** *Textured cardstock:* Bazzill Basics Paper; *Patterned paper:* Cross-My-Heart Cards; *Brads:* DieCuts with a View; *Letter stamps:* Fontwerks; *Stamping ink:* ColorBox, Clearsnap; *Photo corner:* Canson.

Hole-punched Title

I love the depth and subtle texture of a hole-punched title, as well as the hint of color you can add by backing the punched design with either patterned paper or cardstock. It almost has the look of letterset paper. To create a hole-punched title:

① Write your title in pencil. (Or, temporarily adhere a computer-generated title printed on copy paper to your cardstock. Remove it after punching your title.)

② Use two anywhere hole punches in different sizes to create the holes along the pencil lines. Tip: Want smaller holes? Use a paper piercer or large needle.

③ Adhere patterned paper or cardstock in a contrasting color behind the title.

Variation

Try this technique with flowers and other designs, too!

① Choose a piece of floral patterned paper to use as a guide. Temporarily adhere it to your cardstock.

② Use a small anywhere hole punch to punch holes along the lines of the flower on the patterned paper.

③ Remove the patterned paper guide and back the flower with a complementary color of cardstock.
—*Rachel Ludwig, Abbotsford, BC, Canada*

Embossed Clay Accents

To create cool page accents with embossing templates and clay:

 Put the clay through a pasta machine or roll it out with a rolling pin. Press the embossing template into the clay. Tip: Use a stylus to press the edges in deeper and create a more raised image.

2 Very carefully, lift the template off the clay. Press a glass into the clay to make the circle shape.

3 Bake the clay according to its package directions, then let the clay cool before painting it.

 Tip: I wanted the pieces to have a matte finish, so I didn't seal the clay. If you want a shiny finish, coat the painted clay with a dimensional adhesive like Diamond Glaze.

—*Lee Anne Russell, Brownsville, TN*

Make cute clay page accents using an embossing template as a guide. *Page by Lee Anne Russell.* **Supplies** *Patterned papers:* Autumn Leaves, BasicGrey and Scrapworks; *Clay:* Sculpey, Polyform Products; *Embossing template:* Lasting Impressions for Paper; *Acrylic paint, letter ribbon slides and rub-on letters (title):* Making Memories; *Rub-on accents (dots):* KI Memories; *Rub-on numbers (date):* Autumn Leaves; *Zipper pull:* Junkitz; *Ribbon:* May Arts; *Corner rounder:* Creative Memories; *Computer font:* 2Peas Fat Frog, downloaded from www.twopeasinabucket.com.

Budget Work Surface

To avoid damaging my desk or work surface when cutting, gluing or painting, I work on a colorful acrylic cutting board purchased from the kitchen supply area of my local discount store. The cutting boards generally cost under $2 each, so when they get damaged or dirty, I can just throw them away and buy new ones without feeling guilty.

Another plus is that the cutting boards come in fun shapes and colors. One month I bought a daisy. Another, I bought a fish!

—*Kris Gillespie, Brandon, FL*

computer tip

A Little Reflection

My son Connor struggled with acid reflux the first six months of his life, which we both found pretty overwhelming. As Connor was able to get beyond that, he was a much happier baby and I was a much happier mom. I found myself reflecting on how much we need each other and are growing together.

While scrapbooking the relationship, I tried to communicate a sense of reflection in both my writing style and the mirrored shapes and type. To get the mirrored shapes, I photographed Connor crawling in natural light on top of a large mirror in my kitchen. I edited the photos later in Adobe Photoshop to enhance the intensity of the shadows.

Look closely at my mirrored titles and you'll note that the wording is slightly different ("born in love, born to love" and "loving you, loving me"). After creating the first line in each title, I typed the second line and rotated the text upside-down in Adobe Illustrator.

The reflection concept is perfect for people of all ages and topics. Use it with a baby, a teenager, a parent or yourself!

To create white text on a gray background, simply draw a square and color it gray, then type text on top and make it white. A fun variation? Type white text on top and let patterned paper show through from behind.

—Amy Montgomery, Burlington, ON, Canada ♥

Add a sense of reflection with mirrored type and electronically enhanced shadows. *Pages and photos by Amy Montgomery.* **Supplies** *Computer software:* Adobe Photoshop; *Textured cardstock:* Bazzill Basics Paper; *Ribbon and charm:* Making Memories; *Computer font:* Libel Suit, downloaded from the Internet.

super tips

Idea to note: To create an antiqued look, Elsie painted the wire word with two colors of paint.

Adorn your page with darling, easy-to-make flowers. *Page and samples by Elsie Flannigan.* **Supplies** *Textured cardstock:* Bazzill Basics Paper; *Patterned papers:* Autumn Leaves, BasicGrey, Chatterbox, Daisy D's Paper Co., KI Memories, Making Memories, My Mind's Eye and Scrapworks; *Wire word:* Creative Imaginations; *Brads:* American Crafts; *Ribbon:* C. M. Offray & Son; *Epoxy stickers:* MOD, Autumn Leaves; *Acrylic paint:* Making Memories; *Pen:* Pigma Micron, Sakura; *Stamping ink:* ColorBox, Clearsnap; *Other:* Buttons.

Make Cute Flowers

I accented my photo with flowers made from ribbon, brads and patterned paper. Here are three easy ways to create your own:

① Stick a brad through 2–4 short strips of ribbon.

② Cut small "pie" shapes from circles punched from patterned paper. Place a printed epoxy sticker in the center. If desired, write short phrases around the edge of the sticker.

③ Cut flower shapes from patterned paper. Or, if you have a patterned paper with a circle or flower theme, cut out individual shapes and use them as accents. It's a fun way to break up a busy pattern.

Try making these flowers from vellum, felt, fabric or found objects as well!

—Elsie Flannigan, Springfield, MO

Create custom twist ties with fabric stickers and craft wire. *Album by Sandi Genovese for Mrs. Grossman's.* **Supplies** *Textured cardstock, vellum, stickers and fabric stickers:* Mrs. Grossman's; *Rub-on words and safety pins:* Making Memories; *Craft wire:* Artistic Wire Ltd.

Bonus tip from Sandi:

Make a mini book using cardstock, page protectors and fabric twist ties. Trim your cardstock to size and punch ¼" holes along the left-hand edge. Make the book easy to open by creating a fold on the top piece of cardstock approximately 1" from the left-hand edge.

Use refill packs of page protectors either straight from the package or trimmed to size with extra ¼" holes punched in the binding edge. Use the fabric twist ties to bind the album together.

Fabric Twist Ties

Fabric twist ties are inexpensive, take just minutes to make and are so versatile. Use them to bind mini books, embellish pages or close a gift bag filled with cookies (or scrapbook supplies!). With so many options available, you can easily color coordinate the twist ties with your projects. To make a fabric twist tie:

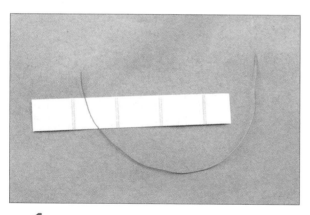

1 Trim a fabric sticker so it's approximately ¾" deep. Cut a piece of wire slightly longer than the fabric sticker strip.

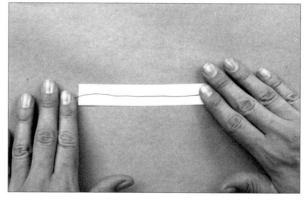

2 Peel off the sticker backing and place the wire down the middle of the sticker (sticky side up).

3 Fold the sticker in half lengthwise, trapping the wire inside.

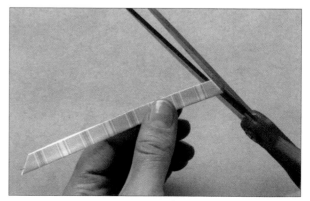

4 Trim each end at an angle. Be sure to cut off the excess wire.
—*Sandi Genovese, Mrs. Grossman's*

Use the negative space left from a sheet of letter stickers or die cuts as an inexpensive alphabet accent. *Page by Stacy Yoder.* **Supplies** *Textured cardstock, patterned paper, printed die-cut letters and tag, ribbon and rub-on flowers:* KI Memories.

Budget Letter Accents

Looking for new ways to use your scrapbooking items? Don't overlook the packaging or leftover pieces. They can be made into pretty photo frames, tags and more.

After I punched the letters from a printed sheet of die-cut accents, I thought it was too cute to throw away. Instead, I backed the punched-out sheet with black cardstock and covered the company's logo along the bottom edge with ribbon. I love how the sheet accentuates this page.

—*Stacy Yoder, Yucaipa, CA*

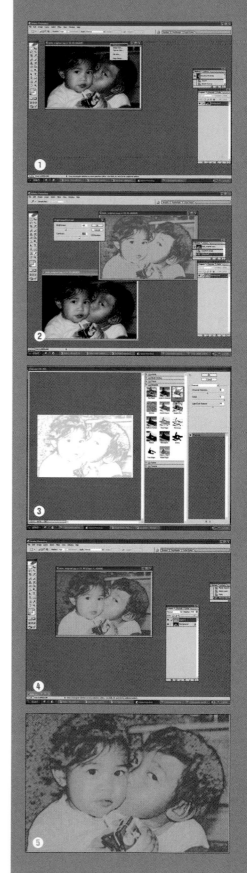

Page by Emelyn Magpoc.
Supplies *Computer software:* Adobe Photoshop; *Textured cardstock:* Bazzill Basics Paper; *Patterned paper:* BasicGrey; *Metal charm, rod and brads:* K&Company; *Ribbon:* May Arts; *Chipboard letters:* Li'l Davis Designs; *Stamping ink:* ColorBox, Clearsnap; *Computer font:* 2Peas Tattered Lace, downloaded from *www.two-peasinabucket.com.*

(original photo)

Charcoal with Color

I love the cool photo effects (like "chalk" and "charcoal") that can be applied with the Sketch filter in Adobe Photoshop. I wanted to create a more "artsy" version of the photo of my children shown here, so I decided to apply a charcoal effect and output the photo on textured cardstock. The challenge? I wanted a charcoal look, but I also wanted to retain some of my photo's original colors. Here's how I achieved that:

1. To create an electronic copy of my original photo, I selected Duplicate from the Image menu.

2. Working with the duplicate copy, I accessed the Filter menu and selected Sketch, then Charcoal, from the descending menu.

3. I selected the charcoal thickness, detail and light/dark balance desired. Next, I accessed the Image menu and its Brightness/Contrast dialog box. I adjusted my settings to achieve the look I wanted.

4. I used Ctrl-A on the keyboard to select the entire duplicate copy, then Ctrl-C to copy the entire image. I pasted the duplicate copy over the original photo by pressing Ctrl-V.
   Next, I adjusted the image's opacity (see the top of the Layers palette). I reduced the percentage to let the background picture show through the sketch.

5. From the Layer menu, I selected Flatten to "fuse" the original and duplicate copies. The result? A classic, artsy look I love. It's also perfect for pages I want to frame and hang on my wall or give as gifts.

—*Emelyn Magpoc, Newark, CA*

Customize letter stickers with rub-on designs. *Page by Cheryl Manz.*
Supplies *Patterned paper, rub-ons and epoxy stickers:* MOD, Autumn Leaves; *Letter stickers:* Chatterbox and SEI; *Ribbon:* foof-a-La, Autumn Leaves; *Patterned paper tape:* Heidi Swapp; *Stamping ink:* VersaMagic, Tsukineko.

Decorated Letter Stickers

Kick up your page titles by decorating your letter stickers! Here, I took a rub-on accent with a circle design and added pieces of it to every other large blue letter sticker. I also layered portions of orange letter stickers over the white ones, trimming things to follow the curve of the paper so the letters would stand out on both patterned papers. For some fun variations on letter stickers (see examples):

- Stamp a design on them with acrylic paint (blue "s").

- Apply a rub-on design, then layer smaller stickers on top (orange "s").

- Rough them up with sandpaper, then adhere small embellishments like paper flowers (red "s").

—*Cheryl Manz, Paulding, OH*

Customize letter stickers with rub-on designs. *Samples by Cheryl Manz.*
Supplies *Letter stickers:* SEI (blue), Scenic Route Paper Co. (large black), Scrapworks (red) and Sticker Studio (small black); *Acrylic paint:* Making Memories; *Flower stamp:* Scrappy Cat; *Stamping ink:* VersaMagic, Tsukineko; *Rub-on design:* Heidi Swapp; *Paper flowers:* Prima.

Stamp an image on cardstock and patterned paper to create a classy image. *Sample by Jenni Bowlin.* **Supplies** *Rubber stamp:* Postmodern Design; *Other:* Vintage book paper and rhinestones.

Rubber Stamp Stencils

I'm always looking for new ways to use my favorite stamps. Recently, I wanted to add a pattern to the openings in an image. After some experimenting, I came up with a way to create a stencil from a stamped image. Here's how:

1 Ink your rubber stamp, then press it on cardstock.

2 Stamp the same image on a scrap of patterned paper.

3 Using a craft knife, carefully cut out the open areas from the stamped image on the patterned paper. Tip: Cut slightly outside of the lines for a more accurate look.

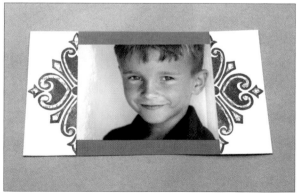

4 Apply a thin amount of liquid adhesive to the open areas on the image stamped on your cardstock. Adhere the cutouts to the image.

—Jenni Bowlin, Mt. Juliet, TN

We were lounging around singing, and I asked Ethan to request the next song. His response was "Wufuded". I had him repeat it. "Sing Wufuded". Ethan was so serious every time he'd say it; I had no idea what he meant. It just made me crack up hysterically! Finally, once the exhaustion from laughing was enough for me, I asked Ethan to sing the song himself. Maybe then I could figure it out. He proceeded with "Oh wufuded is to ride…"! Ah-ha! Jingle Bells!

wufud ed

2 0 0 4   2½

cool tips

Capturing Lights on Film

Wish you could take great pictures of holiday lights? You can! Simply set your SLR camera to manual focus and aim it at your Christmas tree lights. Turn off your flash and adjust your lens so the lights are out of focus.

Unusual? Yes, but this creates an interesting photo that can be used as a page's background element. (See the pattern beneath the title on my page.) Try this with any group of holiday lights!

—Leah LaMontagne, Las Vegas, NV

Pictures of holiday lights brighten a Christmas layout. *Page by Leah LaMontagne.* **Supplies** *Textured cardstock:* Bazzill Basics Paper; *Letter stickers:* American Crafts; *Circle punch:* CARL Mfg.; *Rub-on numbers:* Chartpak; *Stamping ink:* StazOn, Tsukineko; *Other:* Brads.

Beaded Lace

To create gorgeous beaded accents that look like lace, gather two colors of beads, a piece of lace and high-tack, double-sided tape. Then follow these four steps. You can achieve stunning results like those in the page at right by Deb Perry.

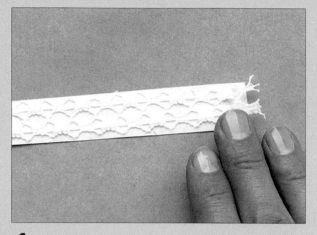

1 Cut a piece of high-tack, double-sided tape to fit your lace strip. Peel back the tape's red protective liner to expose its sticky surface. Place your lace over the exposed tape and press it firmly to secure.

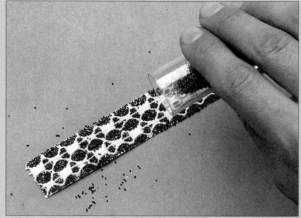

2 Pour your first color of micro bead over the exposed tape. Swirl the beads around with your fingertips to fully cover the tape. Tap the tape on its side to dislodge any excess beads. *Tip:* Work over a large, shallow plastic container to catch excess beads. You can then easily pour them back into your bead container.

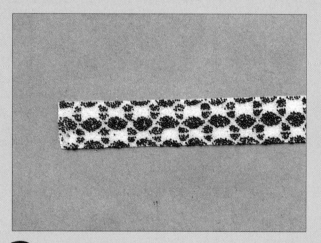

3 Peel the lace off the tape to reveal a lace pattern. Pour your second color of micro beads over the newly exposed tape areas.

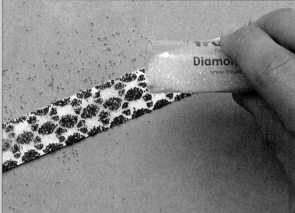

4 Swirl the beads around with your fingertips to fully cover the tape. Tap the tape on its side to dislodge excess beads. Enjoy the lovely look you've just created.

Variation: Try this technique with glitter, colored sand or pigment powder as well!

—Suzanne Chase, Treasure It

Create a beaded lace accent to add an elegant touch. *Page by Deb Perry.* **Supplies** *Patterned paper:* BasicGrey; *Ribbon:* Textured Trios; *Rub-on letters:* KI Memories; *Letter stickers:* Pebbles Inc.; *Micro beads:* Treasure It (clear) and Hallcraft (red); *Pen:* Creative Memories; *Other:* Lace.

Bonus tip from Deb:

I was so excited to try Suzanne's idea! I love how you can get various looks by choosing different color combinations and lace patterns.

Some things I learned while trying this technique? Choose a simple lace design at first, then work up to more intricate designs. When you're comfortable with the technique, consider using more intricately crocheted items like the snowflake on my page.

—Deb Perry, Newport News, VA

label your albums

I like organization and neatness, so all my albums are the same size and color. It used to be that when I tried to find certain pages, I had to open nearly every album to find the one I was looking for. I came up with a great solution: using an eyelet hole punch, brads and a label holder I could make my own spine labels! This costs much less than having the spines embossed, and I can easily change the album titles at will.

—Faith Richardson, Yakima, WA

it's the little things that matter most! ☒

remember

Index Print Layout

I have loads of index prints from the past few years. This page expresses how those little moments all play a part in life's big picture. I like to look at this page, reflect on those details and just be thankful! I've always loved layouts that incorporate index prints as accents—this was an opportunity to focus on the prints instead. I like to use all black-and-white or all-color images for visual unity.

—Elsie Flannigan, Springfield, MO

Put your index prints to good use on a year-in-review layout. *Page by Elsie Flannigan.* **Supplies** *Patterned paper:* K&Company; *Acrylic paint and rub-on word:* Making Memories; *Stamping ink:* ColorBox, Clearsnap; *Other:* Leather strip and buttons.

time-saver

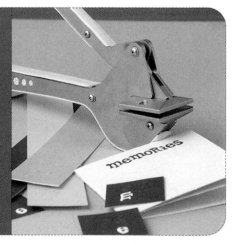

Tired of getting adhesive on your fingers or layout when adhering intricate die-cut letters and shapes? Try QuickStripz, 2" x 12" strips of adhesive-backed cardstock. All you do is die cut your shapes or letters, then peel and stick the cardstock to your page.

—Melany Simpson, QuicKutz

Fresh use for index prints!

how to park straight · that i am beautiful without makeup · how to budget my paycheck · that guys are just as sensitive as girls · to pray without ceasing · not to be overly materialistic · a basic knowledge of lighting and music equipment · to be secure with myself · that i don't know everything · how to air up a tire · that i need to save money · that having a long distance relationship doesn't have to be as hard as it seems · not to procrastinate · the basic rules of baseball · how to dress punk · i can do anything and become anyone if i only have faith in myself · how to park straight · that i am beautiful without makeup · how to budget my paycheck · that guys are just as sensitive as girls · to pray without ceasing · not to be overly materialistic · a basic knowledge of lighting and music equipment · to be secure with myself · that i don't know everything · how to air up a tire · that i need to save

clint · joel · barker

Faith. Over all of our months of dating, the single most important thing you have taught me is to have faith. Not only to have a secure faith in God, but faith in myself. Faith, not just to dream and set goals, but to know deep in my heart that I will fulfill things I never fathomed possible. You have a sincere faith in everything you are doing and where God is leading you everyday. Because you have faith in yourself, you can obtain anything you desire. You will go places and do incredible things because you already believe you can. You have taught me to never discourage or give-up in anything, but to hold strong to my faith. Because of you, I have set my goals higher and I know I will achieve them. Thank you.

baseball · how to dress punk · i can do anything and become anyone if i only have faith in myself · how to park straight · that i am beautiful without makeup · how to budget my paycheck · that guys are just as sensitive as girls · to pray without ceasing · not to be overly materialistic · a basic knowledge of lighting and music equipment · to be secure with myself · that i don't know everything · how to air up a tire · that i need to save money · that having a long distance relationship doesn't have to be as hard as it seems · not to procrastinate · the basic rules of baseball · how to dress punk · i can do anything and become anyone if i only have faith in myself

3 Cool Touches

I knew my "Faith" page would include a lot of text, so I used a few tricks to help. Here's how I created watermark-like words, custom background paper and text that curves:

① **Watermark-like words:** After changing my paper size to 12" x 12" in Adobe InDesign, I created a text box and typed "What you've taught me . . ." I selected a text color slightly darker than the cardstock the text would be output on. I used a large font size and a script font so the text would be easily distinguishable from my foreground text.

  I then made a slightly larger text box and positioned it over the first. I typed my journaling in black and increased the line spacing so it's easier to read "What you've taught me . . ." through the lines.

② **Custom background paper:** I typed the list of favorite qualities on my computer, then output the text to cardstock on a wide-format printer. Again, I chose a slightly darker text color.

③ **Curved text:** I used the Justify Text option to make all the text in the journaling box a perfect rectangle. I then added spaces to the left of each line (I needed to form a concave so my photo would fit in the journaling). I did several test prints on scrap paper to get the shape I wanted.

—*Kayla Schwisow, Elizabeth, CO*

Boost your text's impact with a custom background, screened letters or curves. *Page by Kayla Schwisow.* **Supplies** *Circle punch:* EK Success; *Ribbon:* Making Memories; *Computer fonts:* Liorah BT and Lionel Text Genuine, downloaded from the Internet. *Idea to note:* Kayla placed a dinner plate on top of her main photo, then trimmed around the picture with a craft knife.

Bind mini sheet protectors together with ribbon for an economical gift album. *Sample by Annette Hardy for All My Memories.* **Supplies** *Textured cardstock:* Bazzill Basics Paper; *Patterned paper, ribbon charms, ribbon and epoxy, fabric and vellum stickers:* All My Memories.

Cute, Cheap Gift Albums

Looking for a fast, cute and inexpensive gift album? Try this speedy solution:

① Cut a piece of cardstock to 6" x 2" and fold it in half lengthwise. It will serve as the album's binding.

② Punch holes in the folded cardstock that line up with the holes in your 6" x 6" page protectors.

③ Place the folded cardstock over the left edge of five 6" x 6" page protectors. Thread ribbon through the holes of the cardstock and sheet protectors, then tie it in a double knot on the front of the album. For a more finished look, tie different ribbons all along the binding and cut the ends to 1".

Variation: Create a mini 12-page calendar using this mini-album format and six page protectors. Instead of attaching the page protectors with ribbon, use small key rings.

—Jennifer Haynes for All My Memories

way-cool tips

See-through Layouts

Create a "see-through" layout by connecting different die cuts and punched paper pieces for the background. This is an eye-catching way to display photos and use up leftover punches!

—Jennifer McGuire, Cincinnati, OH

Create a layout with a "see-through" background. *Page by Jennifer McGuire.* **Supplies** *Die cuts:* Sizzix; *Punches:* EK Success; *Textured paper:* Fibermark; *Rub-ons:* Making Memories and Doodlebug Design; *Computer font:* AL Uncle Charles, "Essential Fonts" CD, Autumn Leaves.

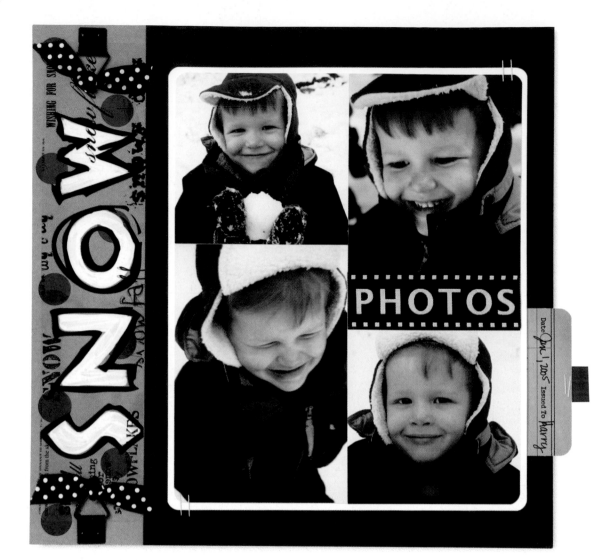

Paint on the back of a transparency sheet. *Page by Kim Kesti.* **Supplies** *Patterned paper, photo hangers and library card:* Daisy D's Paper Co.; *Transparency:* Boxer Scrapbook Productions; *Acrylic paint:* Delta Technical Coatings; *Ribbon:* May Arts; *Other:* Staples.

Transparent Titles

I like filling in transparency titles with acrylic paint to help them stand out, but sometimes it's hard to "paint inside the lines." Now I flip the transparency over and paint on the back. I use a small, flat-edged brush, and I don't worry too much about perfect edges—once I flip the transparency back over, it's perfect!

—Kim Kesti, Phoenix, AZ

new photo angle

A few Christmases ago, we decided to try something a little different for a family photo. We collected everyone at the bottom of the foyer stairs and took a picture from above. It turned out great—and it didn't hurt that looking up creates a very flattering angle for most people.

To duplicate this look, set up the camera well beforehand (I had to tie mine to the railing). Use a helper to define the imaginary "box" people will stand in, and arrange them in the way that works best for relationship, height and more.

Other tips? Use fast film to prevent neck strain in your subjects and know the timer signals on your camera. If you're going to be in the picture, make sure you clear the stairway of obstacles and wear shoes with a good grip!

—Arleigh Jamieson, Vancouver, BC, Canada

Rubber Stamps as Embossing Templates

Want an embossed look but don't have the right embossing template? Use your rubber stamps!
I used this technique to create metal snowflake accents, but you can try this with any shape.

1 Stamp image onto metal with permanent stamping ink.

2 Place stamped metal on a foam mat backed with an acrylic mat, image side up. Use an embossing tool to trace stamped image.

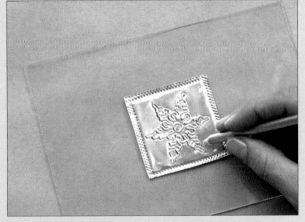

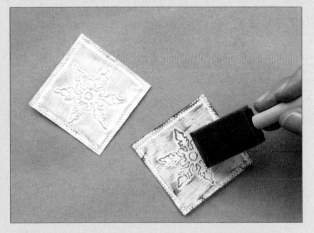

3 Remove foam mat. Place stamped metal on acrylic mat, ink side down, and use embossing tool to further define the image. Decorate edges as desired. (I used a decorative wheel to create a border.)

4 Lightly paint over the embossed image with white acrylic paint. Once the paint is dry, lightly brush dark blue acrylic paint over the white paint.

Some tips for success:

- When using letter stamps, remember to emboss on the correct side of the accent so your letters will face the right direction.

- The simpler the design is, the easier it will be to emboss, so try using stamps with less detail.

- Experiment with different colors of acrylic paint for a new look.

—*Alisa Bangerter, Centerville, UT*

Dress up your winter page accents with stamped metal snowflakes. *Examples by Alisa Bangerter.* **Supplies** *Aluminum metal sheets:* Ten Seconds Studio; *Acrylic stamps:* Close To My Heart; *Stamping ink:* StazOn, Tsukineko; *Acrylic paint:* Plaid Enterprises, Delta Technical Coatings and Ranger Industries; *Texture paint:* DecoArt; *Patterned paper:* Scenic Route Paper Co. and Bo-Bunny Press; *Ribbon:* Stampin' Up!; *Metal bead chain, ribbon charm letters and pins:* Making Memories; *Buckle:* K&Company; *Clear acetate letters:* Heidi Swapp; *Other:* Brads, staples and thread.

AFTER

Cool Photo Look

While in Flagstaff last winter, I took two pretty photographs of red branches emerging from melting ice. The scene reminded me of a butterfly emerging from a chrysalis, and I loved looking at what seemed a harbinger of spring. I hoped to create a layout that would capture the impact and beauty of the moment.

My first attempt (see small page) seemed a bit bland, so I decided to create a lightened version of the smaller photo and insert it behind the bottom block of text. The text is still legible, but the picture adds color and continuity. Here's how to create this effect in Adobe Photoshop:

① Make a copy of your digital photo by highlighting it and selecting Layer, Duplicate Layer, OK.

② From the layers palette, click once on your duplicate photo layer to select it. The layer will be highlighted in blue.

③ At the top of the screen, select Image, Adjustments and Desaturate. The image will become black and white.

④ At the top of the screen, select Image, Adjustments and Color Balance. A box will pop up with slide arrows for Cyan – Red, Magenta – Green and Yellow – Blue.

To get a sepia-colored tone like the one in my layout, pull the slider arrows about halfway to the left toward Cyan, Magenta and Yellow, then move the arrows left or right as necessary to get a color you like.

⑤ At the top of the screen, select Image, Adjustments, Brightness/Contrast. Pull the slider arrow for Brightness all the way to the right (+100). Pull the slider arrow for Contrast far to the left (-75.) This will give your picture a watermark effect. Adjust brightness and contrast to get the look you prefer.

⑥ Select your now-lightened picture in the layers palette. Drag the picture until it's beneath your text box—the text will show up on top of the photograph. If your text doesn't "pop" visually, go back to your photograph and adjust Brightness and Contrast until you can read the text on top of it.

Tip: For greater control over the continuity of line between your original and lightened photos, start with a photo with greater depth of field.

—*Jennifer Weiss, Phoenix, AZ*

Add color and visual interest with a photo behind your text. *Pages by Jennifer Weiss.* **Supplies** *Photo-editing software:* Adobe Photoshop; *Computer fonts:* ParkAveD, Eurostile and Perpetua, all preloaded with Photoshop.

BEFORE

keep that calendar

As I attempted to de-clutter my planner last January, I pulled out all the pages from the previous year and threw them in the trash. I was so sad several days later when I wanted to do a layout about Noah's summer vacation and couldn't remember all of the events and dates that made up those two months. I learned a big lesson: I need to keep my calendars!

This year, be sure to file away old calendars. Not only can they help you recall details of past events, they also speak volumes about who you are, your values and how you spend your time.

—*Jenni Bowlin, Mt. Juliet, TN* ♥

Discovered a surprising shortcut? Have a hot tip or technique to share? E-mail it to *editorial@creatingkeepsakes.com* and put "Tips & Tricks" in your subject line.

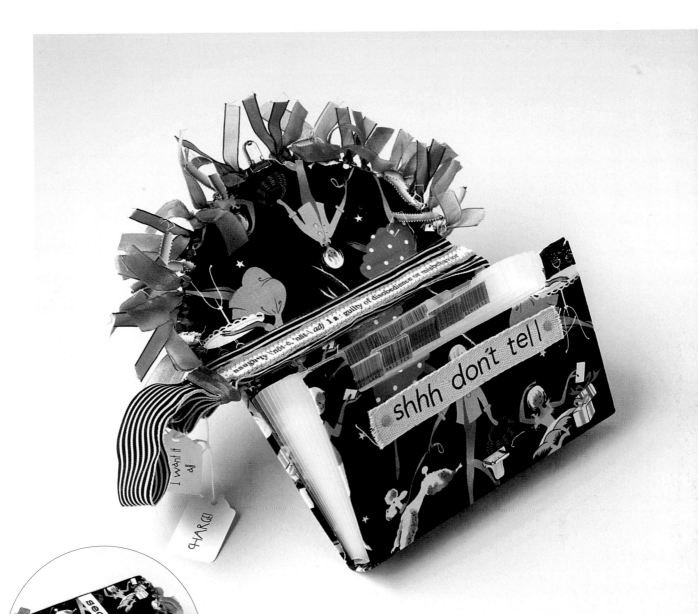

tips you'll love!

Secret Stash

After regularly losing track of punch cards, coupons and receipts from my local scrapbooking store, I decided to create a "scrapper's little black book" to keep track of the items (and conceal my purchases from my husband!).

I purchased a coupon file folder at an office supply store, covered the folder with fabric, and embellished it with scrapbooking supplies. The result is a fashionable, whimsical way to stay organized and on top of the "paper trail."

—Miley Johnson, Omaha, NE　➤

Little Black Book *by Miley Johnson.* **Supplies** *File folder:* Office Depot; *Fabric:* Michael Miller fabrics; *Twill and buckle:* 7gypsies; *Wooden letters:* Michaels; *Brads:* Lasting Impressions for Paper; *Tags:* Avery; *Ribbon:* May Arts; *Computer font:* Barcode, downloaded from the Internet.

Secret Decoder Journaling

I thought it would be fun to create journaling that requires decoding, so I purchased the old Password game by Milton Bradley to see how the decoder envelope worked. I then made a cute decoder by painting the lens of a looking glass with transparent craft paint. Tip: You can make decoders from anything clear, including transparency film.

Next, I encoded my text. Here's how you can do it as well:

1 Create a text box in your word-processing software, then type in your journaling. Select a light color of text so that it will be difficult to read behind the overlay text.

Tip: This technique works best when you choose a font with thin lines.

2 Next, create a second text box on top of your journaling text box and fill it in with your overlay text. Use a tall, plump font with minimal spacing in between the lines. The color of the overlay text should match your looking glass or "decoder" exactly. Tip: To match the "decoder" perfectly to the overlay text, print out several shades of red on one sheet of paper. Place your "decoder" over each color to find the best match. (It will be the color that disappears behind the "decoder.")

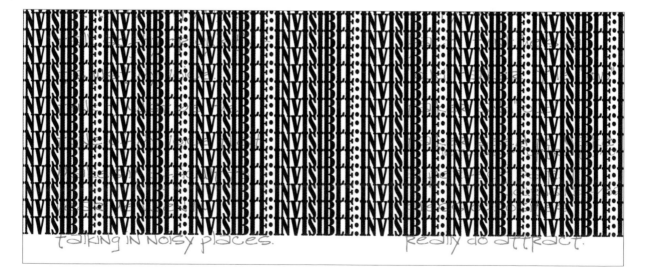

3 Duplicate your text boxes and separate them onto two independent pages. Keep the text boxes in the exact same location on each page. Tip: Microsoft PowerPoint works great for this step. Use the duplicate slide feature.

Use your game decoder envelope, or make a decoder from anything clear—transparency film works!

Sometimes I Feel Invisible. *Page and samples by Laura Stewart.*
Supplies *Patterned paper and tag:* Gartner Studios; *Rub-on letters:* Scrapworks; *Letter stickers:* American Crafts; *Craft paint:* Stained Glass Sheer Color, Krylon; *Ribbon:* C. M. Offray & Son; *Styrene blank:* Plaid Enterprises; *Looking glass:* Manto Fev; *Hole reinforcers:* The Paper Source; *Clear pocket:* Ty; *Corner rounder:* Creative Memories; *Computer fonts:* Bernhard MT Condensed (overlay), Monotype and Reprobate (journaling), downloaded from the Internet; *Patterned paper:* Cut from notecards.

4 Print both text boxes onto the same sheet of cardstock. Print the journaling text box first, then reload the same sheet of cardstock into your printer. Print the overlay text right over the top of the journaling text. (Avoid printing both text boxes at the same time; you won't end up with text layered over text.)

Interested in some variations? Here are three:

- Give a loved one a heart-shaped decoder. Leave secret notes and messages for him or her around the house. These could be as simple as sticky notes on the refrigerator or as elegant as a beautiful card.

- Host a scavenger hunt game at a child's birthday party. Arm the children with "decoders" in different colors and hide messages for them to locate.

- Hide your text behind Andy Warhol-style colored photographs.

—Laura Stewart, Fort Wayne, IN

Twinkling Titles

Recently, I decided to pull out my old jars of fine glitter and make an eye-catching title with foam stamps. I knew the stamping base had to be clear to see the glitter effect on my page, so I used liquid adhesive in place of acrylic paint.

This is my favorite new technique! Simply stamp your title with liquid adhesive, then cover it with glitter, shaking off the excess before the adhesive dries.

—*Jenni Bowlin, Mt. Juliet, TN*

Love to Read by Jenni Bowlin. **Supplies** *Patterned paper:* Treehouse Designs; *Foam stamps, epoxy letter and slider:* Li'l Davis Designs; *Chipboard heart:* Heidi Swapp; *Other:* Rhinestones.

Snow Texture

Use a craft texture medium (I like Snow-Tex by DecoArt) to add wintry details to your cards and pages. You can create everything from snowy looks to fluffy trim to fuzzy bunny ears. Sprinkle on a little glitter while the medium is still wet, or tint it with acrylics to get more fun looks.

—*Heidi Allred, West Jordan, UT*

Accent by Heidi Allred. **Supplies** *Wood frame:* Chatterbox; *Textured cardstock:* Bazzill Basics Paper; *Letter stamps:* PSX Design; *Letter rub-ons:* Scrapworks; *Snowflake stamp, stamping ink and linen thread:* Stampin' Up!; *Acrylic paint:* Delta Technical Coatings; *Texture medium:* DecoArt.

Add a snowy look to your winter cards and pages with a craft texture medium. *Card by Heidi Allred.* **Supplies** *Rubber stamps and stamping ink:* Stampin' Up!; *Acrylic paint:* Delta Technical Coatings; *Snaps:* Doodlebug Design; *Ribbon:* May Arts; *Texture medium:* Snow-Tex, DecoArt.

Use dies to emboss letters into clear styrene accents. *Page by Laura Stewart.*
Supplies *Styrene blank:* Plaid Enterprises; *Patterned paper and ribbon:* American Crafts; *Die cuts:* Sizzix and QuicKutz; *Decorative scissors:* Fiskars; *Stamping ink:* Stewart Superior Corporation; *Computer font:* Keystroke, downloaded from the Internet.

Raised Styrene Letters

Use low-profile dies (like QuicKutz and Sizzix Sizzlets) to emboss letters into shapes cut from styrene blanks. Here's how you can create accents like the "m" and "e" featured on my page:

① Use a die-cut machine to cut a circle from styrene and one from paper. Cut a ring (also from styrene) the same size as the circles.

② Place the styrene circle on a piece of glass. Set a low-profile letter die face-down over the styrene. Cover it with a piece of parchment paper, then use a hot craft iron to "emboss" the letter into the styrene circle. The heat from the iron will be hot enough to let the die cut through, but it won't be hot enough to melt or disfigure your shape.

③ Highlight the embossed letter with solvent-based stamping ink.

④ Place your accent together in the following order: paper circle, styrene ring, embossed styrene circle. Use high-tack tape to hold the pieces together.

Variation: Place beads or other small items inside your accent before adhering the embossed styrene circle over the styrene ring to create shaker boxes.

—*Laura Stewart, Fort Wayne, IN*

Create a Marbled Background

Ever considered making your own marbled paper and transparencies? It's fun and easy with spray paint and a water bath! Simply gather a disposable cake pan or dish tub (I get mine from the dollar store), paper or transparency, a craft stick or toothpick, spray paint, and an old towel or garbage bag. Then:

1 Pour an inch of water into a disposable tray that's slightly larger than the paper you are marbling. Note: The paint will permanently stain your container.

Following the manufacturers' instructions, shake the cans of all spray-paint colors you wish to use. Work quickly—you won't be able to do this once you start applying the paint.

2 Holding the cans about 2" above the water, spray several spots of color on its surface.

 Stir with a craft stick to mix the colors. Work quickly, as the spray paint will surface dry in about a minute.

 Set your paper on the surface of the water. Run a toothpick or craft stick around all edges of your paper, lifting excess paint film off the surface of the water as you go.

5 Lift your paper straight up to remove it (you will not lift one side as shown here—we're simply showing the effects). Set the paper on an old towel or garbage bag to dry.

Some Marbled Looks I've Created

I love to experiment with different combinations to create different effects. While I've made sheets with just one or two transparent colors, I've also had fun combining iridescent finish spray, stained glass paint (transparent), opaque color and metallic silver.

It's always fun to play! You can use the sheets as-is or punch or die cut shapes from them.

I Love You. Supplies *Cover:* Sizzix die, Provo Craft; *Spray paint:* Short Cuts, Paper Finishes, Krylon; *Ribbon:* May Arts (black dot) and unknown ("I love you"); *Brad:* Making Memories; *Other:* Flower.

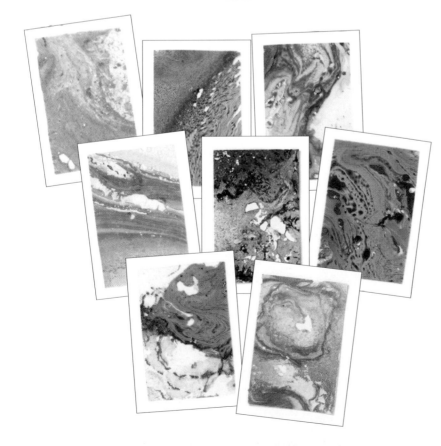

4 Helpful Tips

• If you want to marble multiple sheets, use a shallow container and two buckets, one full of water and one empty. As you create your sheets, you can dump the old water out and pour new water quickly, without too many trips to the sink.

• Spray several spots of your most prominent color first, then fewer and smaller spots of your accent colors. Don't worry about regions without color—they let your background show through.

• While you can use any brand, I like the Paper Finishes line of spray paints from Krylon. They're archivally safe, designed for crafts and scrapbooking, and come in smaller cans.

• For the fastest drying time, use Mylar (transparencies) instead of paper. Mylar won't absorb water like paper will, so it's ready as soon as the paint sets.

—Heidi Stepanova, Centralia, IL

computer tip

AMBERLY
FROGGY & DOGGY
· A TRIO OF FRIENDS ·

g o o d

friends

You can't see him very well in this picture, but Froggy is tucked under your head, where he can usually be found during any rest-time, nap-time or at night. His tummy is no longer plump with stuffing and is flat as a pancake where your cute little head has made a permanent impression. You carry him around all day scrunched between your elbow and your side, so that your hands are free to play. Daddy won him for you at the fair when you were about 11 months old, right before Aiden was born. He truly was your first love... and then along came doggy. I'm not sure how or when the fuzzy duo won you over as a pair, but you certainly do rely on both of them for security and comfort. And neither one will do the trick alone, oooh no! You must have BOTH of them together. It really is very sweet how much you love them and treat them as good friends..

Do a Soft Fade

Create a softer look in your layouts by electronically feathering and brushing away the straight-line edges of your pictures. To achieve this effect in Photoshop, first apply a soft fade vignette to make the outer edges of the picture gradually blend away.

Next, using the Layer Mask tool and a "grungy" or spackled brush, subtly distress the edges. Adobe Studio Exchange has many free downloads for grungy brushes. You can also find a helpful Layer Masks Tutorial (tailored just for scrapbookers) at fotoscrapix.com.

—Kimberly Bee, Tolleson, AZ ♥

Good Friends *by Kimberly Bee.*
Supplies *Photo-editing software:* Adobe Photoshop CS2; *Brush:* Downloaded from Adobe Studio Exchange; *Computer fonts:* Eras Light ITC and Goudy Old Style, Microsoft Word.

Idea to note: To create the circle effects at bottom left, Kimberly used the Marquee, Layer Mask and Custom Shape Tools in Photoshop CS. Using the Path Tool and a small soft brush, she traced around each circle several times, then applied a subtle drop-shadow.

Bubbles by Jennifer Perks. The layout features scattered transparent circles mimicking bubbles, with the word "bubbles" spelled in acetate letters, and a black-and-white photo of a young girl blowing bubbles.

Text on layout: hours (OK, more like 30 minutes) of fun! • catching them, popping • them, watching • an endless supply of bubble liquid + a freshly-turned two-year old = • them float. big bubbles, little bubbles, no bubbles, more bubbles. • ellie had a complete blast just playing with bubbles. april 2005.

ultra-hip tips!

See-through Shapes

I love to use transparent shapes on my layouts as "windows." I used transparent circles here to mimic bubbles, but this technique works well with almost any shape you can imagine. For a clever variation, sandwich a piece of memorabilia or a small photo between two pieces of transparency so they appear to be "floating" inside of the transparent shapes.

—*Jennifer Perks, Round Rock, TX* ❯

Bubbles *by Jennifer Perks.* **Supplies** *Acetate letters:* Heidi Swapp; *Shape cutter and circle template:* Fiskars; *Transparencies:* Office Depot; *Computer font:* Century Gothic, Microsoft Word; *Computer software:* Apple Pages.

So Girly *by Elsie Flannigan.* **Supplies** *Textured cardstock:* Bazzill Basics Paper; *Patterned papers:* Making Memories and Scenic Route Paper Co.; *Flowers:* Prima; *Acrylic paint:* Making Memories; *Stamping ink:* ColorBox, Clearsnap; *White journaling pen:* Uniball, Sanford; *Aluminum duct tape:* Henkel Consumer Adhesives; *Other:* Embroidery thread and buttons.

Faux-Metal Accents

Did you know you can create the coolest faux-metal embellishments with aluminum duct tape? (You can find it at any hardware store.) Soon you'll be creating custom designs that match your layouts perfectly! Simply freehand your design or use a stencil, then follow the steps shown at right. You'll be loving the look!

—*Elsie Flannigan, Springfield, MO*

To Create Elsie's Faux Metal Accents:

1 Draw or stencil your design onto duct tape with a pen.

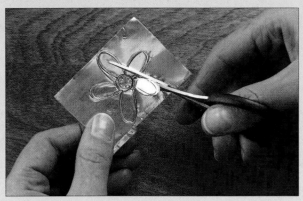

2 Cut out the design with scissors.

3 Cover the design completely with acrylic paint.

4 Once the paint is almost dry, rub the painted surface with a paper towel for a distressed look.

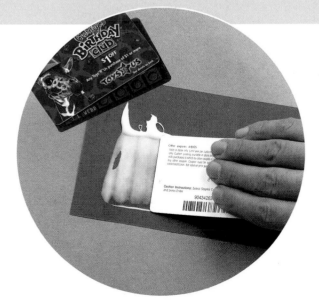

Fantastic Plastic

The next time you get a phony plastic credit card in the mail, keep it! I save these cards—and leftover holiday cards—to use as glue spreaders when I need to apply tacky liquid adhesive on a project.

Whether you're covering the front of an album with patterned paper or creating your own book by hand, this free tool helps you spread a thin, even layer of glue over your surface. After adhering your paper, use a hard rubber brayer to ensure good adhesion and remove any bubbles. After using your card, just wipe it clean and reuse it on other projects.

Another use: Many of these gift cards have interesting designs. You can alter the cards and use them as cool page embellishments.

—Renee Foss, Seven Fields, PA

birthday

turning 24

< a birthday tradition >
one between two siblings

Mom took these photos of me and my younger brother, Mike, in our living room just before the two of us were about to head out the door to the movies. Each year - since Michael's 21st birthday in 2002 - Michael and I have had this "unsung" tradition of treating the other to a movie for their birthday. This year [2004] Mike took me to see the movie *Mean Girls* at the new theater in American Fork. Since my birthday fell on a Tuesday, we had the theater almost all to ourselves. We sat in the very top row, in reclined seats, with our feet kicked up. It was great! If you're gonna watch a movie... that's the way to do it! Neither Mike, nor myself, set out to make this a tradition. But now that it's become that, it's something I've looked forward to each year since we started. It's the one day a year I'm guarenteed special one-on-one time with my little brother. A kid I love, even if I forget to tell him.

Birthday by *Loni Stevens.* **Supplies** *Acrylic paint, photo turn, mini brad, staples, rub-on word ("birthday") and lace trim:* Making Memories; *Circle sticker:* Scrapworks; *Clear photo corners:* Henkel Consumer Adhesives; *Computer fonts:* LB Tino, "Lisa's Favorite Fonts" CD, Vol. 2, *Creating Keepsakes*; AvantGarde and Minion, Adobe Systems.

Acrylic Paint Embellishment

Want another cool use for acrylic paint? Squeeze it on wax paper to make page titles, monogram letters, flowers and other shapes like Loni Stevens did here. After the paint dries, I peel the shapes off and adhere them to my layout. For extra panache, I sprinkle a little glitter on the paint while it's still wet. Tip: For added precision, pour the paint into a small squeeze bottle (such as one for glue).

—*Julie Stella, Newnan, GA*

Two tips from Loni: Use a wax-based pencil to draw the desired shape on the wax paper before you squeeze out the paint. Let the paint dry thoroughly before you remove the accent and glue it to your layout!

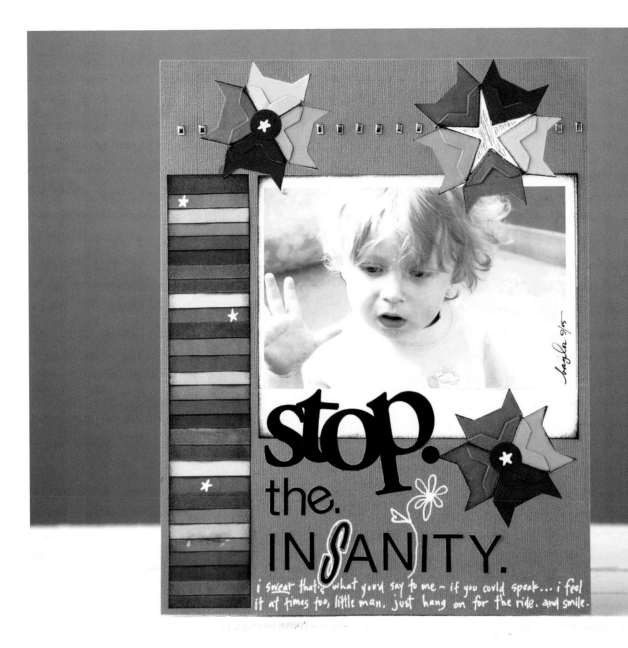

savvy spring tips!

Photo Corner Flowers

Photo corners come in such a variety of colors and sizes. Why not use them for more than just corners? Arrange them together to create flower- or star-shaped accents for your layout!

—*Tia Bennett, Puyallup, WA* ➤

Stop the Insanity *by Tia Bennett.* **Supplies** *Textured cardstock:* Bazzill Basics Paper; *Patterned paper:* Christina Cole, Provo Craft; *Photo corners:* Heidi Swapp; *Brads:* Heidi Grace Designs; *Stickers:* American Crafts, Making Memories and Chatterbox; *Other:* White gel pen and black stamping ink.

Dingbat Mask

While typing a document in Microsoft Word, I discovered a bunch of cute dingbat designs in different fonts. I loved how they could easily be enlarged and trimmed to use as masks (see steps below). For variety, experiment with different sizes or change them to bold or italic before printing. You can even layer different dingbat masks after trimming.

1 Print out a dingbat shape that's been enlarged to 300-400 point size in a word processing program.

2 Trim carefully around the dingbat to create a mask.

3 Place the dingbat mask on background paper and sponge paint over it.

4 Once paint is almost dry, carefully lift the dingbat mask to reveal the image.

—Nic Howard, Pukekohe, New Zealand

Instant Friends *by Maggie Holmes.* **Supplies** *Textured cardstock:* Bazzill Basics Paper and My Mind's Eye; *Patterned paper:* Rusty Pickle; *Rub-ons:* Scrapworks and KI Memories; *Letter stickers:* Scrapworks; *Flowers:* Prima; *Mesh:* Magic Mesh, Avant Card; *Metal flower charm:* Making Memories; *Pen:* Sharpie, Sanford; *Other:* Rhinestones, brads, twill and office clip.

∧ Custom Textured Cardstock

I'm a huge collector of embossing templates, but I recently discovered I can use items from my supply stash that aren't even intended for dry embossing. I especially love using metal charms. Simply attach them face up on a light box with removable adhesive, place your cardstock over the design, and trace around the design with a stylus. You can also use chipboard shapes to achieve the same look!

—*Maggie Holmes, South Jordan, UT*

> **Variation:** Use a straight-edged embossing template or ruler to create background patterns like harlequins and plaids on your layout.

—*Robyn Werlich, St. George, UT*

Unforgettable Moments *by Robyn Werlich.* **Supplies** *Textured cardstock:* Bazzill Basics Paper; *Chipboard letters and "unforgettable" rub-ons:* Heidi Swapp; *"Moments" rub-ons and ribbon:* Making Memories; *Line embossing template:* Fiskars; *Other:* Flower, thread, staples, plastic file folder tab and jewelry tag.

It couldn't have been easy. Taking a second chance on love is nothing short of a leap of faith. But throw into the mix a little girl who already had a daddy she adored and it's got disaster written all over it. Zoe and I came as a package deal. You knew, Nate, that loving me automatically entitled you to a one-way ticket on the parenthood express, with no refunds, no returns, do not pass go, do not collect $200. Can I even begin to tell you how grateful I am that you took that ride, Nate? Slowly, quietly, you formed a bond with Zoe. You may not be her daddy and you may be her parent by default, but you became her friend by choice. You earned her trust. She loves you. She seeks you out each day. For that, and for a million other reasons,

I love you

Package Deal *by Andrea Chamberlain*. **Supplies** *Photo-editing software:* Adobe Photoshop CS2; *Computer fonts:* Garamond, Microsoft Word; Scriptina and Beautiful ES, downloaded from the Internet. *Idea to note:* Andrea wanted to frame this layout for Father's Day, so she created her page with 9.5" x 7.6" dimensions.

Hip and High Key

While I liked this photo of my husband and eldest daughter, Zoe, it was taken at an odd angle and included other distracting elements. Still, I really wanted to scrap it since Zoe avoids any camera like the plague. (You know how that is!) To get the cool results here, I used two techniques:

① **Porcelain Effect.** Following a tutorial from www.myjanee.com, I used layer masks, adjustment layers and blending modes to extract the subjects from the background, turn them black and white and achieve this high-key look. This technique is perfect for less-than-stellar photos (unfortunately, I have quite a few).

② **Two-toned Text.** This dramatic look lends itself so well to the graphic-style layouts I love. It's even fairly simple to achieve. In Adobe Photoshop CS2, simply type text in your choice of color on one layer. Then, with your text layer active, go

into Layer>New>Layer Via Copy to get an exact copy of your text positioned directly over your first layer of text.

On your new layer of text (with your text tool active), change the color of your text. Right-click on your second layer and choose Rasterize Type. Next, use the marquee tool on your rasterized type to select whatever portion of your new text layer you don't want. Hit delete and voila, two-toned text! Here, I flipped my picture horizontally so my two-toned text would fit better.

The colorful sunflower photo by Marjorie Manicke was downloaded from the web site stock.xchang.com. I used Photoshop's magnetic lasso tool to extract the flower from its background for my page. I love the look!

—*Andrea Chamberlain, Penfield, NY*

Today was my conference with Meredith's kindergarten teacher. She had a standard sheet to fill out on each student – notes on their behavior, social interaction, etc. She had just one phrase written on Meredith's: "So Sweet!" I had to laugh. I'm glad that is the side that Meredith is sharing with her teacher. I am well aware, though, that there is a definite flip side. When she is good, she is very good...and we know the rest at home!
Journaling November 9, 2005/ Photos taken on the first day of kindergarten, August 2005

cutie

happy

SO SWEET

So Sweet *by Tracy Miller.* **Supplies** *Patterned paper:* Christina Cole, Provo Craft; *Letters and die cuts:* Scrapworks; *Rubber stamps:* Fontwerks.

Stamped Patterned Paper

I love all of the new shape and design stamps out there, and my favorite way to use them is to enhance patterned paper. Try over-lapping different shapes and colors for a new look.

—*Tracy Miller, Fallston, MD*

easy photo organization

Small three-ring binders (like the sarabinders by Hot Off The Press) are a super easy way to organize your photos. Simply use a square binder to organize your photo CDs and tall binders to organize index prints and negatives.

Label the spine of each binder with what's inside. You can store the binders together on a shelf for easy access when you're ready to scrap.

—*Shauna Berglund-Immel for Hot Off The Press*

computer tip

Love *by Rhonda Stark.*
Supplies *Photo-editing software:*
Adobe Photoshop; *Digital papers,
tags, stitched labels, stitching and
paper clip:* Gina Cabrera,
*www.DigitalDesignEssentials.com;
Computer font:* AL Uncle Charles,
"Essential Fonts" CD, Autumn Leaves.

Alter an Existing Color

While I don't typically create my own digital papers, on
occasion what I've got is not the right color but the pattern is perfect. In those situations I simply use the
Hue/Saturation dialog in Photoshop to customize the
digital paper to meet my exact needs.

As shown, the paper here was originally a darker
green that I adjusted to match perfectly with the background color in the photo. I also adjusted the paper clip
with this method.

To change colors in Photoshop:

① Electronically "copy and paste" the digital paper into
your layout document. Be sure it's the selected layer.

② Select Image>Adjust>Hue/Saturation from the
menu bar.

③ The Hue/Saturation dialog will be displayed. First,
select the colors to adjust by selecting an option
from the Edit list. In this case I wanted to change
them all, so I chose Master.

Move the Hue slider to adjust the color of the image,
the Saturation slider to adjust the saturation (or amount
of color), and the Lightness slider to adjust the amount
of white or black in the color of the image.

④ Make sure the Preview option is selected so you can
see the changes as you adjust your colors. For papers
with multiple colors, you can adjust specific colors by
changing the Edit selection to either Reds, Yellows,
Greens, Cyans, Blues or Magentas.

Give this method a try and you'll expand your selection of digital papers without buying anything additional.
Note: Make sure the digital designer is OK with your
modifying the colors of the images (most are). When
posting the page online, be sure to give credit and note
that the images were recolored.

—*Rhonda Stark, Plymouth, MN* ♥

must-try tips

Make a Pendant

Creating a personal pendant from a layout is quick and easy. Why not make one as a Mother's Day gift for your mom, friend or grandmother? (This idea is also perfect for pins, Christmas ornaments or gift tags.) Turn the page for easy-to-follow steps!

—*Debi Boring, Scotts Valley, CA* >

Pendant *by Debi Boring.* **Supplies** *Memory glass:* Ranger Industries; *Backing paper:* Chatterbox; *Craft wire:* Artistic Wire; *Copper tape:* Venure Tape; *Pen:* Sharpie, Sanford; *Other:* Ribbon, bead and charm.

To create the pendant on the previous page:

1 Scan any square layout.

2 Reduce the scan to the size of a piece of Memory Glass. (I used 1½".) Cut a piece of backing paper to the same size.

3 Bend a 4" piece of wire in half. Twist the bent end into a small loop (to hang on the chain). Bend the ends into "J" shapes. Using adhesive, adhere the ends to the back of the layout with one end of the wire hanging down so you can attach beads or charms.

4 Placing the layout and backing paper back-to-back, sandwich them between two pieces of Memory Glass.

5 Holding the glass together, wrap the edges with copper tape, making sure the glass is centered on the tape. Cut small slits where the tape meets the wire. Pull the wire through the tape. Pinch the sides of the tape onto the glass. Using your thumbnail or a bone folder, press gently on the corners of the tape and gently rub the tape onto the glass.

6 Hang beads or charms on the hanging wire and attach ribbon if desired. Add your chain and wear the pendant with pride!

Tip: To "age" the copper tape and tone down the look, color the tape with a black Sharpie pen, wait a few seconds, then blot the ink off.

Editor's note: As of April 1, 2006, Ranger Industries offers Memory Glass Frames to encase and protect Memory Glass creations. The hinged frames come with pre-soldered, matching jump rings and sport polished chrome, antique copper and black patina finishes. For details, visit *www.rangerink.com.*

Love the luminous beauty of glass accents? Making Decorative Glass Ornamentos from Tilano Fresco is easy and fun. Use the company's kits to create a special touch for any gift or album!

DECORATIVE GLASS
Ornamento Kit

KIT D'ORNAMENTOS
DÉCORATIFS EN VERRE

Tilano Fresco

Turns any image into beautiful ornaments
Transforme toute image en de magnifiques objets décoratifs

computer tip

before **the art of sitting comes the art of**
the LeaN.

The Lean *by Jessica Sprague.* **Supplies** *Photo-editing software:* Adobe Photoshop CS; *Patterned papers:* Cabana White single and Playmates paper pack by Katie Pertiet, www.designerdigitals.com; Brushes: Chick Peas, Pea Blossom, and Swirls Companion kits by Rhonna Farrer, downloaded from www.two-peasinabucket.com; Computer fonts: Marcella, downloaded from www.dafont.com; Variex, downloaded from www.myfonts.com.

Fun with Layer Masks

While playing around in Adobe Photoshop, I discovered two great techniques with layer masks. First, you can use a layer mask to "reveal" parts of digital patterned paper. Second, you can use a layer mask to create an electronic photo overlay for interesting effect.

Before I share more details, a quick note: Layer masks work for a single layer at a time, and hide or reveal only what you specify. The key to understanding them is this: in a layer mask, the only colors that matter are black, white and shades of gray. Black "hides" everything on the object the mask is on, while white "reveals" portions. The shades of gray add a semi-transparent effect.

"REVEAL" TECHNIQUE

To create my "The Lean" page, I followed these steps:

❶ I electronically dragged a whole sheet of striped paper onto my canvas and arranged it behind the photo.

❷ I added a layer mask to the paper (in Photoshop CS, the Layer Mask button is at the bottom of the Layers palette), and then painted the whole mask black with my paint bucket tool. While the striped paper had "disappeared" at this point, it was merely hidden from view.

❸ I chose a swirl brush and stamped directly on the mask with white. The more I stamped, the more portions of paper I could see. I love this technique for digitally "building out" from a basic block of paper in a cool way.

Emerging by Jessica Sprague. **Supplies** *Photo-editing software:* Adobe Photoshop CS; *Patterned papers:* Cabana White single, Sanded overlay and Bear's Life paper pack by Katie Pertiet, *www.designerdigitals.com; Brushes:* Grunge brushes and swirl brush from Pea Blossom kit by Rhonna Farrer, *www.two-peasinabucket.com; Botanical brush from botanical brush set by Katie Pertiet, *www.designerdigitals.com; Elements:* Gear Monogram from Shifting Gears Alpha by Kellie Mize and Postage from Sun Prints Postage by Katie Pertiet, *www.designerdigitals.com; Computer fonts:* Impact and Century Gothic, Microsoft Word.

"PHOTO OVERLAY" TECHNIQUE

For my "Emerging" page, I followed these steps:

1 After cropping my photo to the size I liked, I chose a blue digital patterned paper with words on it and used the marquee tool to select and cut the paper the same size as my photo. With the paper positioned in a layer above the photo, I changed the layer mode in the Layers palette to Overlay to give the paper an interesting semi-transparent look.

2 I wanted the words on the paper to be invisible directly over my son's face, so I created a layer mask on the blue paper but left the mask white (reveal all).

3 I chose the gradient tool and used a circular gradient (which starts at a center point and radiates in a circle from one color to the next) with the center color black and the edge color white. When I drew the gradient on the layer mask, I hid the patterned paper in a smooth "fade" directly over my son's face. (Remember, black "hides" and white "reveals.")

I love the look of layer masks and can't wait to experiment more. Give them a try!

—Jessica Sprague, Cary, NC

Zip, Zip Hooray!

Last summer I watched to see what my neighbor Caroline wore each day, then created an album for her to look back on one day. I took 10 photos of Caroline in 10 different outfits. I asked her to stand in the same place with her hands high on her hips. (I did this so I could cut the pictures at the waist.)

After adhering the photo to page one in the zip album, I cut the picture and the first page. I left just a touch of the photo on the left so the page wouldn't be cut into two pieces. I then cut the rest of the photos before adhering them to the pages.

Another fun idea for a mix-and-match album? Enlarged facial photos where you mix eyes, noses and mouths!

—Shannon Taylor, Bristol, TN

What She Wore by Shannon Taylor. **Supplies** *Patterned paper:* My Mind's Eye; *Acrylic paint:* Making Memories; *Ribbon:* American Crafts; *Rubber stamps:* Hero Arts; *Buttons, brads, jump rings and washers:* Junkitz; *Super tape and foam adhesive:* Therm O Web.

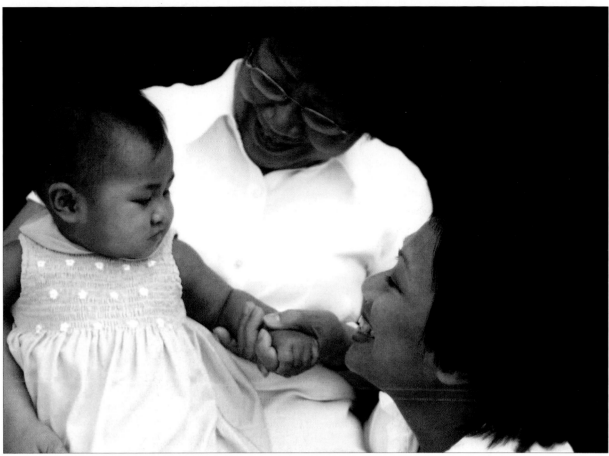

DEE MOORE

4 Tips for Multi-Generation Photos

Want to take a multi-generation photo that captures the warm connection between family members? As owner of Matter of Moments (matterofmoments.com), I take this type of shot often. Here are four tips:

1 Be fully prepared before your subjects arrive so the photo taking can move quickly. Enlist the help of a playful "assistant" who can engage attention as needed. (She might, for example, blow bubbles to catch a child's eye.)

2 Ask the family to dress in the same tones of clothing (lights with lights, darks with darks). Encourage family members to dress in styles that reflect "them."

3 Place your subjects in a position you would naturally see them in. For this photo of CK Hall of Famer Joy Uzarraga and her daughter and mother, I liked the idea of Joy's mom holding the baby while Joy helped get her daughter's attention. This was a spur-of-the-moment shot that ended up being a favorite of everyone. I was glad I had my camera ready!

4 To help relax your subjects, show genuine interest by being friendly and asking them questions. Encourage them to just talk to each other while you check camera settings. Surprisingly, the moment your subjects feel they aren't "under the camera's eye," you can catch the natural reactions you've been hoping to capture.

—Dee Moore, Kansas City, KS

adding a date to digital photos

When I first got my digital photos developed, I noticed my name was printed on the back but not the date. Now, when I get my digital photos developed and the computer asks for my last name, I type that in and add the month and year.

For example, for photos developed in January 2006, I typed OHLSONJANOSIX to specify that the photos were developed in January (JAN) 2006 (OSIX). Now when I flip my photos over, I know the month and year they were developed.

—Wendy Ohlson, Elizabethtown, PA ♥

tool time
sewing machine

Trust in the Lord
with all your ♥ ...
and He shall
direct your paths.
Proverbs 3:5-6

sew creative! | by JENNIFER MCGUIRE

SAY "SUPPLIES," and you and I tend to think of the cardstock, paper and embellishments we use everyday. But what about the tools at the heart of scrapbooking? I'm talking about pens, punches, stamps, stencils—you name it. Not only are they proven performers, they're packed with potential. You can use the tools for basic tasks, or take them to a totally new level by adding creative twists. ›

Visually "connect" elements with sewn lines.

make ya smile? ☑
make ya giggle? ☑
make ya laugh? ☑

yep, he does it all...
samuel, the

joy-bringer
extraordinaire

7.05

Joy-Bringer *by Jennifer McGuire.*
Supplies *Metal letters:* Jo-Ann Crafts; *Buttons:* Buttons Galore; *Rubber stamps:* Paper Inspirations; *Thread:* Coats & Clark; *Computer fonts:* Honey Script and Century 725, downloaded from the Internet; *Title idea:* From Desiree McClellan.

On the
coast of somewhere beautiful,
trade winds blowing through my hair
sunshine dancing on the water,
I wish I was there...

(St. John - 2005)

Coast of Somewhere Beautiful
by Jennifer McGuire.
Supplies *Textured cardstock:* Bazzill Basics Paper; *Rickrack:* Doodlebug Design; *Word charm:* Blue Moon Beads; *Computer fonts:* AL Uncle Charles, "Essential Fonts" CD, Autumn Leaves; Dartangnon, downloaded from the Internet; *Other:* Thread and safety pin.

Mimic a theme with thread—like my sunbeams and waves!

tool time *sewing machine*

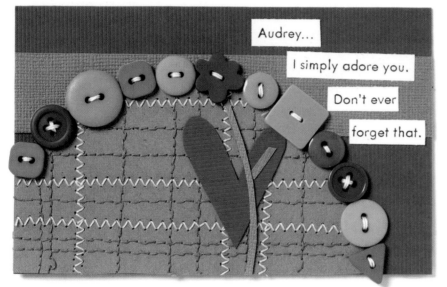

Audrey

Create stripes, plaids or any pattern you like.

Supplies Textured cardstock: Bazzill Basics Paper; Buttons: Doodlebug Design and Buttons Galore; Computer font: AL Uncle Charles, "Essential Fonts" CD, Autumn Leaves; Thread: Singer.

Fringe

Stitch parallel lines and leave the threads untrimmed as "fringe."

Supplies Textured cardstock: Bazzill Basics Paper; Ribbon: May Arts; Flower embellishment: MOD, Autumn Leaves; Thread: Singer.

Balloons

Do "dotted trails" with an unthreaded machine.

Supplies Textured note card and rubber stamp: Hero Arts; Patterned papers: SEI and KI Memories; Epoxy circles: Creative Imaginations; Stamping ink: VersaColor, Tsukineko.

S

Pencil in a shape and
stitch over it.

Supplies Textured cardstock: Bazzill Basics Paper;
Acetate letter: Autumn Leaves; Paper flowers:
Prima; Brads: Making Memories; Thread: Singer.

Life Is Sweet

Stitch die cuts, then rub the
thread with ink.

Supplies Transparency and felt accent:
K&Company; Die-cut machine: Sizzix; Buttons:
Buttons Galore; Stamping ink: VersaColor,
Tsukineko; Other: Thread and printed ribbon.

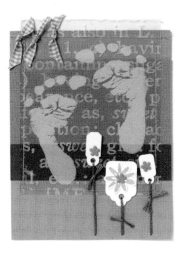

Baby Feet

Secure a transparency with no
glue showing.

Supplies Textured cardstock: Bazzill Basics Paper;
Transparency: Creative Imaginations; Rubber
stamps: Hero Arts; Stamping ink: VersaColor,
Tsukineko; Brads: Making Memories; Ribbon: C.M.
Offray & Son; Other: Tags, string and thread.

Proverbs

Attach journaling or title
strips with ease.

Supplies Patterned papers: Chatterbox;
Chipboard accent: Making Memories; Rub-ons:
Scrapworks (flower) and Autumn Leaves
(stitched heart); Computer font: Century 725,
downloaded from the Internet; Other: Thread.

Roxie

Stitch around the edges
of a simple photo.

Supplies Textured cardstock: Bazzill Basics Paper;
Charm: Flair Designs; Epoxy letters: K&Company;
Thread: Coats & Clark; Safety pin: Li'l Davis Designs.

My Baby

Sew small stitches without
thread, then tear.

Supplies Textured cardstock: Bazzill Basics Paper;
Zipper pull: All My Memories: Thread: Singer;
Rub-ons: Déjà Views by The C-Thru Ruler Co.;
Other: Silk ribbon

tool time
scissors

faith

All who call on God in true faith, earnestly from the heart, will certainly be heard, will receive what they have asked and des... — M...

thank you
thank you
thank you

cute
cuter
cutest

For this Tool Time, I explored new directions with decorative scissors. Not only are they perfect for creating custom edges, they're fab for fringe, fabric and faux stitching looks. See the fun looks I discovered, then come up with your own!

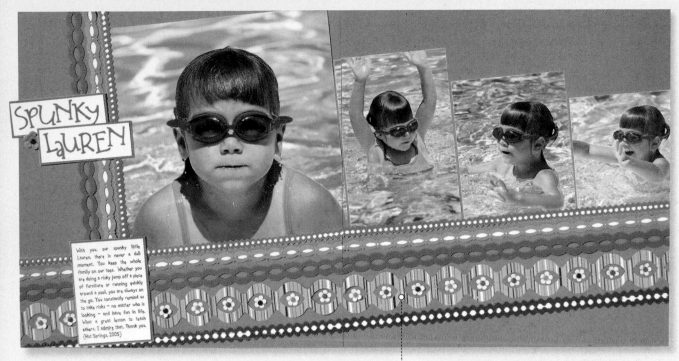

With you, our spunky little Lauren, there is never a dull moment. You keep the whole family on our toes. Whether you are doing a risky jump off a piece of furniture or running quickly around a pool, you are always on the go. You constantly remind us to take risks – no matter who is looking – and have fun in life. What a great lesson to teach others. I admire that. Thank you, {Hot Springs, 2005}

Create a decorative paper chain. Fold a strip in half, then carefully cut both long edges. ---

Spunky Lauren *by Jennifer McGuire.* **Supplies** *Patterned papers:* Doodlebug Design; *Die-cut letters:* Sizzix; *Paper flowers:* Prima; *Brads:* Making Memories; *Decorative scissors:* Fiskars and Provo Craft; *Computer font:* Grumble, downloaded from the Internet.

Give a punched or die-cut accent a ---
new look by altering the ends with
a subtle deco-edge touch.

our dog is not our whole life, but he makes our life whole. {our buddy, 2004}

buddy

Cut the edges of your layout for a little decorative flair.

Buddy *by Jennifer McGuire.* **Supplies** *Textured cardstock:* Bazzill Basics Paper; *Patterned papers:* Autumn Leaves, foof-a-La and Daisy D's Paper Co.; *Rickrack and buttons:* Doodlebug Design; *Letter stickers:* American Crafts; *Decorative scissors:* Fiskars; *Computer font:* Century Gothic, Microsoft Word.

Thank You Card *by Jennifer McGuire.* **Supplies** *Note card:* Hero Arts; *Textured cardstock:* Bazzill Basics Paper; *Patterned paper:* American Crafts; *Brad:* Making Memories; *Charm:* Hobby Lobby; *Flower punch:* EK Success; *Leaf die cut:* Sizzix; *Ribbon:* May Arts; *Decorative scissors:* Fiskars; *Other:* String.

tool time *scissors*

SCALLOP-EDGE SCISSORS

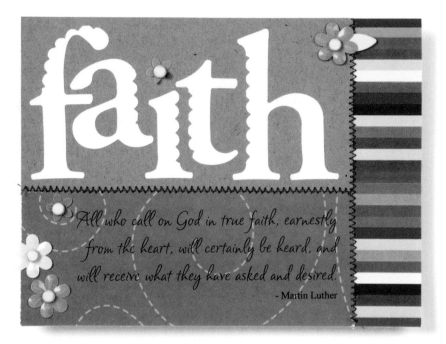

All who call on God in true faith, earnestly from the heart, will certainly be heard, and will receive what they have asked and desired.

- Martin Luther

Faith

Alter part of your letter stickers for a new look.

Supplies Patterned papers: KI Memories; Letter stickers: American Crafts; Sequins: Doodlebug Design; Decorative scissors: Craft Cut; Computer font: Clarissa, downloaded from the Internet; Other: Brads, photo turn and stitching.

Celebrate

Create rickrack in any color.

Supplies Textured cardstock: Bazzill Basics Paper; Rickrack: Doodlebug Design; Metal letters: Making Memories; Buttons: foof-a-La, Autumn Leaves; Decorative scissors: Fiskars; Other: String.

Vasto, Italy...
I can't wait
to return
to you
someday...

Vasto

Cut one edge of your photo, then repeat the edge with paper or cardstock.

Supplies Patterned paper: Daisy D's Paper Co.; Button: Buttons Galore; Decorative scissors: Provo Craft; Computer font: Cantabile, downloaded from the Internet; Other: String and vintage postage stamps.

PINKING-EDGE SCISSORS

Tiny Little Roxie

Get decorative with fabric. Back it with cardstock for stability when cutting.

Supplies Chipboard letter and decorative brad: Making Memories: Paper flower: Prima; Stamping ink: Ranger Industries; Decorative scissors: Fiskars; Other: Fabric, tag, pen and faux flower.

Dream Big

Make fringed accents more noticeable with a deco edge.

Supplies Textured cardstock: Bazzill Basics Paper; Tag: me & my BIG ideas; Flowers: K&Company; Brads: Making Memories; Decorative scissors: Provo Craft; Other: Thread, photo corners and pin.

Cute

Create one-of-a-kind faux postage using photos.

Supplies Textured cardstock: Bazzill Basics Paper; Decorative brads: Around the Block; Ribbon: May Arts; Decorative scissors: Fiskars; Computer font: AL Uncle Charles, "15 Essential Fonts" CD, Autumn Leaves; Other: Thread.

UNEVEN-EDGE SCISSORS

Thank You

Cut decorative edges from cardstock scraps, then use them as masks for inking backgrounds.

Supplies Textured cardstock: Bazzill Basics Paper; Buttons: Hero Arts and Impress Rubber Stamps; Label holder: K&Company; Rubber stamp: Hero Arts; Stamping ink: Ranger Industries; Decorative scissors: Provo Craft; Other: String.

I Love You

Create faux stitching for projects too bulky to fit into a sewing machine. Poke holes with a needle for a more realistic look.

Supplies Textured cardstock: Bazzill Basics Paper; Patterned papers: KI Memories, Anna Griffin and SEI; Tag: me & my BIG ideas; Charm: Blue Moon; Decorative scissors: Fiskars; Other: Safety pin and ribbon.

Happy First Birthday

Cut thin decorative strips, then weave them together in multiple combinations.

Supplies Textured cardstock: Bazzill Basics Paper; Gems, rubber stamp and stamping ink: Hero Arts; Decorative scissors: Fiskars; Other: Ribbon and photo corners.

tool time

punches

you are
the reason
for
MANY
MANY
MANY
of our
smiles.

k

Mo

A tool that I reach for with almost every layout is the hole punch. Whether I use an anywhere or a handheld, hole punches are one of my most useful tools! Have fun stretching your creativity with these 12 ideas.

Give simple letter stickers a hip new look by punching holes in various places before adhering.

The Best View *by Jennifer McGuire.* **Supplies** *Handheld hole punches:* Fiskars; *Letter stickers:* American Crafts; *Patterned papers:* PSX Design; *Pen:* American Crafts; *Computer font:* 2Peas Renaissance, downloaded from www.twopeasinabucket.com; *Other:* Vintage postage purchased from eBay.

Create your own stamps by adhering circles punched from foam to firm plastic.

NZ *by Jennifer McGuire.* **Supplies** *Handheld hole punch:* Fiskars; *Fun foam:* Hobby Lobby; *Acrylic paint:* Delta Technical Coatings; *Gem brads:* Hero Arts; *Computer font:* CongressT, downloaded from the Internet; *Buttons:* foof-a-La, Autumn Leaves; *Other:* Thread.

Punch holes for ribbon weaving—it's simple and fun!

With All My Heart *by Jennifer McGuire.* **Supplies** *Anywhere hole punch:* Making Memories; *Note card:* Hero Arts; *Ribbons:* KI Memories; *Rub-on letters:* Scenic Route Paper Co.; *Corner rounder punch:* EK Success; *Other:* Heart charm.

Ready to try out these ideas?

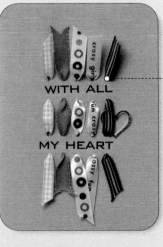

Consider hole punches from these companies:

Anywhere punch
- Eyelet Outlet
- Magic Scraps
- Making Memories

Handheld punch
- Fiskars
- McGill
- Provo Craft

tool time *punches*

I Love You

Ink and stamp over a stencil created with small punched holes.

Supplies Handheld hole punch: Provo Craft; Patterned paper: Making Memories; Rubber stamps: Hero Arts and Rubber Moon; Stamping ink: VersaColor, Tsukineko; Other: Button.

Being a part of the McGuire/ Chapman family means loving time spent boating. On your first adventure, you were hooked. Just more proof that you are the perfect addition to the family.

Our Samuel

Punch through epoxy accents to create dimensional faux brads.

Supplies Handheld hole punch: Fiskars; Epoxy stickers: MOD, Autumn Leaves; Rubber stamps: Educational Insights; Stamping ink: Memories, Stewart Superior Corporation; Ribbon: May Arts; Pen: American Crafts; Computer font: Cafecoco, downloaded from the Internet.

gimme a treat..

Gimme a Treat

Give simple ribbon a new look with punched holes that coordinate with other decorative ribbons.

Supplies Anywhere hole punch: Magic Scraps; Ribbon: American Crafts, KI Memories, May Arts and C.M. Offray & Son; Rubber stamps: Hero Arts; Stamping ink: Memories, Stewart Superior Corporation; Ribbon: May Arts; Other: Staples, tag, brad, bead and wire.

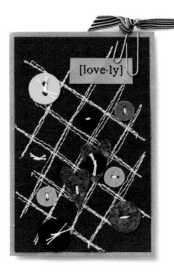

Lovely

Punch two tiny holes in the center of felt, cardstock and cork circles to create faux buttons.

Supplies Anywhere hole punch: Magic Scraps: Die-cut machine (for felt circles): Sizzix; Felt: Hobby Lobby; Cork: Magenta; Heart punch: EK Success; Fabric tag: Jo-Ann Crafts; Ribbon: May Arts; Other: Thread and paper clip.

Keychain

Punch holes in chipboard for a keychain accent.

Supplies Anywhere hole punch and keychain: Making Memories; Chipboard accents: Pressed Petals and Heidi Swapp for Advantus; Rub-ons: Fontwerks (flowers) and Wordsworth (words); Ribbon: KI Memories.

Life

Suspend punched circles between two transparency pieces.

Supplies Handheld hole punch: Fiskars; Patterned paper, button and rub-on: foof-a-La, Autumn Leaves; Ribbon quote: Autumn Leaves; Transparency: Office Depot; Other: Faux flower and thread.

M

Arrange circles punched from adhesive-backed paper to form a letter.

Supplies Handheld hole punch: Provo Craft; Adhesive-backed cardstock and patterned paper: Die Cuts With a View; Tag sticker: Doodlebug Design; Paper flowers: Prima; Other: Brads, thread and ribbon.

K

Punch holes in cardstock, then back it with patterned paper.

Supplies Anywhere hole punch: Making Memories; Chipboard letter: Heidi Swapp for Advantus; Rubber stamp: Hero Arts; Stamping ink: Ranger Industries; Paper flowers: Prima; Computer font: 2Peas Flower Girl, downloaded from www.two-peasinabucket.com; Other: Brads and thread.

Emma Grace

Add interest to scalloped edges.

Supplies Handheld hole punch: Fiskars; Patterned papers: KI Memories and Wild Asparagus, My Mind's Eye; Letter stickers: K&Company; Other: Ribbon and thread

designing with ali

⑦ principles to help improve your pages

As a scrapbooker, my job is to be a visual translator, combining photos, words and creative details, then translating them into a cohesive visual story that will last for generations to come. My book, *A Designer's Eye for Scrapbooking*, defines and explores seven key principles of scrapbook design. These concepts will help you learn how to become a translator of your own memories by first focusing on your overall vision for a page, then asking yourself how you can most effectively communicate your vision. Here's a sneak peek at these seven design principles.

by Ali Edwards

There isn't a right or wrong way to create a layout, but if you stop and think before you begin creating, the result will be more focused. When I begin a new scrapbook page, the first questions I ask myself are: "What is the story I want to tell?" and "What has inspired me to create this layout?"

These questions help me generate a vision for my layout—a mental image, a concept, an idea or a notion. It's whatever motivated me to begin a new page. Having a clear vision will help you make conscious choices about how to most effectively communicate your story. Vision can come from anywhere: a story, a photo, a thought, a song or whatever inspires you.

After you establish your vision, decide how best to communicate the story you want your layout to convey. My top three methods of communicating a vision are to emphasize either the photos, the words or the design.

Next time you begin creating a page, try jotting down a vision and then some options for communicating it.

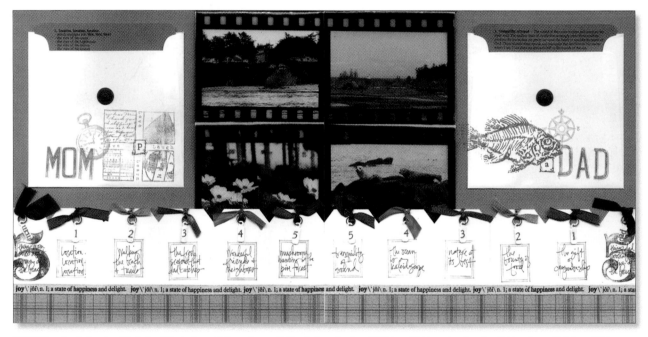

5 Things Supplies *Textured cardstock:* Bazzill Basics Paper; *Patterned paper:* Fiddlerz3; *Accordion tags:* DMD, Inc.; *Mini tags:* American Tag; *Rubber stamps:* Club Scrap (fish), Fontwerks (large letters), Hero Arts (small letters), Ma Vinci's Reliquary (large "5"), PSX Design (numbers), Rubber Stampede (clock), Stampabilities (compass) and Stampa Rosa (rectangle); *Stamping ink:* VersaColor, Tsukineko; *Jump rings and decorative brads:* Making Memories; *Ribbon:* May Arts and 7gypsies (yellow); *Large negative strips:* Creative Imaginations; *Printed twill ("Joyz"):* 7gypsies; *Computer font:* Garamond, Microsoft Word; *Other:* Square envelopes.

□ **vision:** To detail my parents' top five reasons they love living on the coast.

□ **communication:** I asked both my parents to e-mail me five reasons they love living at the beach. I used the small accordion tag because it had six homes for journaling: one for a small title and the others for supporting information. I also included the full version of my parents' words tucked inside the large square envelopes. On this layout, my vision is communicated through words.

Ali's Notes

1. Cut the top off a string envelope to create a simple pocket for additional journaling.

2. Ask your parents, siblings, children or friends to supply you with journaling. Having different voices in your scrapbooks produces depth and adds interest.

3. When dealing with supplies, sometimes it's fun to ask yourself, "How could I use this product differently?" Rather than using the accordion tag folded up, I stretched it across the width of my cardstock so it became a home for my journaling.

4. The stamped collage on the outside of each envelope represents ideas about my parents that came to mind as I was putting this page together.

Building a strong foundation

After I've established my vision (and how best to communicate it), I create a basic structural framework called a foundation. A foundation is a place where you'll build your layout. It gives your photos, journaling and embellishments "homes." Foundations tend to be in the background, giving stability and balance to your page. On your foundation, you may choose to add several embellishments or just a single photo.

Simon Was Here Supplies *Textured cardstock:* Bazzill Basics Paper; *Stamping ink:* VersaColor, Tsukineko; *Rubber stamps:* Fontwerks ("S") and PSX Design ("04"); *Ribbon:* Michaels; *Square tag:* Creative Imaginations; *Computer font:* Eurostile, Microsoft Picture It!.

□ **vision:** To record how Simon always likes to leave little mementos here and there.

□ **communication:** This page began with the photo of the small bird and marbles. To make the page complete, I used that photo to illustrate how Simon transports his toys around the house and yard.

Ali's Notes

1. You can create foundations using a variety of mediums: paint, pens, embellishments, pre-made page designs and more. For this layout I rubbed small inkpads directly onto the cardstock, creating three distinct homes for my journaling and photos.

2. Use a pen to create an additional frame around the main elements on your layout. Include words at breaking points within the line to reinforce concepts and words from your journaling.

3 Gathering together

As you begin building a page on your foundation, certain design concepts can help you better communicate your vision. One of my favorites is to gather elements and place them in close proximity. This creates harmony and unity through repetition. Repeated elements such as photos, embellishments or punched squares of patterned paper reinforce the idea of an underlying structure.

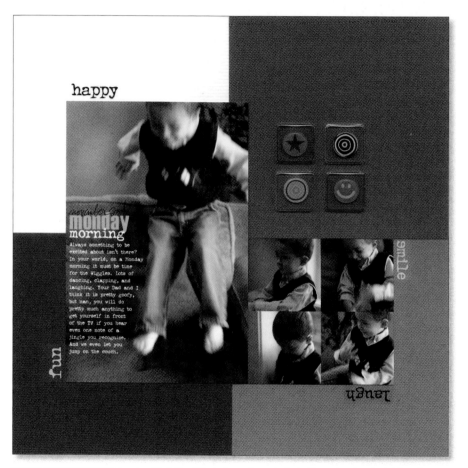

Monday Morning Supplies *Textured cardstock:* Bazzill Basics Paper; *Computer fonts:* Ghostwriter, downloaded from the Internet; Haettenschweiler, Microsoft Word; *Acrylic circle and square accents:* KI Memories; *Word stickers:* Bo-Bunny Press; *Pen:* American Crafts.

☐ **vision:** This page began with the blurred photo of Simon jumping on the couch.

☐ **communication:** Because I was working with an enlarged blurred photo, I felt it was important to create a very structured, clean page around it. Comprised of four different gatherings, the repetition of shape gives an overall feeling of order and unity. The small, colorful embellishments keep the page from feeling too stiff—they add just the right touch of whimsy, which is also repeated in the journaling.

Ali's Notes

1. Note how the gathering of four square elements is repeated several times within the design:
   • The foundation, comprised of four quadrants
   • The four small photos
   • The four embellishments

   Plus, I emphasized the square foundation by placing together the large photo (counting as two squares), the group of embellishments and the group of four small photos.

2. Add journaling directly to your photo with a photo-editing program.

Go with the flow

Flow is a page characteristic that directs your viewer where to look first, second and so on within your layout. Flow can move horizontally, vertically, around a page in a circle, or zigzag back and forth. Strips of patterned paper easily guide the eye from one place to the next.

Gack Birthday Supplies *Textured cardstock:* Bazzill Basics Paper; *Patterned paper:* KI Memories; *Letter stickers and pen:* American Crafts; *"Happy Birthday" accent:* Making Memories; *Circle tags:* EK Success; *Circle accents:* Scrapworks.

□ **vision:** To record and celebrate birthday gifts given to me by friends.

□ **communication:** The flow of this layout follows the traditional western movement from left to right. Note how you first look at the circle accent, then the "gack" title, then the area bordered by the striped strips and finally at the photo.

Ali's Notes

1. Photograph gifts you receive on your next birthday and document them on a layout. You can also include cards and other flat memorabilia. Don't be afraid to trim them to fit on your page.

2. Type can be just as effective vertically as horizontally. Try a different type orientation on your next layout.

3. I love to create layouts that exist within a frame created by the cardstock foundation. When I design layouts in this manner, I tend to have one or more embellishments that break across the frame's borders. On this layout, notice the circle tag in the lower right section of the second page. By breaking across the border, the embellishment helps visually ground the content portion (rather than having it appear as if it's "floating" on top of the cardstock).

5 Charm school

Charm is simply the power to delight. When I design a layout, I want certain elements to be almost irresistible: the colors, a photo, my words or maybe the typography. Charm attracts attention. Something on the page needs to draw viewers in and make them want to envelop themselves in the content of the page. It's maximizing an element within your vision to most effectively tell your story.

McDougall Memories Supplies *Textured cardstock:* Bazzill Basics Paper; *Patterned paper:* 7gypsies and Mystic Press; *Patterned transparency:* My Mind's Eye; *Plastic "M" accent:* Making Memories; *Mini frames:* DieCuts with a View; *Acrylic paint:* Making Memories; *Computer fonts:* 2Peas Hot Chocolate, downloaded from *www.twopeasinabucket.com*; Cezanne and Garamouche, P22 Type Foundry.

□ **vision:** I wanted to create a page featuring short, specific memories of my grandparents.

□ **communication:** I began this layout by jotting down the memories I wanted to include. Next, I looked through my photos to find something with the power to charm. I chose a photo of my grandparents from a family vacation.

To emphasize the photo, I enlarged it, making it the largest single element on the layout. I wanted to include additional photos that supported the memories in my journaling, so I gathered these together on the second page. My journaling found homes within the frames along the bottom of the layout.

Ali's Notes

1. Customize metal embellishments to match the colors within your layout. On these pages, I painted the frames red.

2. One of the things I love about scanning my old photos is that photo paper makes a great writing surface. Next time you print photos at home, consider writing specific details directly on the photo with a photo-safe pen.

3. Note how the foundation of this layout includes patterned paper and elements that touch all edges. Some of the elements, such as the journaling frames and the smaller photo on the first page, break out of the foundation to add interest.

4. Transparencies are a great design tool. When I was close to finishing this layout, I felt like it was missing something. The red frames along the bottom seemed to be taking me right off the page. To counteract that effect, I printed enlarged parentheses on a transparency and attached one to each end of the layout. This seemed to help keep my eye more within the boundaries of the layout.

6 Give and take

Give and take is simply the process of creating balance on your layout. If you add an element to one side of the layout, you need to add an element to the other side of the layout. If you take away an element from one side, you need to take an element away from the other side. Your goal is to achieve a feeling of harmony.

One of my favorite ways to achieve balance on a two-page layout is to create a foundation on the first page, then simply apply that foundation to the second page and rotate it a quarter turn or upside down. This is a very simple way to create a balanced layout.

Seattle Simon Supplies *Textured cardstock:* Bazzill Basics Paper; *Patterned paper:* EK Success; *Patterned vellum:* My Mind's Eye; *Leather circle accents:* Heidi Grace Designs; *Word circle accents:* Scrapworks; *Transparency:* Hammermill; *Rub-on letters:* Li'l Davis Designs; *Brads:* Making Memories; *Circle stamp:* Club Scrap; *Stamping ink:* VersaMark, Tsukineko; *Computer font:* Optima, Linotype Library.

☐ **vision:** To celebrate Simon's weekend adventure in Seattle with my parents.

☐ **communication:** As I was looking through the photos from this event, I fell in love with the ones featuring my dad and Simon. I knew they would be the charming elements for my layout. Note how my foundation is reversed on the second page to include additional photos and tell more of the story.

Ali's Notes

1. Print journaling on a transparency and place it over two different patterned papers (soft prints work best). The transparency is attached behind the photos.

2. Create the photo frame by attaching all the photos together, then overlaying a piece of cardstock the same size as the interior section of the foundation. For correct line placement, cut the photos with a craft knife.

3. Three is definitely my favorite number when it comes to adding embellishments to my layouts. Note how each page features three leather circle embellishments. These help unify the layout and keep your eye within the content of each page as you view it.

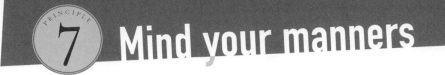

7 Mind your manners

PRINCIPLE

Manner is the way you infuse your personality into your layouts. The layouts you create are a direct reflection of you, your family, your memories and your style. What type of scrapbook page do you love? Single-photo layouts focusing on the charm of the photos? Layouts with extensive journaling? I believe that if you go with what you truly love, your pages will be filled with genuine feeling and emotion.

My manner combines technology and traditional scrapbooking. I like the freedom to choose either or both styles as I create my pages. I'm inclined to line up elements (especially photos) and accent them with circle elements, creating visual triangles on almost every page. I love gathering elements—repetition of shape and pattern is a key part of my scrapbooking manner. Developing your manner is deciding what you love, what you are skilled at, and then running with those ideas.

Kisses from You Supplies *Textured cardstock:* Bazzill Basics Paper; *Patterned paper:* Chatterbox; *Patterned vellum and circle stickers:* American Crafts; *Circle punch:* The Punch Bunch; *Ribbon:* May Arts; *Slide mounts:* Adorama; *Computer fonts:* AL Softhearted, "Script" CD, Autumn Leaves; Myriad, Linotype Library.

□ **vision:** To create a page celebrating Simon's loving nature.

□ **communication:** This page stemmed from three photos of Simon giving kisses. Note how I repeated circle embellishments: three punched circles backed with patterned paper and three circle stickers placed on top of the slide mounts. ♥

Ali's Notes

1. Cover slide mounts with patterned paper. Connect them with coordinating ribbon.

2. Use paper tearing as a method of establishing flow throughout your page.

3. Achieve unity on your layout by repeating patterns and shapes.

IT'S hip TO BE SQUARE

SCRAP FASTER WITH A GRID

Look around and you'll see grids everywhere—on everything from windowpanes to bathroom tile. While they're used for support and structure, guess what? Grids work great on scrapbook pages, too! They're a handy design formula I turn to again and again to speed up my scrapbooking. Each square creates a place for a photo, title, accent or journaling. I can say goodbye to the fuss and hello to getting more of my memories scrapbooked! BY TRACI TURCHIN

4 Big Benefits

Grids may not be "sexy," but they're hot, hip items on my scrapbooking list. Why?

❶ They're simple to use, flexible, and they speed up the design process.

❷ Grids can be modified to fit a layout of any size, with any number of photos and embellishments.

❸ Working with several colors and themes? Grids create a cohesive look.

❹ Grids can make you taller, thinner and more attractive. OK, maybe they can't turn you into a movie star, but they *can* make your pages more attractive.

{2004} by Traci Turchin. **Supplies** *Patterned papers:* 7gypsies and Chatterbox; *Textured cardstock:* Bazzill Basics Paper; *Stickers:* American Crafts and Creative Imaginations; *Acrylic paint:* Making Memories; *Computer font:* Century Gothic, Microsoft Word. *Idea to note:* To tie everything into the black, white and pink color scheme, Traci used pink and white acrylic paint around the edge of each photo and paper square.

Even a mix of colors and themes can look like they belong together!

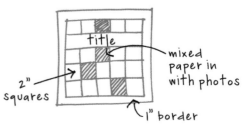

What You'll Need

If you're thinking you'd better add graph paper to your grocery list, put that pencil away. You don't need special tools to create a grid.

Traditional scrappers can plan their grids on scratch paper. Digital scrappers can overlay "lines" on top of their layout with their software's guide tool. Regardless of the method you choose, you'll need to do a little math. A calculator could come in handy!

Leave empty squares— or break the pattern with photos—to catch the viewer by surprise!

ASK 3 QUESTIONS

Before I start calculating, I consider page elements since they'll affect grid size. I ask:

1. What will work best for my photos? I can use large grid spaces for a few key photos or smaller grid spaces for multiple supporting photos.

2. What will work best for my journaling? I decide how much text to include and whether to place it inside or outside of the grid.

3. Do I plan to include accents or memorabilia that will require grid space?

Perfect Hike by Traci Turchin. **Supplies** *Photo-editing software:* Adobe Photoshop CS; *Computer fonts:* Century Gothic, Microsoft Word; Postmaster, "Typewriter Fonts" CD, Autumn Leaves. *Idea to note:* Traci created her grid electronically, then left a few empty squares as visual "resting places."

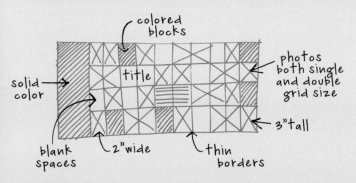

Sketch Your Grid

After deciding the following, sketch the results on paper or create a grid electronically.

- What size is the layout?

- Will it have a border around the outside of the grid or within it?

- Will the grid be square or rectangular? How will this affect the borders around the outside? (If I decide to use a square grid on a rectangular layout, I'll need to have a large border on one side. I could place a title, journaling or accents in this space.)

- Will I be making a square grid out of rectangles? A rectangular grid out of squares? Which shape will best showcase my photos?

- How many spaces will the grid include? What sizes will they be?

Tip: A quick and easy grid for a 12" x 12" page is a "three across and three down" grid with 3" squares and a 1½" border around the edge. (See "Celebrate" below.)

Kelly's 17th birthday, 1 June 2003. The traditional "family" party, with Kelly's boyfriend Joe, too. We always had a family party and a kid party.

guess it doesn't matter so much now. What does matter is that I'm glad now she was always there. And I was glad to celebrate 17 with her.

The family party had the good presents, the kid party had the fun. Sleepovers usually, in little sleeping bags. Kelly and I always invited each

other to our parties. I know that half of the time it was a genuine invitation, half the time...not so much. I wish it had always been genuine. I

Celebrate *by Traci Turchin.* **Supplies** *Textured cardstock:* Bazzill Basics Paper; *Photo-editing software:* Adobe Photoshop CS; *Computer font:* Century Gothic, Microsoft Word. *Idea to note:* To create transparent text, Traci typed on top of each photo in Photoshop. She lowered the opacity of the text layer to let the photo show through.

Wrap your journaling around your grid!

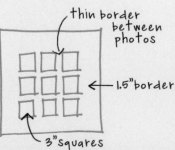

thin border between photos

1.5" border

3" squares

Making the Grid Your Own

To add a distinctive touch, try one or more of the following:

- Create a grid with unusual shapes.

- Use a corner rounding punch on the corners.

- Add borders. Leave space between grid squares, lay strips of patterned paper across seams, or simply edge each photo or accent with paint or ink.

- Add texture to your layout with textured paper, paint, or ink.

- Use embellishments in grid spaces or let them creep off the grid into the layout's border.

- Think outside the grid. Combine grid spaces to create a larger area for journaling, cut photos to take up multiple spaces, or leave parts of the grid empty to create "white space."

Friend *by Traci Turchin.* **Supplies** *Patterned papers:* Anna Griffin, KI Memories, Imagination Project and Sandylion; *Textured cardstock:* Bazzill Basics Paper; *Flower and letters:* Making Memories; *Button:* KI Memories; *Acrylic paint:* Luminarte; *Computer font:* Century Gothic, Microsoft Word. ♥

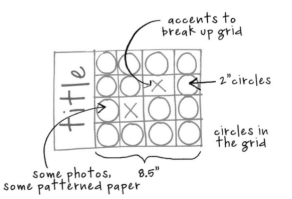

accents to break up grid

2" circles

circles in the grid

some photos, some patterned paper

8.5"

Squares too stuffy?
Use circles!

favorite
first
photos

4" x 6" scrapbooking

Save time with these sketches for standard prints

I'LL CONFESS—after my sweet daughter Claire was born, I couldn't resist capturing hundreds of photos of her. From her sweet smile to her tiny fingers and toes, I didn't want to miss a single moment of her first year of life.

Before I knew it, I had dozens of pictures of baby Claire that needed to be scrapbooked. As the busy mom of a newborn baby and a preschooler, I needed a quick and easy solution. How could I create memorable pages in a minimum of time?

My solution was to create a series of scrapbook page sketches that feature 4" x 6" prints. I use the prints straight from the photo lab or my digital printer—no cropping or enlarging required! > > >

by becky higgins

If you're like me, I bet you have plenty of 4" x 6" prints at home that you'd love to scrapbook in a way that's fast, easy and beautiful. I'm excited to share my favorite 4" x 6" sketches with you, along with a few creative ways to scrapbook those standard-sized prints right now. Let's get started!

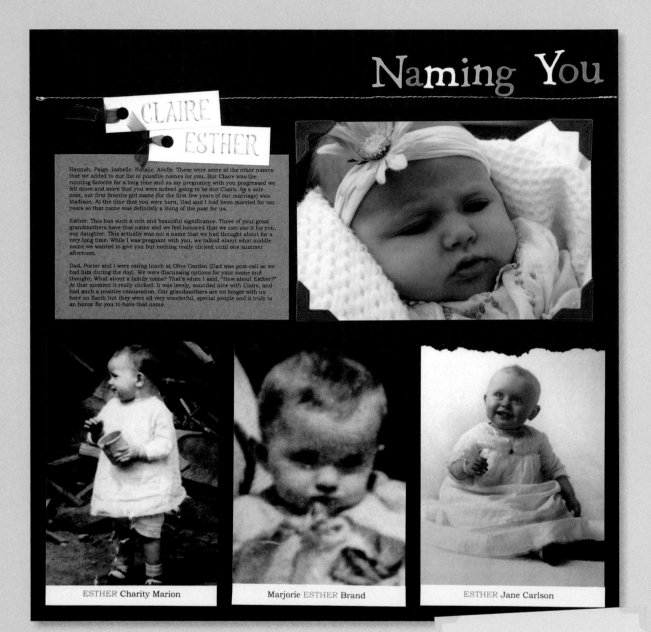

Naming You *by Becky Higgins.* **Supplies** *Letters:* QuicKutz; *Ribbon:* Magic Scraps; *Stamping ink:* Clearsnap; *Computer fonts:* Bookman Old Style (journaling), Microsoft Word; Omatic ("Claire Esther"), downloaded from the Internet; *Hole punch:* Marvy Uchida; *Photo corners:* Heidi Swapp for Advantus; *Other:* Thread.

Turn to page 241 to see Becky's sketches on one easy-to-copy page!

Expecting Claire *by Becky Higgins.* **Supplies** *Cardstock:* Bazzill Basics Paper; *Patterned paper and letter stickers:* Chatterbox; *Chalk:* Stampin' Up!; *Corner rounder punch:* McGill; *Bookplate:* Making Memories; *Pen:* EK Success; *Brads:* Lasting Impressions for Paper.

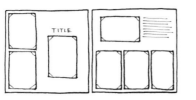

4" x 6" is a common size for photos from a photo shoot. Show the prints off in style!

Turn your 4" x 6" photos into recipe cards! Use the photo on the front with the recipe on the back.

Food *by Becky Higgins.* **Supplies** *Foam letter stamps:* Creative Imaginations; *Acrylic paint:* Making Memories; *Computer font:* Rockwell, downloaded from the Internet.

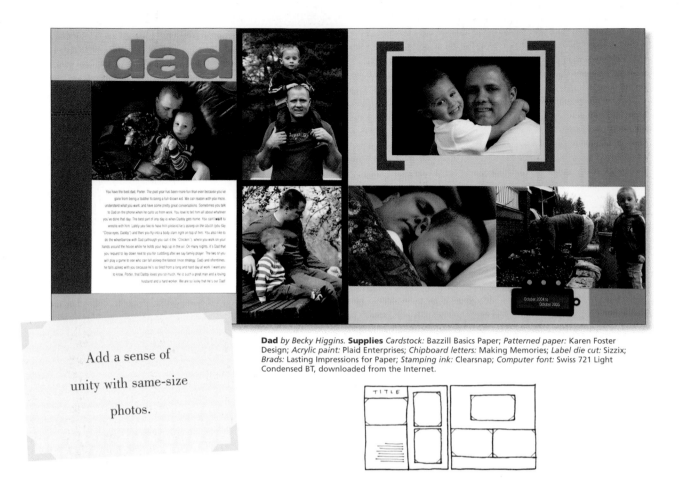

Dad *by Becky Higgins.* **Supplies** *Cardstock:* Bazzill Basics Paper; *Patterned paper:* Karen Foster Design; *Acrylic paint:* Plaid Enterprises; *Chipboard letters:* Making Memories; *Label die cut:* Sizzix; *Brads:* Lasting Impressions for Paper; *Stamping ink:* Clearsnap; *Computer font:* Swiss 721 Light Condensed BT, downloaded from the Internet.

Favorite First Photos *by Becky Higgins.* **Supplies** *Cardstock:* Bazzill Basics Paper; *Patterned paper:* Chatterbox; *Ribbon:* Li'l Davis Designs; *Letter stickers:* SEI; *Flowers:* Prima (small) and purchased at Pat Katan's (large); *Brads:* Lasting Impressions for Paper; *"C" foam letter stamp:* Making Memories; *Acrylic paint:* Plaid Enterprises.

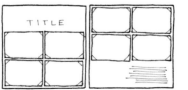

10 Great Sketches for 4" x 6" Photos

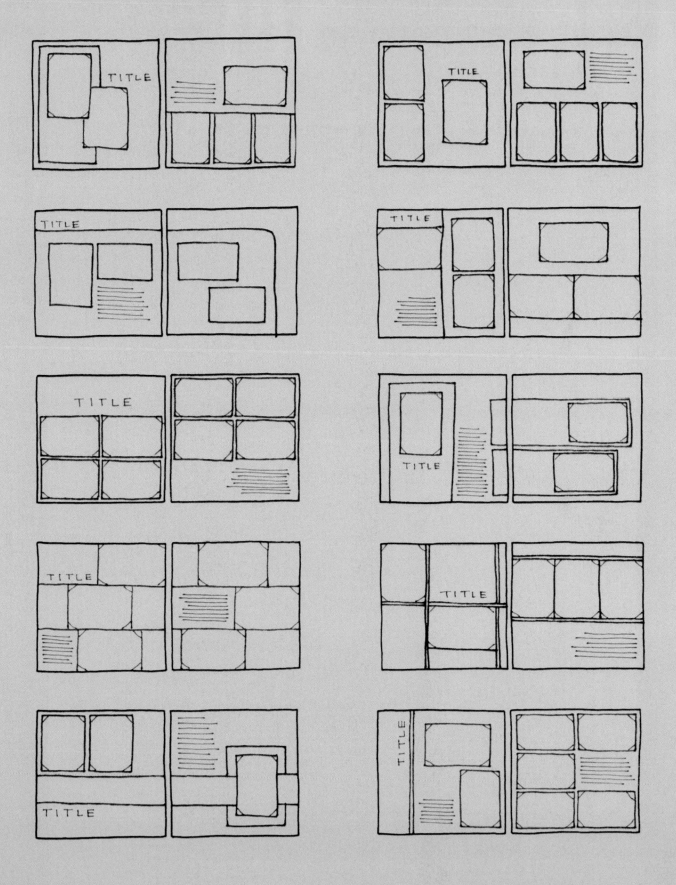

SEPTEMBER 25, 2005
EUMUNDI, QUEENSLAND

My darling Abi, you are at the
sweetest age at the moment. You
are really taking great pleasure in discovering the world
around you. You want to try everything Olivia does, and
you want to explore everything — you seem so fearless. At
the playground you want to go on all the rides, including the
slide, and your favourite is the see-saw. You always have
so much fun playing and exploring your world. I love you

digital
and *loving* it

YOU CAN BE, TOO, WITH THESE TIPS AND EASY BASICS

WHEN I FIRST CONSIDERED making a digital page, I was hesitant. I'd used Adobe Photoshop before, but for the past two years I'd only used it to view and alter photos. I felt intimidated. Then I was asked to create a brochure for the school where I volunteer. "OK," I thought, "I'll just dig in and figure this out."

I wanted my design to be fresh and hip, so I installed Photoshop Elements, found a helpful tutorial CD to learn the basics, and set to work. Before long, I felt empowered. I could actually do this! Sure, I might not be as fast as seasoned digiscrappers, but creating things digitally was fun, and I love how the brochure turned out. I only wish I'd taken the plunge to create digital designs sooner.

Have you considered making a digital layout but delayed because you're not sure where to start? Here's the help you need to get started! I'll share the tips that help me create a basic design, then show you easy ways to embellish your pages. I did it—so can you!

BY BRITTANY BEATTIE

the basic page

To make a digital page, start with these basic steps:

1 **Open a New Document**. To open a new document, select the **File** menu, **New**, then **Blank File**. A pop-up box will appear. Give the document a Name (this does *not* save the file; see step 7, "Save Your Work," on page 245). Choose **Custom** for the Preset, then select your desired page Width and Height (you can switch the measurement from pixels to inches). Choose your Resolution (at least 300 pixels/inch), select "RGB Color" for the Color Mode and decide which Background Contents mode you prefer (I usually select "Transparent"). (For more on selecting the best options, see "Getting Started" on page 247.)

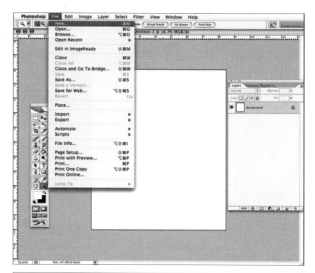

2 **Color the Background.** Create a new layer by selecting the **Layer** menu, **New**, then **Layer** (or use the shortcut keys Ctrl + Shift + N). Select your desired color in the **Set Foreground Color** tool from the toolbar (it looks like two squares overlapping each other). Your desired color should be in the box on the top.

When you click on the top box, a pop-up box with a spectrum of colors will appear. Find your desired color gradient and click on it, then click **OK**—the color will automatically appear in the top box of the **Set Foreground Color** tool. Select the **Paint Bucket** tool from the toolbar, then click your mouse on the background of your layout and the layer will be filled with color.

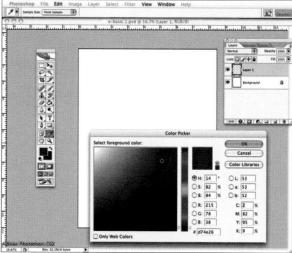

3 **Import Your Photos.** Open a photo in Photoshop and it will appear in a new document. Select the **Move** tool from the toolbar (it looks like a mouse arrow with two crossed lines in a "t" shape below it), then click on the photo and drag it to the thumbnail of your layout at the bottom of the screen. *Note:* If you can't see the thumbnails, look for a small blue bar with an upward-facing arrow at the bottom of the page, then click on the arrow and the thumbnails should appear.

Return to your layout. Make sure **Show Bounding Box** is checkmarked in the **Move** palette. *Note:* Whenever you select a tool from the toolbar, its palette will appear on-screen, generally directly above your layout.

To resize the photo, move your mouse arrow to a corner of the bounding box until it appears as two arrows. Then hold down your shift key (it will maintain the correct proportions of your photo when it's resized), click on your mouse and drag the photo to the desired size. To move your photo to a new location, click inside the photo, hold down the mouse button and drag the photo into place.

4 **Create a Journaling Box.** Create a new layer in your file. Select the **Rectangular Marquee** tool from the toolbar (it looks like a rectangle with dashed lines). Click the mouse on your layout, then drag it to create your desired rectangle size. When the size is correct, release the mouse.

Select the **Edit** menu, then **Fill Selection**. In the **Use** box, select **Color**. A pop-up box will appear that lets you choose your desired color for the journaling block. Select the desired color gradient, then click **OK** and the box will fill with the selected color. Use the **Move** tool to reposition the box as desired.

5 **Print Your Text.** Select the **Horizontal Type** tool (it looks like a "T") from the toolbar. Click the mouse on your journaling box where you want the text to appear. When the cursor appears, type your text.

You can adjust the font and size in the appropriate boxes in the **Type** palette. (Highlight the text first like you would in a word-processing program.) If your text extends beyond the edge of your layout, use a hard return—Photoshop will not wrap the text automatically. Use the **Move** tool to reposition the text as desired.

6 **Add Shadows.** Shadows will make your digital page look more like a traditional scrapbook page. To add a shadow to an element, select that element in your **Layers** palette, then find the **Styles and Effects** palette near the right-hand edge of your screen. Click on the left-hand box in the palette (the default is set to **Effects**) and choose **Layer Styles**.

Click on the right-hand box (the default is set to **Bevels**) and select **Drop Shadows**, then select your desired shadow—**Low** and **Soft Edge** usually produce the most realistic looks. When you select your desired drop shadow, the shadow will automatically appear on the layout.

7 **Save Your Work.** Don't forget to save the page you created! Select the **File** menu, then **Save**. Type in your desired file name, then select **Photoshop (.PSD)** for the format. (For more on file formats, see the "Getting Started" section on page 247.)

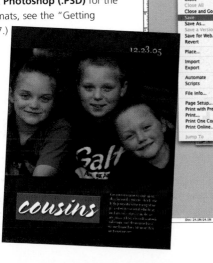

easy-to-make looks

Once you've made a basic page, it's time to start embellishing your layout. With a few straightforward steps, you can create great looks just like those on your traditional pages. Check out these five ideas to get you started.

∨ Add Decorative Frames

Use the Brush tool to create photo frames with a distressed feel.

Ireland by Katie Pertiet. **Supplies** *Software:* Adobe Photoshop; *Patterned papers:* DesignerDigitals.com; *Computer fonts:* AL Highlight, "15 Essential Fonts" CD, Autumn Leaves; Carlotta and Trade Gothic, downloaded from the Internet.

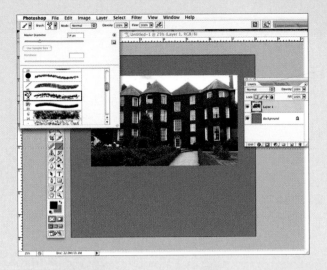

1 Add a photo to your layout as desired (see step 3, "Import Your Photos," on page 244).

2 Select the foreground color (see the top square of the **Set Foreground Color** option from the toolbar) you want to use for your frame.

3 Click on the **Brush** tool from the toolbar. Select a brush from the box in the **Brushes** palette that appears when you choose the **Brush** tool.

4 Decide the style and size of the brush in the **Brushes** palette (for options, use the drop-down menu for each box). *Note:* You will need to select a fairly large brush size for the frame to appear.

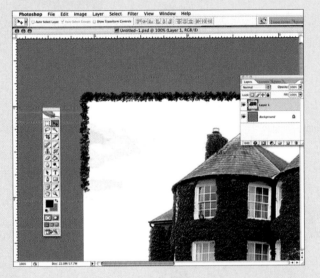

5 Position your mouse arrow near the edge of the photo. Hold down the shift key to ensure a straight line, then move your brush along the side of the picture until the edge is covered. *Note:* If you made your brush mark beyond the edge of the photo, select the **Erase** tool from the toolbar, then use it to clean up the undesirable edge.

6 Repeat for each side of the photo.

getting started

If you're new to the digital realm, remember these basics about the type of file you create.

File Size: If you plan to print your digital pages, use at least 300 dots per inch (dpi) for the file size when you create a new document. (This will provide the level of resolution you need for quality results.) Verify that the page size is large enough for the size you plan to print, such as 12" x 12" or 8" x 8".

Layers: Digital layouts are composed of multiple layers you can overlap, cut and rearrange on a layout. (Think of how you layer with cardstock, stickers and photos.) Every time you add a new element, such as patterned paper, create a new layer for it first.

You can always merge layers later, but you'll want to start with each item on a separate layer so it's easier to make changes to individual elements as you go. You can switch between the layers as you work by clicking on each element in the **Layers** palette in your program.

Toolbar: Want to create a new block for a border? Need to change the color of a page element? Use a tool from the toolbar. For example, the **Shape** and **Rectangular Marquee** tools both let you add a new block of "paper" to your design.

File Types: When you create a new document, save it as a ".psd" (Photoshop document) file to maintain the highest quality and let you create multiple layers. Once you finalize your layout, you can flatten the layers (select the **Layer** menu, then **Flatten Image**) so it can be imported into another document by saving it as a ".tif" file.

If you want to share the layout with someone via e-mail, save a *copy* of it as a ".jpg" file. (This will be easier to view since the file size is smaller, but it will decrease the file's resolution slightly.) You can also downsize the size of the copied file for easier e-mailing by selecting the **Image** menu, **Resize**, then **Image Size.** A good file size for sharing layouts is 150 dpi at a 4" x 4" image size.

∨ Create Patterned Paper

Customize your designs by creating your own patterned paper with the Brush tool.

Grandpa and Grandma

I
look
at you,
smiling
down the
bright years,
and it strikes me
that I am your future.

I am the partial sum of
your dreams - me, and
thousands who you
touched during
your lives.

And it all
began
with
love.

Photo: June 1940

Love

You have a reason to smile, and I hope you are.

Love *by Jessica Sprague.* **Supplies** *Software:* Adobe Photoshop CS; *Brushes:* Chick Pea and Pea Blossom, downloaded from *www.twopeasinabucket.com;* Miss M, downloaded from *www.rebel-heart.net; Computer fonts:* P22 Cezanne ("Love" and "Grandpa and Grandma") and Shannon Book (remaining text), downloaded from *www.fonts.com.*

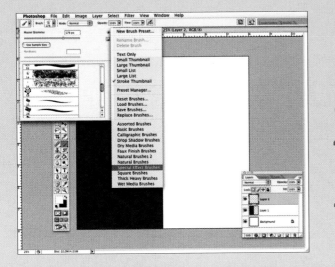

1 Create the box you want to use for the patterned paper on a new layer using the **Rectangular Marquee** tool (see the instructions in step 4, "Create a Journaling Box," on page 245).

2 Select white for the foreground color from the toolbar using **Set Foreground Color** in the toolbox.

3 Select the **Brush** tool from the toolbar. Decide the style and size of the brush in the **Brushes** palette (for options, use the drop-down menu for each in the **Brushes** palette). Create a new layer and stamp your brush to create your desired pattern over the layer created in step 1.

4 Check the **Layers** palette to make sure the layer with your brush stamp is selected; if it's not, click on it to select it. Look in the **Layers** palette and click the arrow in the **Opacity** box to reveal a slider, then use it to decrease the opacity of your brush to create the two-tone look of your patterned paper.

Note: Adjust the **Opacity** box in the **Layers** palette—not the **Brushes** palette—if you want the opacity of the brushed image to change.

ADDITIONAL IDEAS:
- To keep the brushed image from overlapping your photo, make sure the photo layer is above the brush layer in the **Layers** palette.
- If you want a multicolored patterned paper instead of a tone-on-tone look, select a color for the foreground color of the brush instead of white in step 2 and do not adjust opacity as directed in step 4.

troubleshooting Q&A

Once you start working with Photoshop, you'll no doubt experience a few situations that give you pause. Here are three common questions and their answers.

Q **I made a change to my layout, but it appeared on a different layer. How do I input it in the correct layer?**

A Each time you make a change, confirm that you're on the right layer (see the **Layers** palette). If not, select the desired layer from the **Layers** palette by clicking it once. *Note:* If you do make a change to the wrong layer, be sure to undo it. Select the **Edit** menu, then **Undo . . .** (the name of the change will appear after "Undo"), or use the shortcut keys (Ctrl + Z).

Q **I placed an element on my layout, but I can't find it. Where did it go?**

A Check the **Layers** palette. The element may be hiding below another layer or element. Once you find the layer you want, click it once and hold down, then drag the layer up in the palette until the element appears in your layout.

Q **I want to move one element, but another element keeps moving with it. How can I move just one element at a time?**

A More than likely, you've placed two elements on a single layer (unfortunately, this keeps them from being moved separately). Remember, when you move part of a layer, it moves everything on the layer. The best solution is to plan ahead. If you want to move elements as you go, make sure you create a new layer for every element so it can be moved independently of the others.

⌄ Stamp Titles

Think rubber and foam stamped looks are just for traditional pages? Think again.
You can easily create a stamped look digitally.

So Happy *by Kimberly Lund.* **Supplies** *Software:* Adobe Photoshop Elements; *Patterned papers, ribbon and tag:* Heather Ann Designs; *Computer fonts:* Dream Orphan, downloaded from *www.dafont.com*; 2Peas Spread Sunshine, downloaded from *www.twopeasinabucket.com*.

1 Create a new layer on the layout. Do not fill in a color—leave the layer transparent. *Note:* The background and other layers can be filled with color—only the new layer needs to be transparent.

2 Click the **Horizontal Type** tool from the toolbar, then select your desired font and size using the boxes in the **Type** palette that appears.

3 Place your cursor in the desired spot on the layout and click once. When the cursor appears, type your text. *Note:* If you want to move your text, select the **Move** tool from the toolbar once the text is added.

4 Make sure the text layer is selected in the **Layers** palette. Select the **Layer** menu, then **Simplify Layer**.

5 Select the **Filters** menu, **Artistic**, then **Plastic Wrap**. Choose the following settings from the pop-up menu that will appear: Highlight Strength: 15; Detail: 9; Smoothness: 7. Click **OK**.

6 Select the **Filters** menu, **Brush Strokes**, then **Sprayed Strokes**. Choose the following settings from the pop-up menu that will appear: Stroke Length: 20; Spray Radius: 5; Stroke Direction: Right diagonal. Click **OK**.

7 Click the arrow in the **Opacity** box in the **Layers** palette to reveal the slider, then use it to decrease the opacity of the text until you achieve your desired stamped look.

tools to know

If you've decided to test the water with digital scrapbooking but aren't quite sure where to begin, read on! I've compiled descriptions of some commonly used tools from Photoshop Elements Help to guide you.

Brushes: The **Brush** tool (see the paintbrush in the toolbar) creates soft or hard strokes of color and patterns. Adobe offers a library of existing brushes, but you can also create your own from an image.

Filters: Filters (see the **Filters** menu) let you easily alter the appearance of a page element by applying effects like blur, diffuse and fresco.

Layers: A layer (see the **Layer** menu) is simply a transparent blank canvas. You can stack multiple layers over the locked "Background" (original image) to create changes without altering the original.

If you want two layers to move as a single unit on your layout, you can link them together (in the **Layers** palette, click on the empty box next to the eye icon on the layer you want to link to the current layer selected).

If you want to combine two elements onto a single layer, merge them (select the **Layer** menu, then **Merge Down**). Keep in mind that once elements are merged, they can't be separated.

Opacity: As its name says, the opacity function (see the **Layers** palette) lets you change the opacity of layers, filters and effects so that more (or less) of the underlying image shows through. A layer with 1% opacity is nearly transparent, while one with 100% opacity is completely opaque.

Palettes: Palettes provide information on a variety of aspects and offer more options for added control when applying a particular tool. Some palettes, such as **Layers**, are always visible and appear on the right-hand area of your screen. Palettes for specific tools, such as the **Move** tool, appear above your layout only when the tool is selected from the toolbar.

Select/Deselect: To make changes to an isolated element on your layout without affecting the entire layout, select an area (see the **Select** menu). When an area is selected, a dotted line (often called "marching ants") will appear. To deselect, go to the **Select** menu, then choose **Deselect**.

Marquee: The **Rectangular Marquee** tool (see the dotted rectangle shape from the toolbar) draws a square or rectangular selection, while the **Elliptical Marquee** tool draws a round or elliptical selection.

Text Tools: Use the **Horizontal Type** or **Vertical Type** tools (see the "T" shape in the toolbar) to create and edit text. Each added text element creates a new layer. The **Type Mask** tools let you shape the text as well as create different effects along with font, style, size and color of the type.

Make a Monogram

Jazz up a monogram by making it look like it's cut from patterned paper.

SEPTEMBER 25, 2005
EUMUNDI, QUEENSLAND

My darling Abi, you are at the sweetest age at the moment. You are really taking great pleasure in discovering the world around you. You want to try everything Olivia does, and you want to explore everything — you seem so fearless. At the playground you want to go on all the rides, including the slide, and your favourite is the see-saw. You always have so much fun playing and exploring your world. I love you.

A *by Suzy Nunes.* **Supplies** *Software:* Adobe Photoshop Elements; *Patterned papers:* The Digi Chick; *Computer fonts:* Times New Roman ("A"), Microsoft Word; Journaling Hand and Hootie!, downloaded from the Internet.

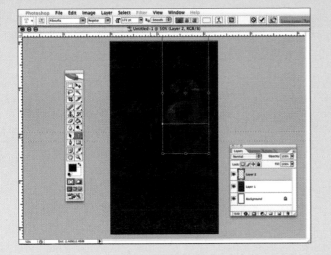

1 Open your patterned paper in a new document. (If you haven't downloaded any patterned papers from the Internet, make your own with the instructions in "Create Patterned Paper" on page 249.)

2 Select the **Horizontal Type Mask** tool from the toolbar. *Note:* This tool is different from the **Horizontal Type** tool. To select it, look in the **Horizontal Type** palette for the transparent "T" icon with the dotted outline around it.

3 Choose your font style and size in the boxes in the **Type** palette.

4 Position your cursor over the desired section of patterned paper, click your mouse, then type your monogram letter.

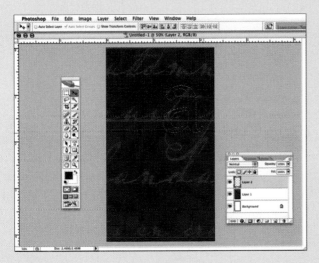

5 Click on the **Move** tool from the toolbar and the "marching ants" selection will appear around the letter.

6 Copy the letter (use "Ctrl + C" on your keyboard), then paste it in the file with your layout (use "Ctrl + V" on your keyboard).

7 Add the white border by selecting the **Edit** menu, then **Stroke (Outline) Selection**. *Note:* Make sure the layer with your monogram is selected in the **Layers** palette. Choose the following settings: Width: 10; Color: White; Location: Inside. Click **OK** to apply the effect.

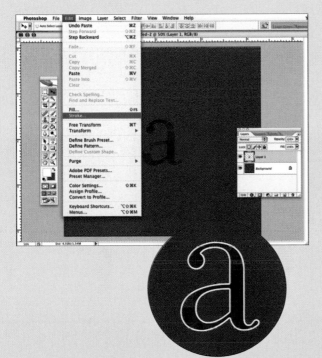

helpful web sites

Ready to get your feet wet in the world of digital scrapbooking? Check out these sites to find digital papers, embellishments and more:

- *www.designerdigitals.com*
- *www.digitaldesignessentials.com*
- *www.digitalscrapbookplace.com*
- *www.heatheranndesigns.com*
- *www.matterofscrap.com*
- *www.promos4digiscrappers.com*
- *www.scrapartist.com*
- *www.scrapbook-bytes.com*
- *www.scrapbook-elements.com*
- *www.shabbyprincess.com*
- *www.thedigichick.com*
- *www.twopeasinabucket.com/digital.asp*

∨ Create Rows of Patterned Squares

Add a pattern to an entire row of shapes with a single sequence.

I Love You 100 *by Robin Carlton.* **Supplies** *Software:* Adobe Photoshop Elements; *Patterned papers:* The Digi Chick; *Computer fonts:* Helvetica, Adobe Systems; 2Peas Rock Star, downloaded from *www.twopeasinabucket.com*; Susie's Hand and School Bully, downloaded from the Internet.

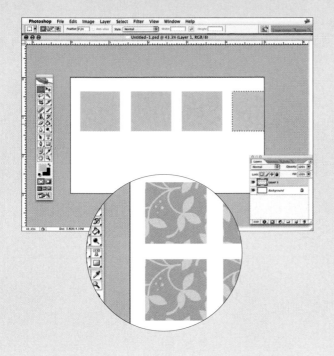

1 Create a new layer. Click on the **Rectangular Marquee** tool from the toolbar and use it to create one row of shapes *on a single layer* as desired. *Note:* Fill in each shape with a color to make sure the shape is added.

2 Open the file with your patterned paper, then select a portion that fits over the row of squares using the **Rectangular Marquee** tool from the toolbar. While the area is still selected (you should see the "marching ants"), select the **Move** tool, then drag the selected area and drop it over the row of shapes on your layout.

3 Make sure the patterned paper is selected in the **Layers** palette. Select the **Layer** menu, then **Group with Previous**—the shapes will fill with the patterned paper.

4 Repeat steps 1–3 for each row of shapes.

products to help you

From tutorials to software to ways you can store your finished layouts, numerous products can help you enter the world of digital scrapbooking. Here are some great options to get you started.

TUTORIALS

The Scrapper's Guide to Adobe Photoshop Elements 4.0
MSRP: $29.95
Web site: www.scrappersguide.com

In this instructive CD made specifically *for* scrapbookers *by* a scrapbooker, video instruction will walk you through each step of the digital process. Learn how to easily manage Adobe Photoshop Elements 4.0 while gleaning practical digital scrapbooking tools along the way. The videos are a great resource for visual learners. CDs are also available for Adobe Photoshop Elements 3.0.

Do It Digital (The I "DID" It Network) Tutorial Kits
MSRP: $6.95 per kit
Web site: www.scrappydoodlekits.com

Do It Digital (The I "DID" It Network) tutorial kits from *www.scrappydoodlekits.com* make digital scrapbooking with Corel Paint Shop Pro 8 a snap. Each step in the tutorial is clear and simple and includes details such as what size the photo should be, how to create a new layer and how to flatten an image. In a readily accessible way, the tutorial helps users become more intimate with Paint Shop Pro. Each kit also includes a complete set of digital elements to create the featured project in the training.

SOFTWARE

Adobe Photoshop Elements 4.0
MSRP: $99
Web site: www.adobe.com

Corel Paint Shop Pro X
MSRP: $99
Web site: www.corel.com

To make a layout, you'll need a photo-editing program that lets you create with a wide selection of tools. Both Adobe Photoshop Elements 4.0 and Corel Paint Shop Pro X are great options. You're sure to love the new features offered in Adobe Photoshop Elements 4.0, including automatic red-eye removal, skin tone corrections for photos and a magic selection brush. And with Corel Paint Shop Pro X, you'll even receive free video tutorials to make the digital creation process easier. ♥

10

TIPS FOR BETTER PHOTOGRAPHY

Get rave results with these fun twists

I was at a photography store dropping off my film when one of the assistants asked if I was Candice. "Yes, I am," I answered. "How do you know my name?" "We all know who *you* are," she replied. "We love your pictures, and we always look forward to seeing what you'll bring in next!"

The woman next to me in line said she wished people were waiting for *her* photos. They always came out so "blah." I started thinking about why two people with the same camera, subject and setting can walk away from a photo shoot with such different results. Following are my top 10 tips to help every scrapbooker improve his or her photography. With a little practice, you may find that the next time you go to pick up your pictures, the developer will greet you by name! →

BY CANDICE STRINGHAM

Locations for your photos can be found in unexpected places. By simply cropping out the distracting elements, you have a beautiful setting for a photograph.

1 **Find your creative eye.** The key to loving the pictures you take is knowing what you love. Look through magazines and tear out pictures you like. Tape the pictures to the wall or in a place where you can live with them for a while.

After a few days, analyze the similarities. Have you chosen all black-and-white pictures, or are you attracted to bright colors? Do the pictures show the subject's location, or are they extreme close-ups? Are they weighted on the left side or the right? This exercise will help you prepare for that perfect picture before you even start taking pictures. You'll know what you like and what your eye is attracted to.

2 **Keep a notebook.** Fill a notebook with ideas and sketches of the photos you want to take and it will help you shoot faster. For events, take a tip from wedding photographers: Have a list of pictures you want to take. For

example, on the Fourth of July I want to take pictures of the following:
• Kids with a flag
• Family watching a parade
• Husband at the grill
• Mom with her famous apple pie
By using this list, you'll be more aware of what you want and less worried about missing that shot you needed.

3 **Watch for location, location, location.** Look at the world around you with new eyes. Go on an afternoon drive, or take a walk around your neighborhood. Even small areas can make great photos: a patch of ivy climbing up a fence, a brightly painted wall or a fun park. Also search the Internet for information about local sites. It was years before I realized I was only a short drive away from national parks, sand dunes, salt flats and architectural wonders that all made great backdrops for photos.

4 **Crop with your camera.** A picture of your child playing in the front yard is cute. A picture of your child in the front yard with the neighbor's 1973 rusty Gremlin in the background is not so cute.

The next time you pick up your camera, take a picture from where you're inclined to stand. Take another picture a few steps closer, then one even closer. When you get the results back, take a good look. You might just like what you see!

After setting up your shot, get several steps closer to minimize distracting backgrounds.

By getting above or below your standing height, you can create a wide variety of moods.

5 **It's all about the angle.** Using different angles while shooting can really help your pictures look more professional. Remember the neighbor's ugly car? Well, shooting the photograph from above would eliminate the car, resulting in a backdrop of beautiful green grass. Try standing on a chair, table or ladder or lying down on the ground to take your photo.

Choosing the right light can be the most important part of taking a great photo.

6 Find the right natural light.

Photographers recommend two times of the day for shooting outside: early in the morning (sunrise) and late in the afternoon (sunset). This is because your subject is illuminated by a nice, soft sidelight instead of harsh overhead lighting.

Sunrise gives off a soft bluish light, while sunset gives off a warm-toned light—flattering to just about anyone. The time I most like to shoot outside? On a cloudy day, just before a storm. The clouds gently wrap your subject with soft light.

Slightly tilting your camera can add drama to your photographs.

7 **Try a lateral tilt.** One of the major things professional photographers do that amateurs don't is *lateral tilting*. This means holding your camera vertically, then tilting the camera slightly to the left or right to get an angled look. Lateral tilting is one of the simplest things you can do to create more visual interest in a photo.

The rule of thirds can help you compose more interesting, vibrant shots.

8 **To center or not to center?** That is the question. Look at your subject through the camera, center it, then move the camera around so the subject is on the left, then the right. Place the subject low, then high. You've got several choices when it comes to placing the main subject of your photo, and the center isn't always the best. Try new placements.

When in doubt, trust the *rule of thirds*. Think of imaginary lines dividing the picture into thirds horizontally and then vertically. You should place your subject at the intersection of these lines. Still, remember: the most important thing is not what the rules say but what you like.

Consciously decide what emotion or mood you want to capture with your photo, then shoot with that end in mind.

9 **Think outside the box.** Sometimes it's the idea, not the technique, that makes a photo great. So, think creatively when planning to take pictures. I usually start the creative process by asking myself a few questions: Who is the person I'm photographing? What do they love? How can I show that? What emotion do I want to show? What style of photography will help me get my point across? By thinking creatively, you may find yourself taking a lot more photos that you love.

10 **Shoot lots of pictures.** Most professionals do. Fashion photographers will shoot rolls and rolls of film just to get one perfect shot. Think of it like this: you have a better chance of winning the lottery if you buy more than one ticket.

striking seasonal settings for your photographs

HOW MANY TIMES have you gone to an expensive photo studio and watched them set up a backdrop for your photo? Beachfront scenes, fall leaves, a roaring fire in a fireplace … has it ever occurred to you that you have access to all of these "backdrops"—right outside your front door?

The four seasons provide amazing settings for photos of you and the ones you love. If you start viewing the world as "one big backdrop" for your photographs, you'll be stunned at the quality of your photos and how much real life they capture.

To help you get started, here are photo ideas, tips and examples from each of the four seasons. The next time you take a walk, keep your eyes open for perfect photo settings that capture the richness and beauty of your photo subject *and* the world around you. →

ARTICLE BY CATHERINE SCOTT

Spring

As the world emerges from its winter thaw and people emerge from the world of the indoors, take advantage of the gentle spring sunlight, which seems to tint photos with a soft, fresh green. Here are some spring moments and settings to take advantage of:

Rainstorms

Since when do we sit inside when it's raining? Don your raincoats and waterproof boots and head for the streets to dance in the rain. Bright colors contrasted with the dark storm clouds add a playful touch to photos. Don't forget to zoom in on especially endearing scenes:

◆ Rain boots stomping through puddles
◆ A chubby hand gripping the handle of an umbrella

◆ An innocent face turned toward the raindrops
◆ Raindrops running off a brightly colored coat

Have you ever noticed the amazing light as a storm begins to clear? The world is cast in a greenish-golden light, and scenes you've glimpsed a hundred times before seem to change before your very eyes. Grab your camera and take pictures of your house, your street, your sidewalk and your kids in the vivid new light.

New Growth

Have you witnessed the miracle of snow melting away to reveal bright green grass? A fragile new bud pushing up through frozen ground? It's easy to find inspiration in the miracles of spring.

Don't let these moments of discovery and wonder pass you by:

◆ Green buds pushing through tree branches
◆ Flowers unfolding into bursts of color
◆ Birds carrying nest-making materials through the air
◆ Fragrant blossoms fluttering from trees to the ground

Take advantage of any opportunities to fill the frame of your camera with spring scenes (or scenes from any season): a field of tall grass, daffodils or tulips, or a lilac bush in full bloom. Positioning a person in the midst of the scene will provide a striking seasonal photo.

The world is in full bloom, the sun is high and school is out. Relive your childhood days by spending lazy days outside and discovering new ways to capture the season on film. Be sure to use a great color film to capture the colors of the season—and watch for these guaranteed great photo settings:

Water

Water is everywhere during the summertime! From the swimming pool to the ocean, the backyard sprinkler to the tall glass in someone's hand, capture the refreshing quality of water in your photos. Try capturing scenes like these:

◆ Faces showing the surprise of the transition between the hot summer sun and a cool ocean wave
◆ Goggled faces emerging from under-water in the swimming pool
◆ A line of children in bright bathing suits standing in front of a sprinkler's spray of water
◆ A hot, sweaty little one gulping a glass of ice water

When shooting photos involving water, remember to add interest by capturing complete reflections when possible and paying attention to glare from the sunlight, which may affect your photos.

Summer's Bounty

Nature is absolutely splendid during the summer: white puffy clouds, brilliant blue skies, grass-covered hills and plentiful fruits, veggies and flowers. No matter where you go in the summertime, bring your camera along and get ready for photo ops at every turn. Here are a few you won't want to miss:

◆ Hands carefully selecting vivid fruits and vegetables at the farmer's market
◆ Wide-open fields of green grass or golden wheat against a clear sky
◆ Children standing in, collecting, holding and wearing flowers
◆ Faces against the green, leafy treetops

Use a fill flash to photograph subjects in bright sunlight, or better yet, move your subjects to an area of full shade to eliminate dark shadows on faces. The best times to take summer photos are early morning (which will cast a slightly blue light on your subjects) or early evening (which can create a gorgeous "halo" of golden sunlight on your subjects' hair).

Fall

The crisp air is invigorating, the colorful leaves are inspiring, and harvest time is here. Enjoy the outdoors in cozy sweaters and soft corduroys—which also look great in photos! Use your camera to catch the changing light and preparations for winter. Try these ideas:

Country Bliss

There's no better time than fall to head for the country! The rustic settings, gorgeous weather and open space are the perfect spot to take the yearly family photo or capture outdoor portraits of those cuties you adore. Watch for opportunities like:

- A weathered barn to provide a textured backdrop for smiling faces
- Kids running through a crowded pumpkin patch

- An adventurous grin smiling from a tree heavy with apples
- Hands clasping the treasures of the season: a colorful leaf, a ripe apple, a huge sunflower or a miniature pumpkin

Make sure you capture just the shot you want by taking one shot of the grand fall scene and one that's zoomed in on your subject. Then, take your pick of which photos capture your desired effects.

Falling Leaves

You can't escape the yearly chore of raking the yard, but you can turn the work into a fruitful photo session! Fall's splendor is found in the dazzling colors of leaves, both on trees and off. Grab your rake *and* your camera, and make the

most of your hard work by capturing:

- A small child sitting in the middle of a huge pile of leaves
- A precious face framed by a branch of colorful leaves pulled gently into the picture
- Children throwing leaves into the air and watching them float on the fall breeze
- Rosy cheeks shining after a morning of hard work in the yard

Fall colors are beautiful in photos. Make sure your subject doesn't fade into the background by dressing him or her in a color complementary to the colors outside; denim looks terrific against the browns, reds, yellows and oranges typical in fall scenes.

The world is quiet under a blanket of fresh snow. Smoke drifts from chimneys, traffic slows, and the world looks clean again as winter introduces itself once more. Find charming scenes for photos indoors and out this season as you and your loved ones celebrate each other. Here are some scenes to watch for:

Snow

Clean, white snow is a beautiful backdrop for photos—the uniformity and brightness help your subject shine as the star of the show. Here are a few moments you won't want to miss:

- Mitten-covered hands rolling snowballs
- Kids laughing as they make snow angels in the snow
- A hat- and scarf-bundled smiling face
- Wonder-filled eyes sparkling with the magic of the first snow

Because snow is white, bright colors work well in snow photos. Keep your winter photography plans in mind when buying winter hats, mittens, scarves and coats!

Cozy Home

Don't let the cold weather put a halt to your photographs! Remember that heading indoors is a ritual of the winter season; be sure to capture the moments you share with the ones you love in your cozy home. Here are a few ideas:

- A loved one enjoying a moment warming by the fire
- Savoring comfort foods served for lunch and dinner
- Donning your home with decorations for the winter holidays
- Children wrapped in soft blankets to fend off the chill

Consider using a faster-speed film when shooting photographs indoors where lighting may be softer than the outdoors. Also, remember that indoor flash photography can cast harsh shadows behind your subject, so turn on a lamp first for adequate lighting.

As the seasons turn, look at the world around you with fresh eyes—the eyes of a photographer in search of the perfect seasonal scenes. Return to your favorite photo-taking spots to take advantage of the beauty around us. And, most importantly, always remember: The world is your (free) backdrop! ❤

TAKE A
SELF-PORTRAIT
TODAY

It's easy, with these expert tips

PEOPLE ASK if I've always been comfortable in front of the camera. Heavens, no! In fact, years ago, whenever someone pulled out a camera, I pulled a goofy face. No, I wasn't hamming things up for fun—instead, I was hoping to distract people from my unstyled hair, the big zit on my chin or the extra weight I was carrying once again.

Oh sure, I still hate it when a photograph reveals my extra chin(s!), but working at CK for nearly nine years has taught me an important lesson. After seeing *thousands* of layouts that rarely feature *you*, I've realized that, zit or no zit, I need to be in front of the camera—and often. You do, too.

So, hand your camera over to someone else at parties and events. Even better, spend a little one-on-one time with your camera. Yep, I'm suggesting a (gasp!) self-portrait.

BY TRACY WHITE

the basics

Zit and chin issues aside, taking a self-portrait can be a little challenging. After all, if you're in front of the camera, how do you know you're taking the right shot? My best advice is to take lots of photos—I know I do! Even with the immediate feedback offered by today's digital cameras, you'll enjoy having several options to choose from when looking for that "right" shot.

I chatted with cute Elsie Flannigan and got a few of her helpful self-portrait tips. What's cool is you don't need any special equipment—just you and your camera!

ELSIE'S PORTRAIT TIPS

Instead of simply holding your camera at arm's length, choose a unique angle. Experiment with holding the camera out on a table, like Elsie did in the photo below. How about shooting from above or to the side? Keep playing with angles until you discover one that accentuates your best features.

You don't have to look into the camera. Try looking down or to the side. Experiment with different expressions and see what you can capture that communicates emotion and personality.

Don't worry about your photo being perfect. Elsie mentioned that hers is a bit blurry, but it really captures the feel she was going for. A little imperfection can add character and charm!

Favorite Color *by Elsie Flannigan.* **Supplies** *Patterned papers:* KI Memories, Scenic Route Paper Co., K&Company, BasicGrey, Making Memories and Chloe's Closet; *Photo tape and chipboard letters:* Heidi Swapp for Advantus; *Other:* Buttons and thread.

a little more advanced

I'm defined by so many working parts—my values, education and environment are just a few. Since you've committed to taking a self-portrait (you did commit, didn't you?) consider including your environment. It'll reveal a side of you that would be missed in a basic "head and shoulders" shot.

I chatted with talented photographer Candice Stringham and she shared handy tips for composing an environmental self-portrait. So, look around. Where do you work? What's your favorite spot at home? Do you have a place to cuddle up and relax at the end of the day? Keep these thoughts in mind, then grab a camera and a tripod and follow these easy tips from Candice:

① Tape a blank sheet of paper where you'd like your head to be in the photo.

② Place the camera on a tripod and compose the shot. The sheet of paper will help you determine the distance and focus for the photo. Remember to be purposeful in deciding what you want to include in your self-portrait.

③ Set the camera's timer, remove the piece of paper, then get in position before the camera takes your picture. Voila—you've made a self-portrait! If you're using a digital camera, check your results and make adjustments. If not, don't be afraid to take plenty of images.

Rustic Elegance
by Candice Stringham.
Supplies *Textured card-stock:* Bazzill Basics Paper; *Patterned papers:* foof-a-La, 7gypsies, Making Memories, BasicGrey and K&Company; *Letter accents, foam stamps and jewels:* Making Memories; *Other:* Book cloth, glass beads and a pearl from a necklace.

THE RULE OF THIRDS
Kick up the composition of any photo by using the rule of thirds. Here's what I mean: Imagine placing a tic-tac-toe grid over your viewfinder. By placing your subject along one of the lines—especially where two lines intersect—the subject is in the most visually dynamic and appealing spot.

try something different

I love moody images and an easy way to create mood is through movement. For this shot I placed my camera on a tripod, slowed down my shutter speed, then moved my head as the timer released. I love the feeling of reflection and movement this technique created.

Want another variation? Consider jumping, twirling or swaying in front of the open shutter. It's fun to play!

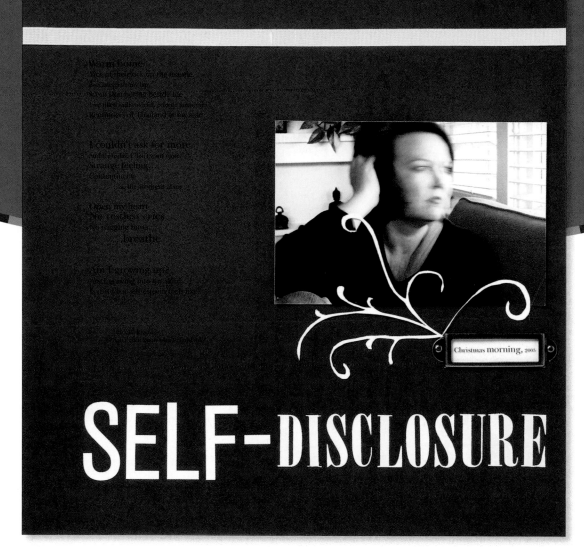

Self-Disclosure *by Tracy White.* **Supplies** *Letter stickers:* American Crafts; *Book label, ribbon and letter rub-ons:* Making Memories; *Computer font:* Baskerville, Apple.

WHAT? TAKE A SELF-PORTRAIT?

Raise your hand if you're caught up with your scrapbooking.

   [Silence. Cricket chirping somewhere in the background.]

See? No hands, and yet I'm proposing that you take more photos and they're of you. Do you know why? You're amazing. Yes, you. Your family wants to see you in your scrapbook. They want to know you and remember you. So, take a deep breath and get in front of the camera!

more than just a pretty face

Who ever said a self-portrait has to be of your face? Becky Higgins wanted to celebrate her hands and all they do for her family. What part of you do you love? Your eyes? That gorgeous smile?

Getting a portrait of a body part can be tricky. Becky's advice? First, get the zoom exactly where you want it before you start snapping. Second, since it's sometimes difficult to move the camera, Becky and her son moved their hands to different positions.

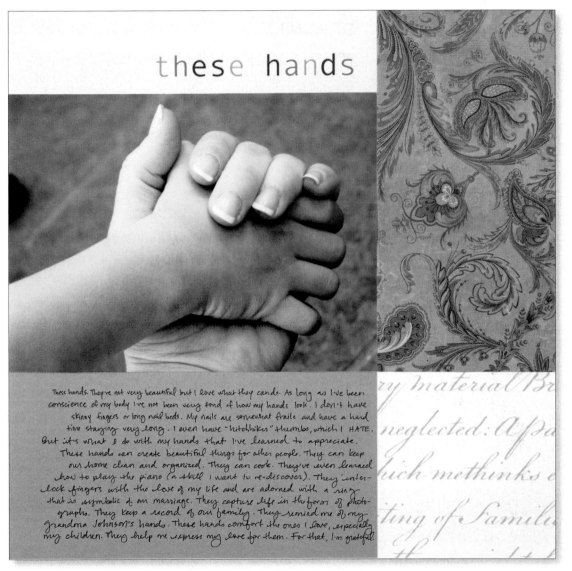

These Hands *by Becky Higgins.* **Supplies** *Patterned paper:* Anna Griffin; *Computer font:* Verdana, Microsoft Word.

QUICK TIP FROM THE PRO

Skylar Nielsen, long-time CK photographer, has this tip to share: For great lighting that's even and neutral, **position yourself beside a window** that's shaded from direct sunlight. To reduce contrast and shadowing, **hang a white towel** on the side of you opposite the window to reflect the light back onto your face.

lessons learned from a default self-portrait photographer | by teri fode

I really, truly don't take self-portraits because of vanity! I stumbled onto them because I'd abused my own family with my love of photography. I was simply desperate for a human being who would cooperate with my endless hunger to learn about photography, my camera and portrait-style photos.

Spending hours experimenting with lighting, shutter speed, aperture, ISO settings and the mysterious white-balance of digital photography really paid off. Fiddling with my camera is what really helped me understand digital photography—even though I had to use myself as a subject!

One of the greatest benefits of practicing on yourself? You can take tons of photos and delete those you hate until you find one that passes your scrutiny. And that's really something—a photo of you that you actually like!

HERE ARE SOME TIPS I've learned through my journey of "self-photography." I'll also share a technique I use that doesn't even require a tripod!

- First, I always use my compact digital camera when taking self-portraits because it isn't bulky like my digital SLR. That's important because I hold my camera with one hand, arm extended.

- Remember, it's all in the angle of your arm to get the most natural pose! Make sure you extend your arm all the way out, elbow straight and slightly raised (not too much) so your hand is just at or above eye level. Experiment until you achieve the angle that's most flattering for you.

- Experiment with digitally cropping your photos. Depending on the mood you want to create in the photo and your layout, don't be afraid to use creative cropping for an artistic look.

- Catchlights are the reflection of the light source that shows up in the subject's eyes. It gives a natural twinkle to the eyes. Want to capture catchlights in your own eyes? Position yourself so you're facing the light source. If you can see the gleam of the lights in your eyes when previewing your photo, you've captured catchlights. In this shot, I was near a window on a cloudy day.

some final notes

- Great lighting matters.
- Get to know your camera by experimenting with settings like aperture, shutter speed, ISO and white balance.
- Use self-portraiture as your own photography class.
- Try posing candidly for varied shots. For example, smile, don't smile, look sullen, look happy, lean your head on your hand or arm, angle your head and more.
- If the rule of thirds enhances your final shot, use it when cropping your photos.
- Crop out your extended arm, almost to your shoulder, to look the most natural.
- Use Photoshop or another software program to touch up the photos to your liking.

Use photo-editing software to enhance and perfect your photos.

ORIGINAL PHOTO

< how to | Lighten a dark photo

I snapped my photos with a bright background, leaving my subject in shadow. While the best solution would have been to set up the photo correctly before I took the shot, it just didn't happen. I used photo-editing software to lighten the subject while keeping the background details intact. Here's how:

① Select the subject in shadow with an outline tool like Magnetic Lasso.

② "Feather" the selection to soften the edges between the area you are brightening and the background.

③ Use Levels (in Photoshop CS) or your software's brightening adjustment tools to lighten the subject. Start by lightening the shadows and then the midtones (in Levels, use the middle slider to adjust shadows).

④ If you want to adjust the background a bit, you can select Inverse and make adjustments on this area.

⑤ If you want to add some contrast back into the subject you just lightened, apply contrast adjustments to the entire photo; otherwise you may get a defined border between the subject and the background.

—*Debbie Hodge*

ICE CREAM SHOPPE by Debbie Hodge
Supplies *Textured cardstock:* Bazzill Basics Paper; *Patterned papers:* Scenic Route Paper Co.; *Stickers:* A.C. Moore; *Ribbon:* May Arts and unknown; *Hinge:* Ives; *Snaps and colored staples:* Making Memories; *Computer fonts:* Bookman Old Style (journaling), Microsoft Word; CAC Shishoni Brush (subtitle) and Casablanca Antique (date), downloaded from *www.scrapvillage.com*; Otherwise, Adobe Photoshop, Adobe Systems; *Other:* Thread and photo turn.

BONUS TIP FROM DEBBIE:
If you have your digital photos printed professionally and you have altered your photos with photo-editing software, ask them to print your images with no corrections. You should also stick with the same developer because after a few rounds, you'll come to understand the correlation between your equipment and theirs, and your adjustments will be increasingly successful.

Shoot a Still Life Today

[*Be an artist with your camera*]

If you're like a lot of people, you savor the lovely flowers, cards and candy boxes of Valentine's Day, then discard them. Wait—not so fast! Why not take photos of these inanimate objects (also called "still lifes") when you first get them and capture the beauty for your scrapbook pages? Still-life photos are simple to capture, and they're a stunning way to reinforce a page or card theme. Unleash your inner artist!

by Jennifer Weiss

What You'll Need

Gather the following:

① A **camera with flash** (off-board* is best)

② A **diffuser**** (or make your own with tissue or vellum)

③ Several sheets of **colored poster board** or **cardstock**

④ The object or **objects to be photographed** (here's your chance to buy flowers and chocolates!)

⑤ A **tripod** or something similar

⑥ **Masking tape**

Additional **props**

* An off-board flash can be adjusted by twisting it in different directions.

** A diffuser is an item that scatters light and is used to soften shadows.

Create a Backdrop

ONCE YOU'VE GATHERED THE ITEMS NEEDED:

① **Scout out your desired setting.** For the best photos with natural lighting, shoot them next to an open door or a large window when the sun is overhead and light is streaming in gently. If shadows are a problem, twist your off-board flash so it faces the ceiling. Use a reflector (foil will work) opposite the area receiving light to fill in shadows.

② **Push a table** or horizontal flat surface against the wall.

③ **Take a sheet of poster board** and bend it gently so half rests on the wall and the other half rests on the table.

④ **Tape the top** of the poster board to the wall and the bottom to the table. You should now have a curved backdrop that looks almost like a skateboarding ramp. The curved shape is ideal for still-life shots since there's no distracting shadow line or delineation between "floor" and "wall." All you and others will see is your background color. (See black background on "Valentine" page below.)

Valentine *by Jennifer Weiss.*
Supplies *Metal-rimmed vellum tag, metal XOXO and eyelet mesh hearts:* Making Memories; *Wooden cutouts in photograph:* Michaels; *Rhinestone brad:* Scrappin' Creations; *Computer fonts:* Book Antiqua ("Valentine"), Microsoft Word; ParkAveD, downloaded from the Internet; *Other:* Metal eyelet heart.

5 Sweet Shots for Valentine's Day

Sure, you can take wonderful still-life photos year-round, but don't miss your opportunity to shoot the following this Valentine's Day:

- **A box of chocolates** with the lid off so people can see the delicious treats inside. Prop the box at an angle for easier viewing.

- **Pre-painted wooden cutouts** in heart and flower shapes. (I picked mine up for around 50 cents each at Michaels.)

- **Homemade cards** that match your colors, shapes and theme. Or, ask your kids to make special cards for the photo shoot!

- **One or more roses** arranged next to candy and a card. You don't need a dozen roses to get a lovely picture (although that's fine, too). For a romantic look, pull off leaves or petals and scatter them around the base. They'll add visual weight to your picture. (See "Love" page.)

- **Hershey's kisses,** conversation hearts or rose petals arranged in a heart shape on colored cardstock or poster board. Take a picture standing directly above.

What's Up with White?

*You can use white poster board, but be aware that it tends to appear gray in photos unless your light sources are studio quality. **Two tips?** Before the photo shoot, position your curved poster board against a window lit by bright sun. After the photo shoot, use photo-editing software to brighten dark backgrounds or remove unwanted elements.*

Note: You can "push" your camera reading up two f-stops to get a white background, but this generally alters the color of the foreground as well. Take three shots, one with your camera on automatic and two where you've kept the same shutter speed but have gone up or down one aperture setting.

To my dear husband: Amado, I love you so very much. Be mine always!

Love *by Jennifer Weiss.* **Supplies** *Photo-editing software:* Adobe Photoshop, Adobe Systems; *Pink vellum:* Paper Pizazz; *Ribbon letters:* Scrappin' Creations; *Computer fonts:* Arial, Aeolus and NimbusSanT, Microsoft Word.

Steady, Now . . . Shoot!

Now that you're ready to photograph your favorite objects in unforgettable ways:

① **Check to see if your camera has a close-up or macro mode** (usually represented by a flower image). If it doesn't, you can simply stand a few feet away from the subject and take a close-up shot with your zoom lens.

② **Arrange the still-life object** on the part of the poster board that rests on the table. If desired, add simple props like scattered leaves.

③ **Position your camera on a tripod** in front of the object and adjust the height. No tripod? Use any stable surface (even a bag of dried beans!) to hold your camera steady. Or, put your camera into "timer" mode so it takes the pictures 5–20 seconds after you gently press the shutter release button.

Note: You'll find "image stabilization" and "vibration reduction" built into many of today's digital cameras. While these features help avoid blurry pictures, don't expect to get sharp pictures when holding the camera for ¹⁄₁₅ or even ¹⁄₃₀ of a second.

④ If your camera has an adjustable flash, try twisting it upward to **soften or eliminate shadows**. Or, put a diffuser over your flash for the same effect. No diffuser? Try taping a piece of tissue or vellum over your flash and take a few test shots.

⑤ Now comes the fun part. Once you've confirmed that the item and props are all contained within the backdrop area, **take several pictures**, adjusting zoom and camera angle each time. **Experiment!** Try the following angles:

• Straight on (stand directly in front)

• One or two steps to the side (left or right)

• Downward (stand on a journal, phone book, ladder . . .)

• Upward (lie on the floor or crouch)

• Sitting position on a counter

• Zoom in, zoom out

Get in the Mood

For a more intimate photo, switch your camera to aperture-priority mode and play with depth of field (this affects how much of your photo is in focus). When shooting a rosebud, for example, select a smaller f-stop to keep the rosebud in focus and the stem out of focus. Select a larger f-stop to keep both the rose and the stem in focus.

You are the

Apple LOVE

of my life
of my eye

Sometimes I'm struck by the pure beauty of everyday objects. The reds and golds of these apples glinting in the light caught my eye -- startled, a bit, I looked with enjoyment. Love seems the same way, sometimes. Every so often I stop, taken aback with how deep my love is for my husband, how very wonderful he is. It just amazes me.

How did I get so lucky? I ask myself in wonder and with thanks. On Valentine's Day, I'm glad to look beyond the typical and expected roses and flowers and find beauty in other places, like these apples. And it reminds me never to forget about the many loves of my life that exist right in front of my eyes, every day! Amado, I love you so so much!

Apple Apfel Manzana

My Sweet Valentine

Use the magnetic lasso in Photoshop to remove unwant—ed elements in a jiffy.

Love of My Life
by Jennifer Weiss.
Supplies *Photo-editing software:* Adobe Photoshop, Adobe Systems; *Computer fonts:* Myriad and Shannon, Microsoft Word.

See how the angle and zoom can make a world of difference? That's the beauty of still lifes—they're an invitation to turn the mementos of today into visual masterpieces for tomorrow! ❤

> Mini Album and Tin

Use just one piece of 12" x 12" cardstock to create this tiny mini book, which makes the perfect gift in an altered mint tin! Here's how:

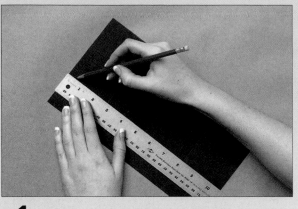

1 Cut a piece of cardstock to 6" x 10⅝"; score it into 12 sections, measuring 2" x 2¹¹⁄₁₆" each. (See diagram below).

2 Cut along cutting lines.

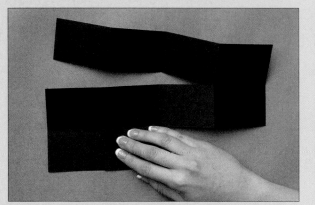

3 Accordion fold the bottom row in numerical order (1, 2, 3, 4). Tuck the pages under number 5. Accordion-fold the next row in numerical order (5, 6, 7, 8). Tuck the pages under number 9. Accordion-fold the last row. This makes the "inside pages" of the booklet.

4 Cut and fold the book cover out of cardstock, measuring 2¼" x 6". Also cut a strip to create the slider for the cover.

5 Adhere the first and last pages of the booklet to the inside pages of the cover. Score and fold the strip into a slider and decorate it as desired. Complete your booklet with photos and journaling.

9	10	11	12
			cutting line
8	7	6	5
cutting line			
1	2	3	4

6"

10 ⅝"

Bonus tip from Teri

Cut out the index prints that you receive from
the photo lab for your mini album. Or, create
your own mini photos using the index print
feature from your photo-editing software.

Mini Album by Teri Fode. **Supplies** *Patterned paper:* 7gypsies; *Heart punch:* EK Success; *Brad:* Doodlebug Design; *Computer font:* Bradley-Hand ITC, downloaded from the Internet; *Other:* Charm.

> ### Altered Mint Tin:

① Paint the lid and bottom of your tin. For best
results, use metal paints.

② Embellish the lid with torn patterned paper and
then treat it with a crackle medium, following the
manufacturer's directions.

③ Let it dry then embellish it.

④ Insert your mini album for a perfect album-in-a-
box gift!

Altered Mint Tin by Teri Fode. **Supplies** *Mint tin:*
Altoids; *Patterned paper:* 7gypsies; *Mesh:* Maruyama,
Magenta; *Metal paint:* DecoArt; *Acrylic paint:* Delta
Technical Coatings; *Crackle medium:* Duncan
Enterprises; *Decoupage medium:* Mod Podge, Plaid
Enterprises; *Tag:* Making Memories; *Stamping ink:* PSX
Design; *Computer font:* Bradley-Hand ITC, downloaded
from the Internet; *Other:* Charm and ball-chain.

Bonus tip from Teri

When adhering paper to a tin, use a decoupage
medium for best results. To prevent bubbling, apply
one coat over the paper and let it dry before applying
the paper to the tin. Apply a second coat of decoupage
medium over the paper and tin for a shiny finish.

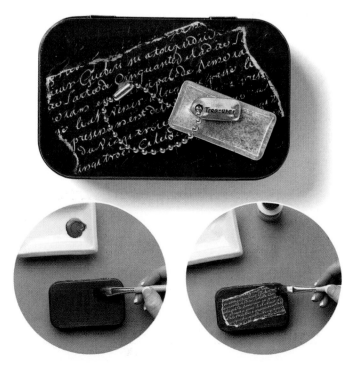

Sis by Teri Fode. **Supplies** *Mint tin*:
Altoids; *Metal paints*: DecoArt; Acrylic
paint: Delta Technical Coatings;
Crackle medium: Duncan Enterprises;
Decoupage medium: Mod Podge,
Plaid Enterprises; *Flower accent and
heart punch*: EK Success; *Patterned
paper*: Doodlebug Design; *Tag*:
Making Memories; *Stamping ink*: PSX
Design; *Mesh*: Maruyama, Magenta;
Computer font: Bradley-Hand ITC,
downloaded from the Internet;
Other: Charm and ball-chain.

Sis **Mini Book** by Teri Fode. **Supplies**
Cardstock: National; *Patterned paper*:
Doodlebug Design; *Heart punch*: EK Success;
Brad: Doodlebug Design; *Computer font*:
Bradley-Hand ITC, downloaded from the
Internet; *Other*: Charm.

Variations: Simply change the colors and
embellishments for a completely different
look. Consider themes such as Mother's Day,
holidays and birthdays. They also make
excellent thank-you gifts!